PRINCIPLES OF MANAGEMENT

M. Govindarajan
Formerly, Assistant Professor
Department of Mechanical Engineering
Anna University, Chennai

S. Natarajan
Formerly, Professor and Head
Department of Mechanical Engineering
Anna University, Chennai

PHI Learning Private Limited
Delhi-110092
2026

In fond memory of ***Shri Asoke K. Ghosh*** *(October 1942 – February 2024), Founder Chairman and Managing Director of PHI Learning, whose vision endlessly inspires.*

The Legacy Continues....

Published by Pushpita Ghosh, PHI Learning Private Limited, Rimjhim House, 111, Patparganj Industrial Estate, Delhi-110092 and Printed by Gopsons Printers Pvt. Ltd., A-14, Sector-60, Noida, Gautambudh Nagar, Noida, Uttar Pradesh-201301.

₹550.00

PRINCIPLES OF MANAGEMENT
M. Govindarajan and S. Natarajan

ISBN-978-81-203-2843-3 (Print Book)
ISBN-978-93-5443-045-9 (e-Book)

The export rights of the book are vested solely with the publisher.

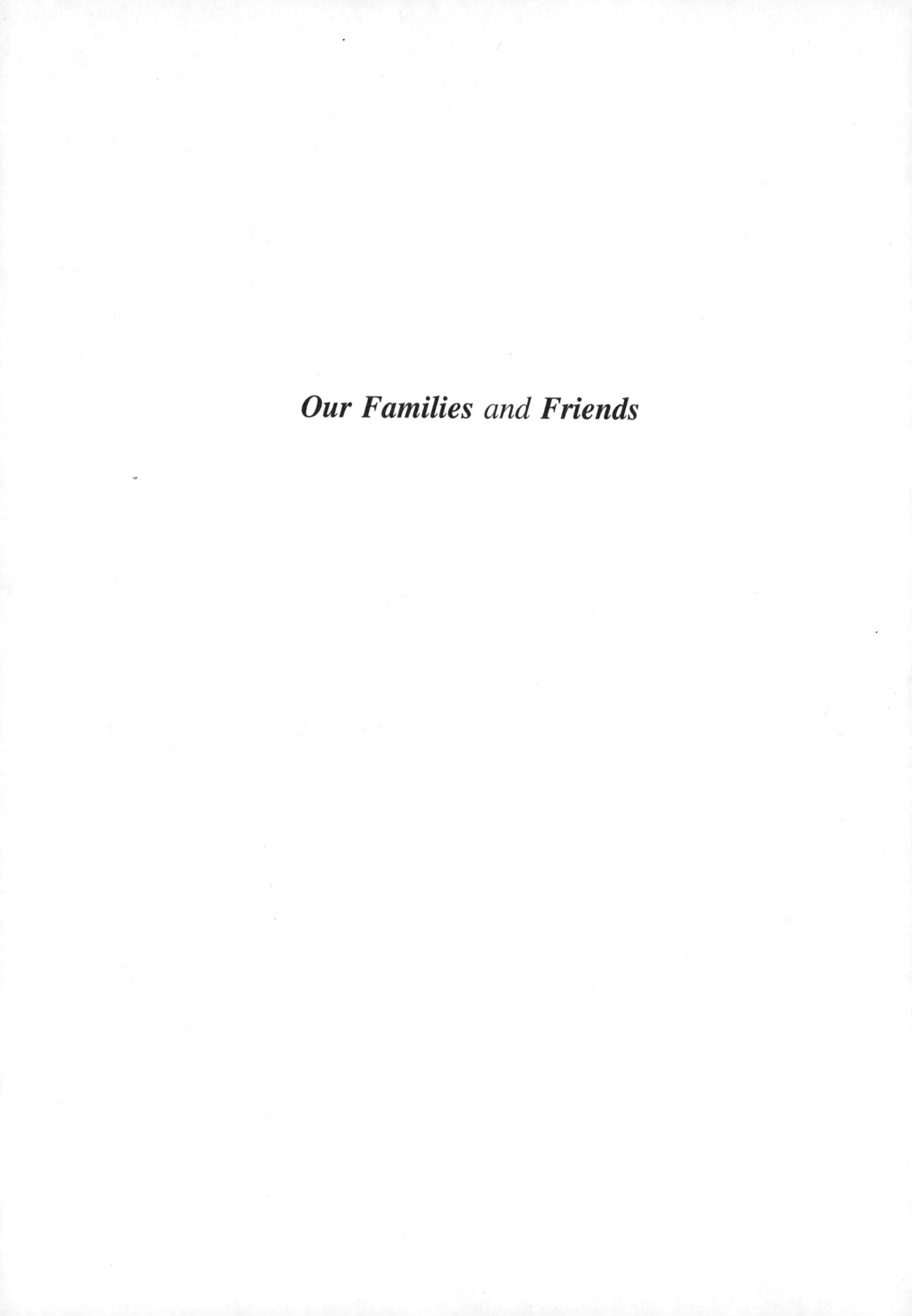

Our Families** and **Friends

Contents

List of Figures

Preface

Much water has flowed down under the bridge since F.W. Taylor put forth his theory of scientific management. Then appeared on the scene, a galaxy of management stars who further expanded the frontiers of managerial knowledge and gave it a separate identity. The collective wisdom of the management scientists, over a period of time, acquired the status of a discipline for long-term study, namely, *Management*. The modern management gurus have taken the concepts and practice to dizzy heights and to the pinnacle of glory. Simultaneously, the work on functional areas of management was also progressing. Each area became a separate subject of study and hence, a plethora of books dealing with different areas of management appeared on the bookshelves. Rest is history.

'Principles of Management' is a prerequisite course for pursuing higher studies in management. This book is written in 10 chapters with emphasis on readability and user-friendliness. We have taken care not to clutter the subject-matter with too many details, and to maintain its smooth and logical flow from one chapter to another. The end of each chapter carries review questions and caselets. The final chapter carries a primer on modern management and outlines 14 new concepts. Some of them may be in a nascent stage of development but their importance cannot be ignored. Thus, with a syllabus-wise coverage and an examination-oriented approach, this text provides a 'little more' that makes it distinguishable.

We take this opportunity to sincerely thank Mrs. Rajalakshmi and Mrs. Prabha, for writing and typing the manuscript and without whose help it would not have seen the daylight.

We also owe a deep sense of gratitude to Mr. V.S. Senthil Kumar for the enthusiasm shown and physical help provided by him. At the same time we would like to acknowledge the help rendered by Mr. G. Mukundan in providing the sketches needed for this book.

Our special thanks are due to Mr. Srinivasan for taking the photocopies and helping to improve its general layout.

We are grateful to Prentice-Hall of India for bringing out a sleek edition of this book.

M. Govindarajan
S. Natarajan

Sow an action and you reap a habit
Sow a habit and you reap a character
Sow a character and you reap a destiny

William James
American Psychologist

CHAPTER 1

Introduction

The term 'business' signifies individual and group activities directed toward wealth generation through exchange of goods and services. Business, as a system, uses various inputs like men, material, machinery, information and energy to create goods and services as output to meet the needs of the consumers. Business involves risks and the profit gained is the reward for risk-taking. The common risks are changing technology, changes in consumer preferences, competitive threats, and government polices. Business influences the living standard of people and is the leading indicator of the development of any nation.

1.1 OBJECTIVES OF BUSINESS

The objectives of business are two-fold: economic and social.

(i) Economic objectives include:
   (a) Ensuring a satisfactory return on investment (ROI).
   (b) Growth of business through diversification, merger, or acquisition.
   (c) Product innovation on a continuous basis.
   (d) Ensuring profitability by gaining strong market position.

(ii) Social objectives include:
   (a) Prevention of environmental pollution and ecological imbalance.
   (b) Overall development of the locality where the business is situated.
   (c) Development of backward areas.
   (d) Promotion of ancillary and small scale industries.

1.2 ESSENTIALS OF GOOD BUSINESS

The essentials of good business are:

1. A business must have well defined and attainable objectives.

2. It should follow a proper planning procedure based on up-to-date, reliable, and adequate information.
3. It should have a proper layout and location so as to ensure minimization of costs and maximization of profits.
4. A business should have a responsive and adaptive management.
5. It should hava a sound organization structure ensuring effectiveness.
6. A business should have a customer-focused marketing system.
7. A business should also have sound personnel policies.

1.3 CONCEPT OF MANAGEMENT

Managing is the art of getting things done through people in formally organized groups. Management can thus be defined as the art or skill of directing human activities and physical resources in the attainment of predetermined goals. The ability to manage is an attribute quite apart from any technical skill. A manager can take advice from technical or functional experts, consider the information given by them, and come to a conclusion that results in a management decision. Management is practised with the help of five basic functions: planning, organizing, staffing, directing and controlling.

1.4 MANAGEMENT AND ADMINISTRATION

The features of management and administration are briefly discussed below.

1.4.1 Management Process

1. Management is the process of planning, organizing, coordinating, leading, motivating and controlling the resources (including human resources) of an organization in the efficient and effective pursuit of specified organizational goals.
2. A manager is a person who plans, organizes, leads, and controls human, financial, physical, and information resources in the efficient and effective pursuit of specified organizational goals.
3. Planning is the management function of developing a futuristic frame of reference from which to identify opportunities and threats that lie in the future and to take immediate action to exploit the opportunities and counter the threats.
4. Organizing is the management function of assigning duties, grouping tasks, establishing authority, and allocating resoures required to carry out a specific plan.
5. Staffing is the management function of recruitment, selection, placement, approval, and development of people to occupy the roles in the organization structure.
6. Leading is the management function of influencing, motivating, and directing human resources towards the achievement of organizational goals.
7. Controlling is the management function of monitoring organizational performance towards the attainment of organizational goals.

1.4.2 Administration

Administration describes not only the activity of implementing policy decisions, but also the activity of regulating the day-to-day operations of a section of an organization, such as the office. During the evolutionary stage of management there were three views regarding the difference between administration and management as discussed below.

1. *Management and administration are the same:* The term administration is used for the higher executive functions in government circles while the term management is used for the same functions in the business world.
2. *Administration is above management:* Administration is the function concerned with the determination of corporate policy; the coordination of finance, production and distribution; and the settlement of the complex structure of the organization under the ultimate control of the executive, while management is concerned with the execution of policy setup by administration for the particular objects before it.
3. *Administration is part of management:* Management is the general term used for the total process of executive control while administration is that part of management which is concerned with the installation and following of the procedure by which the progress of activities is regulated and checked against plans.

1.4.3 Management Skills

Three basic kinds of skills—technical, human and conceptual are needed for a manager. *Technical skill* is the ability to use the procedures, techniques, and knowledge of a specialized field. For examples, surgeons, engineers, and accountants all have technical skills in their respective fields. *Human skill* is the ability to work with, understand, and motivate other people as individuals or in groups. *Conceptual skill* is the ability to coordinate and integrate the organization's goals and activities.

1.4.4 Management Levels

The term levels of management refers to a line of demarcation between various managerial positions in an organization. There are generally four levels of management (Figure 1.1) namely: (1) top-level management, (2) upper middle management, (3) middle management, and (4) lower-level or first line management.

1.4.4.1 Top-Level Management

Top-level management consists of a small group of people and is responsible for the overall management of an organization. These people are called executives. The various functions performed by the top management are as follows:

1. Laying down the objectives of the enterprise.
2. Preparing strategic plans and policies for the enterprise.

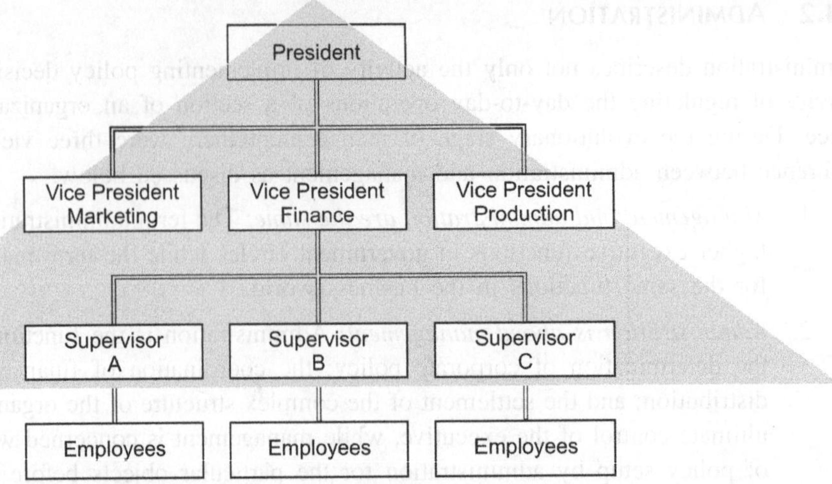

FIGURE 1.1 Levels of Managements

3. Issuing necessary instructions for the preparation of departmental budgets, schedules, procedures and so on.
4. Appointing executives for the middle level.
5. Coordinating the activities of all departments with the help of reports, memoranda, and so on.
6. Maintaining public relations.

1.4.4.2 Upper-Middle Management

The upper-middle management consists of heads of various functional divisions. The heads of functional divisions are in constant touch with the top management. They are responsible for the effective performance of their functional divisions.

1.4.4.3 Middle Management

The middle management can consist of more than one level in an organization. The principal responsibility is to direct the activities in such a way that the organization's policies are implemented and its goals are achieved.

1.4.4.4 Lower-Level Management or First Line Management

The first-line (first level or front-line) managers direct employees at non-managerial levels i.e. they do not supervise other managers. For example, foremen or production supervisors in a manufacturing plant. The important functions of a supervisor include the following:

1. To plan and organize the activities of the group.
2. To arrange for necessary materials, machines, tools, etc. for workers and to provide them with the necessary working environment.
3. To provide training to the workers.

4. To supervise and guide the subordinates
5. To solve the problems of workers.
6. To communicate employees problems to the higher management.

1.5 MODERN MANAGER

The Industrial Revolution which began in the eighteenth century transformed the job of a manager from owner-manager to a professional, salaried manager. The inventions, machines, and processes of the Industrial Revolution transformed business and management (such as, the use of fossil fuels as sources of energy, the railroad, the improvement of steel and aluminium metallurgical processes, the development of electricity, the discovery of the internal combustion engine etc.). With the industrial innovations in factory-produced goods, transportation, and distribution, big businesses came into being. New ideas and techniques were required for managing these large-scale corporate enterprises. The church and the military served as examples of control for these new managers. Many of the management terms and techniques used today have their origin in ecclesiastical and military authority (for example, superior, subordinate, strategy, mission etc.).

1.5.1 Information Age

An interesting description of the modern era is the Information Age that describes the general use of technology to transmit information. Managers realized that they could profit from immediate knowledge of relevant information. The telegraph was the first instrument to transform information into electrical form over long distances. The computer and telecommunications industries continue to converge and have resulted in advances in two-way pagers, digital cellular services, desktop video-conferencing, portable satellite phones, mini-dishes and high-speed internet access. The Information Age implies a time for a revolution in the information environment for business and management. The changes that are taking place may be more significant to management than the Industrial Revolution. Managers provide guidance, implementation, and coordination so that organizational goals can be realized. The modern manager encourages employees of the organization to develop teamwork spirit, which effectively helps to fulfill their needs and achieve organizational objectives. The modern manager provides an atmosphere of empowerment by letting workers make decisions and inspiring people to boost productivity.

1.6 SCIENCE, THEORY AND PRACTICE OF MANAGEMENT

Managing means acting or reacting in the light of the reality of a situation. Managers can work better by using the organized knowledge about management. It is this knowledge that constitutes a science. Thus, managing as practice is an art; the organized knowledge underlining the practice may be referred to as a science. The essential feature of any science is the application of the scientific method to the development of knowledge. Thus, science comprises clear concepts, theory and other accumulated knowledge developed from hypotheses, experimentation and analysis. Theory is a systematic grouping of interdependent concepts and principles that gives a framework to, or ties together, a significant area of knowledge. The role of theory is to provide a means of classifying significant and pertinent management knowledge. Principles are fundamental truths, explaining relations between two or more sets of variables. Techniques are essentially ways of doing things or methods of accomplishing a given result. Techniques normally reflect theory and help managers undertake activities most effectively.

1.7 WHY STUDY MANAGEMENT THEORY

Theories are perspectives with which people make sense of their world experiences. A theory is a coherent group of assumptions put forth to explain the relationship between two or more observable facts. *First,* theories provide a stable focus for understanding what we experience. A theory provides criteria for determining what is relevant. For example, to Henry Ford, a large and compliant workforce was one relevant factor that he theorized about his business. In other words, his theory of management included, among other things, this assumption about the supply of labour. *Second,* theories enable us to communicate efficiently and thus move into more and more complex relationships with other people. *Third,* theories make it possible to keep learning about our world. By definition, theories have boundaries *i.e.* there is a limited field that can be covered by any one theory.

1.8 MANAGERIAL OBJECTIVES

Management is the process of designing and maintaining an environment for the purpose of efficiently accomplishing selected aims. Managing is an essential activity at all organizational levels. However, the required managerial skills vary with organizational levels. To achieve the basic purpose, managers pursue the following objectives.

1. Efficient use of resources: The factors of production are utilized in a way that effort, energy and waste of time are minimized. The focus is on higher productivity.

2. Customer satisfaction: Customer satisfaction is important for the survival and growth of business.

3. Adequate return on capital: The company must achieve a reasonable rate of return on the amount invested and the risk taken by the owners of business.

4. Satisfied workforce: Satisfied workers are assets to a company. They contribute effectively to the goals of the organization.

5. Improved work conditions: Fair wages for the work, security of employment, and good working conditions for the workforce will result in higher standard for living for the employees.

6. Building supplier relationship: Management should seek to achieve good relations with the suppliers of raw material and capital so as to continue to be in the market.

7. Contribution to national goal: Careful use of scarce resources will lead to improvement of the locality where the company is located.

1.9 MANAGERIAL ROLES

To fulfill the multifarious functional reponsibilities, managers assume multiple roles. A role is an organized set of behaviours. Henry Mintsberg has identified ten roles common to the work of all managers. The ten roles are divided into three groups: *interpersonal, informational* and *decisional.* The informational roles link all managerial work together. The interpersonal roles ensure that information is provided. The decisional roles make significant use of the information. The requirements of these managerial roles can be fulfilled, or these roles can be played, at different times by the same manager and to different degrees depending on the level and function of management. The ten roles are described individually, but they form an integrated whole (Figure 1.2).

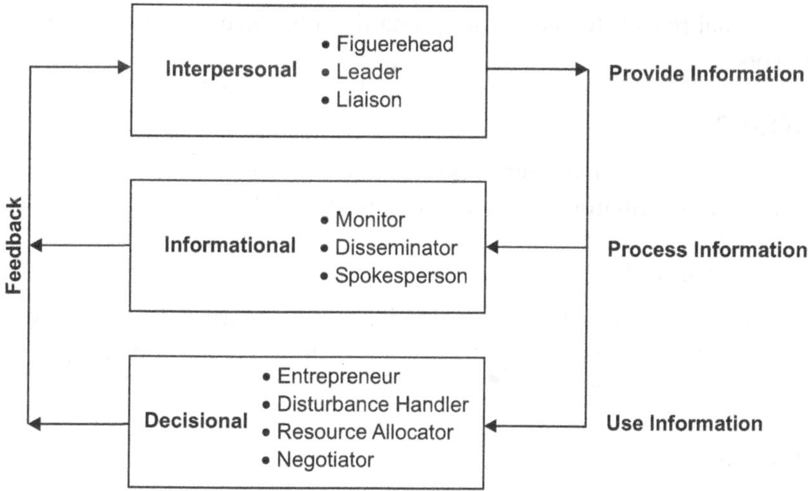

FIGURE 1.2 Managerial Roles.

1.9.1 INTERPERSONAL ROLE

A manager, in order to be effective, has to assume different roles at different points of time as demanded by the call of duty. The three interpersonal roles are primarily concerned with interpersonal relationships.

1.9.1.1 Figurehead Role

In the figurehead role, the manager represents the company legally and socially to those outside of the organization. Every manager has to perform some ceremonial duties such as attending the wedding of employees, entertaining dignitaries and so on. These may or may not have any real substance. The supervisor represents the work group to higher management and higher management to the work group.

1.9.1.2 Liaison Role

In the liaison role, the manager interacts with peers and people outside the organization. The top level manager uses the liaison role to gain favours and information, while the supervisor uses it to maintain the routine flow of work. For example, becoming member of social club and professional bodies.

1.9.1.3 Leader Role

The leader role defines the relationship between the manager and the employee. The direct relationship with the people in the interpersonal roles places the manager in a unique position to get information. He must motivate and direct the activities of his subordinates towards accomplishment of organizational objectives.

1.9.2 INFORMATIONAL ROLE

The three informational roles listed below are primarily concerned with the information aspects of managerial work.

1.9.2.1 Monitor Role

In the role of a monitor, the manager receives and collects information. The information collected, by scanning the environment, facilitates managerial decision-making function.

1.9.2.2 Disseminator Role

In the role of a disseminator, the manager transmits special information into the organization. The top level manager receives and transmits more information from people outside the organization than the supervisor.

1.9.2.3 Spokesperson Role

In the role of a spokesperson, the manager disseminates the organization's information into its environment. Thus, the top level manager is seen as an industry expert, while the supervisor is seen as a unit or departmental expert. The manager informs and satisfies various people who influence organization's goals. Thus, he advises the shareholders about financial performance and assures consumer groups that the organization is meeting the social obligations.

1.9.3 DECISIONAL ROLE

The unique access to information places the manager at the centre of organizational decision-making. There are four decisional roles.

1.9.3.1 Entrepreneur Role

In the entrepreneur role, the manager initiates change. The manager seeks and identifies opportunities to promote the needed change. He is also involved in the development and implementation of change strategy.

1.9.3.2 Disturbance Handler Role

In the disturbance handler role, the manager deals with threats to the organization. This role equips the manager to take corrective actions needed to resolve important, unexpected disturbances. He must seek solutions to various unanticipated problems like strike, accidents and so on.

1.9.3.3 Resource Allocator Role

In the resource allocator role, the manager chooses as to where the organization will expend its efforts. This role deals with allocation of scarce resources to various requests. Specific activities include developing and monitoring budgets, forecasting future resource needs and handling problems in acquiring them.

1.9.3.4 Negotiator Role

In the negotiator role, the manager negotiates on behalf of the organization. The top-level manager makes the decisions about the organization as a whole, while the supervisor makes decisions about his or her particular work unit. For example, a manager might represent the corporation to negotiate a trade union contract, a joint venture and so on.

1.9.4 Supervisor's Role

In the role of a supervisor, the manager performs the managerial roles but with different emphasis than higher managers. Supervisory management is more focused and short-term in outlook. Thus, the figurehead role becomes less significant and the disturbance handler and negotiator roles increase in importance for the supervisor. Since leadership permeates all activities, the leader role is among the most important of all roles at all levels of management.

1.10 SOCIAL RESPONSIBILITY

Social responsibility is the set of obligations an organization aims to fulfill. For example, to protect and enhance the social context in which it functions.

1.10.1 Areas of Social Responsibility

Managers should pay particular attention to their social responsibility that can be grouped under eight headings as follows.

1. *Ecology and Environmental Quality*
   (a) To maintain a pollution-free environment

   (b) To ensure dispersion or spread of industries
   (c) To ensure beautification and proper land use
2. *Consumption*
   (a) To provide true and fair business dealings
   (b) To provide product warranty and service
   (c) To ensure control of harmful products
3. *Community Needs*
   (a) To provide expert service for local problems
   (b) To ensure healthcare facilities and education
4. *Government Relations*
   (a) To encourage restriction on lobbying
   (b) Controls of business through political action
5. *Minorities and Backward Communities*
   (a) To provide training to the unemployed
   (b) To provide equal employment opportunity
   (c) To locate plants and offices in minority areas
   (d) To encourage minority business by purchasing from them
6. *Labour Relations*
   (a) To maintain improved occupational health and safety
   (b) To ensure provision of day-care centres
   (c) To provide options of flexible working hours
7. *Shareholder Relations*
   (a) To take care of shareholders' interests
   (b) To make improved financial disclosures
8. *Corporate Philanthropy*
   (a) To provide financial support for promotion of arts and culture
   (b) To arrange for special scholarships and gifts for the education industry
   (c) To provide financial support for charities

1.10.2 Managerial Ethics

Managerial ethics are the standards of behaviour that guide individual managers in their work. These ethics guide the thinking and decision making with respect to what is good and what is bad. There are three basic areas of concern, namely, the relationship of the firm to the employee, employee to the firm, and the firm to other economic agents.

How the organizations treat their employee is reflected by the following elements:

- Recruitment and termination
- Working conditions
- Wages and incentives
- Individual respect as human beings

How employees treat their organization is reflected by the following parameters:

- Conflicts of interest
- Secrecy maintained by the employee
- Honesty shown in expense accounts

How the organization treats economic agents is reflected by the opinion of the following

- Customers
- Competitors
- Share holders
- Suppliers
- Dealers
- Unions

1.10.3 Personal and Business Ethics

Managers should pay close attention to the values that guide people in their organizations, the corporate culture that embodies those values, and the values held by people outside the organization. It is important to distinguish between personal ethics and business ethics, although there is not always a clear boundary between the two. Personal ethics deals with how we treat others in our day-to-day affairs. Professional (business) ethics often involves choices on an organizational level rather than on a personal level. Many of the problems will seem different because they involve relationship between two corporations, between the company and the government, or between corporations, companies and groups of individuals.

1.11 DEVELOPMENT OF MANAGEMENT THOUGHT

The following factors have contributed to the development of management thought in the present era.

Impact of world wars (1914–1918; 1939–1945): The two world wars demanded the factors of production to work harmoniously and with efficiency. The Great Depression (1930) that followed the First World War and the New-Deal that followed the Second World War emphasized the effective utilization of resources and efficient management to handle group activities.

Growing competition: The severe competition in the market has come from factors such as technological innovations, huge capital investments, economic liberalization and globalization of market, buyers sovereignty and increasing obsolescence.

Complexities of business: The complexities in business have been generated by the increasing size of organizations, high degree of specialization, increase in government regulations and control, trade union activities, and pressure of various conflicting interest groups. This has resulted in the divorce of ownership and management.

1.11.1 Evolution of Management Thought

The roots of management thought can be traced back to early periods as exemplified below.

Management in antiquity: Early Egyptian Papyri (1300 BC) indicates the recognition of the importance of organization and administration in the bureaucratic states of antiquity. Similar records (Confucius parables) are found in China also.

Roman catholic church: The most effective formal organization in the history of Western civilization has been the Roman Catholic Church. The development of the hierarchy of authority, with its scalar and territorial organization, the specialization of activities along functional lines, and the early, intelligent use of the staff device are examples of these techniques.

Military organizations: Some of the most important principles and practices of modern business management may be traced to military organizations. However, they failed to put much theory to use before the past two centuries.

Cameralists: The cameralists were a group of German and Austrian public administrators and intellectuals. They believed that to enhance the position of the state, it was necessary to maximize material wealth.

Industrial revolution (Mid 19th century): Earlier to the Industrial Revolution, commerce was conducted on a limited scale and organizations were relatively small. With the development of the economic discipline and technologies of manufacturing, both commerce and organizations grew rapidly.

1.11.2 Contribution by Management Scientists

Scientific management is that kind of management through which business is conducted according to the standards established on the basis of facts gained through systematic observation, experiment or reasoning. A framework for the study of the evolution of management thought is shown in Figure 1.3. The following are some of the individuals who were instrumental in the development of scientific management.

Charles Babbage (1792–1871): He was a proponent of the specialization of labour. He advocated that managers should conduct time studies to determine how long it should take for each specialized task.

Fredrick Winslow Taylor (1856–1915): The principles of scientific management as enumerated by F.W. Taylor are:

- Develop a science for each job with standardized work implements and efficient methods for all to follow.
- Select the workers scientifically with skills and abilities that match each job, and train them in the most efficient ways so that they may accomplish tasks.

- Ensure cooperation through incentives and provide the work environment that reinforces optimal work results in a scientific manner.
- Divide responsibility for managing and for working, while supporting individuals in work groups for what they do best.

Frank (1868 –1924) & Lillian Gilbreth (1878 –1972): The husband and wife team developed time and motion study, referring to each motion as '*therblig*' (anagram of 'Gilbreth'). Their classification design covered such motions as grasping, moving, and holding, to name a few. Lillian devoted most of her research to the more human side of management. She was the first to introduce rest pauses in an 8-hour work.

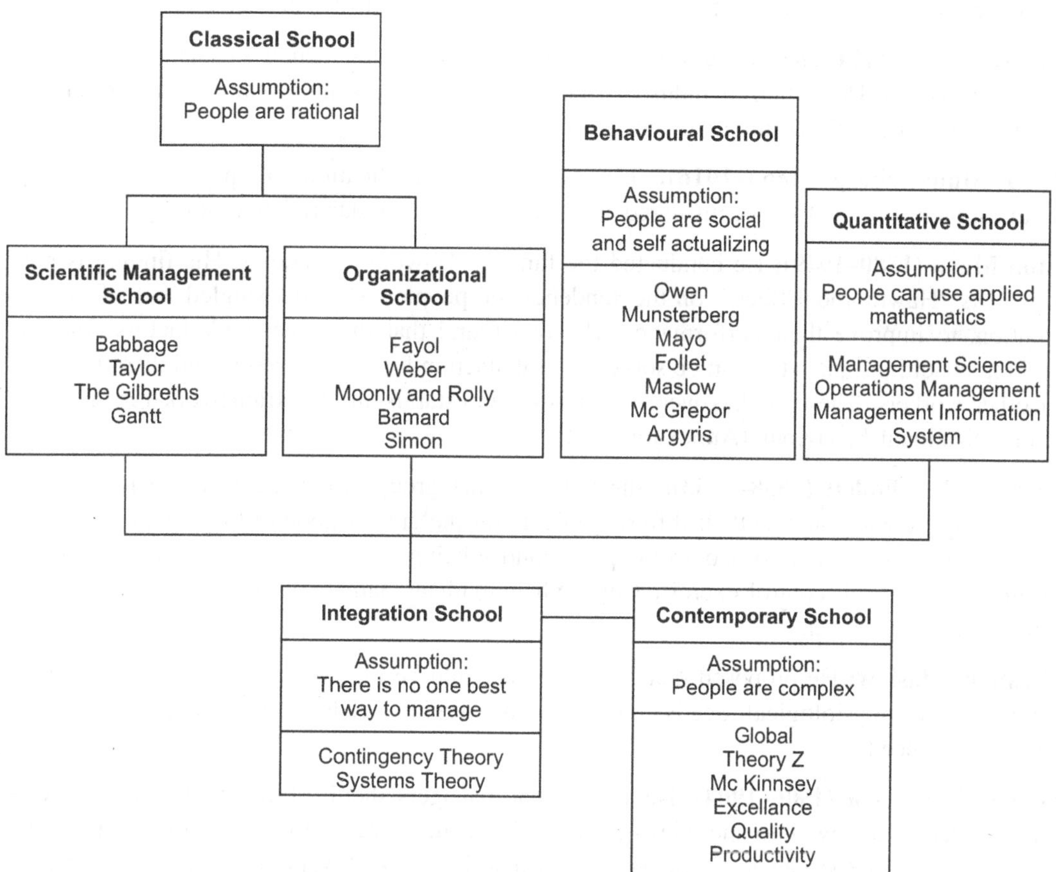

FIGURE 1.3 Framework for the Study of Evolution of Management.

Henry Gantt (1861–1919): He developed the Gantt Chart that provides a graphic representation of the flow of work required to complete a given task (progress of work). The Gantt Chart is the precursor of CPM and PERT. He also developed work quota systems, complete with bonus system for workers who met or exceeded quotas.

Henri Fayol (1841–1925): He was the first to envisage a function process approach to the practice of management. According to him, all managerial tasks could be classified under either of the categories – Technical, Commercial, Financial, Security, Accounting or Administrative. He developed the 14 principles of management (Annexure 1).

Chester Barnard (1886–1961): He believed that organizational success required individuals who were willing to accept the authority of others. He also developed a set of working principles by which organizational communication systems can maintain final authority.

Herbert Simon: He believed that a manager is an administrative man and not an economic man, who makes decisions amid bounded rationality and selects not the maximizing alternative but selects the first alternative that meets some minimal level of achievement.

Robert Owen (1771–1858): He was the first to speak out on behalf of the organization's human resources. He criticized industrialists who spent huge sums of money on production machines but did little to improve the lot of the people.

Hugo Munsterberg (1863–1916): He studied the application of psychology to the organizational setting. He is considered to be the father of industrial psychology.

Elton Mayo (1880–1949): He conducted the famous 'Hawthorne' studies. His finding is now known as 'Hawthorne Effects' or the tendency of people, who are singled out of special attention, to improve their performance. He also found that the same work factors (such as working conditions, pay etc.) can be sources of satisfaction for some workers and dissatisfaction for other workers. These studies were a milestone in establishing the framework for the study of organizational behaviour (Annexure 2).

Mary Parker Follett (1868–1933): She believed that groups were the mechanisms through which people could combine their differing talents for the greater good of the organization. The Follett Behavioural Model of Control depicts control being sponsored by and oriented towards the group, while self-control exercised by both individuals and the group ultimately result in both sharing the power.

Abraham Maslow: He proposed that man's needs could be placed in a 'Hierarchy of Needs', ranging from physiological needs, safety needs, social needs, esteem needs, and self-actualization needs.

Douglas McGregor (1906–1964): He argued that managers should shift their traditional views (Theory X) to a new humane view (Theory Y) concerning employee-work relationship. According to him, the views of Theory X, that man is lazy and wants to avoid work are both pessimistic and counterproductive while the views of Theory Y that man wants to work and work was good is positive, and should become the standard for humanizing the work place.

Peter Drucker: Drucker is a profound thinker and a prolific writer. His contributions include specifying the functions of management in more objective terms, popularizing MBO and emphasizing time management. He has written a number of books outlining and developing his thoughts on management.

1.11.3 CLASSICAL APPROACH TO MANAGEMENT

The bureaucratic model of organization dominates the classical approach. Max Weber (1864–1920) presented an ideal organization structure called a bureaucracy. He believed that rationalization was the most persistent cultural value of Western society. On an organizational level, the bureaucracy represented a completely rational form. All characteristics of a bureaucracy are built around the framework of large scale administrative tasks. Large businesses, industries, churches, hospitals, and military educational government organizations are bureaucratic in nature. Max Weber recognized certain conflicts inherent in bureaucracy. He stressed the functional attributes but never properly considered the significant dysfunctions in his analysis.

The characteristics of an ideal bureaucratic organization are:

(i) Specialization and division of labour: The importance of having the authority and power to carry out assigned duties is recognized. In addition, the bureaucrats must know the precise limits of their sphere of competence so as not to infringe upon that of others.

(ii) Positions arranged in hierarchy: Hierarchy is the natural order of things. Bureaucracy forces control over every member in the structure.

(iii) A system of abstract rules: A rational approach to organization requires a set of formal rules to ensure uniformity and coordination of effort.

(iv) Impersonal relationship: An ideal official should be dominated by "a spirit of normalistic impersonality, without hatred or passion and hence without affection or enthusiasm". Another important aspect of ideal bureaucracy is that employment is based on technical qualifications. The bureaucrat is protected against arbitrary dismissal, and promotions are made on the basis of on seniority and/or achievement.

1.11.4 BUREAUCRATIC DYSFUNCTIONS

The Weber model can serve equally well in analyzing either the functional or the dysfunctional ramifications of classical organization structure. For example, specialization leads to increased productivity and efficiency but also creates conflicts between specialized units to the detriment of the overall goal of the organization. Specialization may impede communication between units. The management team of a highly specialized unit may not fully communicate with units above, below or horizontal to it. The functional attributes of a hierarchy are that it maintains unity of command, coordinates activities and personnel, reinforces authority, and serves as the formal system of communication. In theory, the hierarchy has both a downward and an upward orientation, but in practice, it has often turned out to have only a downward emphasis. Thus, individual initiative and participation are often blocked, upward communication is impeded, and there is no formal recognition of horizontal communication. Personnel who follow only the formal hierarchy may waste a great deal of time and energy.

1.12 APPROACHES TO THE STUDY OF MANAGEMENT

There are different schools of thought regarding the study of management. They are briefly explained.

1. Empirical or case approach: This method analyses management by studying experience, usually through cases. It is based on the belief that, through the study of managers' successes and mistakes in individual cases and their attempts to solve specific problems, students will come to know how to manage effectively in similar situations. Also, cases can provide an artificial laboratory situation for experiencing, explaining, and testing management knowledge. The approach has serious limitations because experience has definite limitations in a subject as complex and broad as management.

2. Interpersonal behaviour approach: This method is based on the idea that managing involves getting things done through people and therefore, its study should be centered on interpersonal relationships. Variously called the human relations, leadership or behavioural science approach, this school concentrates on the human aspect of management. Motivation, psychology, leadership and human interactions form bulk of the theory.

3. Group behaviour approach: This approach is concerned primarily with the behaviour of people in groups rather than behaviour of individuals. Many of the problems in managing stem from group behaviour patterns, attitudes and desires. It is based on sociology and social psychology, rather than on individual psychology. The group behaviour approach varies from the study of small groups with their cultural and behavioural patterns to the study of behavioural composition of large groups.

4. Cooperative social systems approach: This approach is concerned with both the interpersonal and the group behavioural elements. Interaction between personnel leads to systems of cooperation. This approach is broader than the field of management but it overlooks many concepts, principles, and techniques that are important to managers.

5. Socio-technical systems approach: Personal attitudes and group behaviour are influenced by the technical systems and must be made harmonious, otherwise changes are made usually in the technical systems. Wherever technology has a great effect on group behaviour pattern, the orderly analysis and coordination of social and technical systems can have great managerial benefits.

6. Decision theory approach: It is believed that since managing is characterized by decision-making, the central focus of management theory can be on decision–making and the rest of the management thought can be built around it. If goals are clear, adequate information is available, and the organization structure provides a clear understanding of responsibility for decisions, then the actual making of a decision is fairly easy. In fact, managers report that they spend a very small percentage of their time in actually making decisions.

7. Systems approach: A system is essentially a set or assemblage of things interconnected, or interdependent, so as to form a complex unity. There are planning systems, organizational systems and control systems. Within these, there are many subsystems, such as systems of delegation, network planning, and budgeting. Emphasis on systems approach has forced many managers to consider more perceptively the various interacting elements affecting management theory and practice.

8. Mathematical or management science approach: The primacy focus of this approach is mathematical model. Mathematics provides a powerful and logical tool for simplifying and solving complex problems. However, it is difficult to see mathematics as a separate approach to management.

9. Contingency or situational approach: This approach emphasizes the fact that what managers do in practice depends upon a given set of circumstances (a contingency or a situation). Contingency theory takes into account not only given situations but also the influence of given solutions on behavioural patterns of an enterprise. For example, an organization structured along the lines of operating functions, such as finance, engineering, production and marketing might be most suitable for a given situation. It may foster patterns of group loyalty to the functions rather than to company.

According to the contingency approach the manager's task is to identify which technique will in a particular situation, under particular circumstances, and at particular time best contribute to the attainment of management goals. Where workers need to be encouraged to increase productivity, for example, the classical theorist may prescribe a new work-simplification scheme. The behavioural scientist may instead seek to create a psychologically motivating climate and recommend some approach like job enrichment—the combination of tasks that are different in scope and responsibility and allow the worker greater autonomy in making decisions. If the workers are unskilled and training opportunities and resources are limited, work simplification would be the best solution. However, with skilled workers driven by pride in their abilities, a job-enrichment program might be more effective. The contingency approach represents an important turn in modern management theory, because it portrays each set of organizational relationships in its unique circumstances.

10. Managerial roles approach: This approach is to observe what managers actually do and from such observations come to conclusions as to what roles do managers play—whether interpersonal role, informational role or decision role.

11. Mckinsey's 7–S framework: The 7-S's are strategy, structure, system, style, staff, shared values and skills. However, the terms used are not precise and hence this approach is of limited use.

12. Operational approach: This approach draws together concepts, principles, techniques and knowledge from other fields and managerial approaches. The attempt is to develop science and theory with practical application. It distinguishes between managerial and non-managerial knowledge and develops classification system built around the managerial functions of planning, organizing, staffing, leading and controlling.

1.13 BUSINESS ENVIRONMENT

Just as human beings live in, influence and get influenced by an environment, similarly, businesses, also affect and get affected by the environment in which they operate. These environments may be classified in four groups:

(i) Economic
(ii) Social
(iii) Political
(iv) Legal

1.13.1 ECONOMIC ENVIRONMENT

It is sometimes thought that the economic environment is of concern only to businesses whose socially approved mission is the production and distribution of goods and services that people want and can pay for. But it is also of the greatest importance to other types of organized enterprises. A government agency takes resources usually from tax payers and provides services desired by the public. A university takes resource input from students and other contributors and transforms these into educational and research services.

The factors affecting an economic environment are dicussed below.

1.13.1.1 Capital

Almost every kind of organization needs capital—for machinery, buildings, inventories of goods, office equipments, tools of all kinds and cash. Some of these may be produced by the organization itself. Cash resources may also be generated within an organization to buy capital items outside, as when business profits are used to purchase equipment. Organized enterprises are usually dependent for capital requirements on various suppliers whose job is to provide materials and other items of capital that an organization requires for its operation. Thus,, capital is an important economic factor that influences the business.

1.13.1.2 Labour

Another important factor affecting the economic environment is the availability, quality and price of labour. In some societies untrained common labour may be plentiful, while highly trained labour may be in short supply. Engineers may be scarce at one time and plentiful at another, as has occurred in the ups and downs of the defense and space operations. However, supply of labour is itself influenced by the status of economy.

1.13.1.3 Price Levels

The input side of an enterprise is clearly affected by the price level changes. If prices go up fairly rapidly, the turbulence created in the environment on both the input and output sides can be severe. Inflation not only upsets businesses but also has highly disturbing influences on every kind of organization through its effect on the costs of labour, materials, and other items.

1.13.1.4 Government Fiscal and Tax Policies

Another important input to enterprise is the nature of government fiscal and tax policies. Although, these are, strictly speaking, aspects of the political environment, their economic impact on all enterprises is tremendous. Government control on the availability of credit through fiscal policy has considerable impact not only on business but also on most non-business operations. Similarly, Government tax policy affects every segment of society. The way taxes are levied is also important not only to business but also to the people generally. For example, if taxes on business or profits are too high, the incentive to go into business or stay in it tends to drop, and investors will look elsewhere to invest their capital. If heavy taxes are placed in real estates, people may find it too expensive to own a house and may go to cheaper less comfortable living quarters.

1.13.1.5 Customers

Without the customers, the business cannot exist. But to capture customers, a business must try to find out what people want and are willing to buy. To be sure, the expectations and demands of the various public served by organized enterprise are influenced by non-economic as well as economic factors in the environment. The principle ones are people's attitudes, desires and expectations, many of which arise from cultural pattern in the social environment. Another factor in the market is the appearance of substitute products. For example, publishers of magazines saw their market eroded when advertisers shifted to television. Also, people desire for different products with passage of time. The needs of industrial buyers change as their products change, as new processes are developed, and as different equipments and materials come in the market. In the long run, any enterprise has to serve the different and changing needs of customers. To do otherwise is a sure road to enterprise failure.

1.13.1.6 Technology

One of the most pervasive factors in the environment is technology. It is science that provides knowledge, and it is technology that uses it. The term technology refers to the sum total of the knowledge we have, of ways, to do things. It includes inventions, techniques, and vast stores of organized knowledge about everything. But its main influence is on ways of doing things–on how we design, produce, distribute, and sell goods as well as services. The impact of technology is seen in new products, new machines, new tools, new materials, and new services. A few of the benefits of technology are greater productivity, higher living standards, more leisure time, and a greater variety of products.

1.13.2 Social Environment

The social environment is made up of the attitudes, desires, expectations, degrees of intelligence and education, beliefs, and customs of people in a given group or society. The concept of social responsibilities requires organizations to consider the impact of their actions on society. The ethical environment, which could well be included as an element in the social environment, includes sets of generally accepted and practiced standards of personal conduct. These standards may or may not be codified by law, but for any group to which they are meant to apply, they sometimes have virtually the force of law.

1.13.3 Political Environment

The attitudes and actions of political and government leaders and legislators do change with the ebb and flow of social demands and beliefs. In many communities, strong sentiments about air and water pollution control subsided only when plants that were unable to meet new standards had to be shut down. Government affects virtually every enterprise and every aspect of life. It promotes business by stimulating economic expansion and development by providing financial assistance. Finally, government is also the biggest customer of goods and services.

1.13.4 Legal Environment

Every manager is encircled by a web of laws, regulations, and court decisions not only on the national level but also on the state and local levels. Some are designed to protect workers, consumers, and communities. Others are designed to make contracts enforceable and to protect property rights. Many are designed to regulate the behaviour of managers and their subordinates in business and other enterprises. There is relatively little that a manager can do in any organization that is not, in some way, concerned with, and often specifically controlled by, a law or regulation. Managers are expected to know the legal restrictions and requirements applicable to their actions. Thus, it is understandable that managers, especially in business and government, usually have a legal expert close at hand as they make their decisions.

1.14 SOCIAL ATTITUDES, BELIEFS, AND VALUES

Managers of various enterprises have been criticized for not being responsive to the social attitudes, beliefs, and values of particular individuals, groups or societies. But attitudes and values differ among workers and employers, rich and poor people, college student and alumni, accountants and engineers. This variety makes it difficult for managers to design an environment conducive to performance and satisfaction. It is even more difficult to respond to these forces when they are outside the enterprise.

1.14.1 Arguments for Social Involvement of Business

1. Public needs have changed leading to changed expectations. Business received its charter from society and has to respond to the needs of society.
2. The creation of a better social environment benefits both society and business. Society gains through better neighbourhoods and employment opportunities while business

benefits from a better community, since the community is the source of its workforce and the consumer of its products and services.

3. Social involvement discourages additional government regulation and intervention. The result is greater freedom and more flexibility in decision-making for business.
4. Business has a great deal of power and should be accompanied by an equal amount of responsibility.
5. Modern society is an interdependent system and the internal activities of the enterprise have an impact on the external environment.
6. Social involvement may be in the interest of stockholders.
7. Problems can become profits. Items that may once have been considered waste (for example empty soft drink cans) can be profitably used again.
8. Social involvement creates a favourable public image. Thus a firm may attract customers, employees and investors.
9. Business should try to solve the problems that other institutions have not been able to solve. After all, business has a history of coming up with novel ideas.
10. Business has the resources. Specifically, business should use its talented managers and specialists as well as its capital resources to solve some of society's problems.
11. It is better to prevent social problems through business involvement than to cure them. It may be easier to help the hard core and unemployed than to cope with social unrest.

1.14.2 Arguments Against Social Involvement of Business

1. The primary task of business is to maximize profit by focusing strictly on economic activities. Social involvement could reduce economic efficiency.
2. In the final analysis it is the society that pays for the social involvement of business through higher prices. Also, because social involvement would create excessive cost for business, it cannot commit its resources to social action.
3. Social involvement can create a weakened international balance of payments situation as the cost of social programs would have to be added to the price of the product.
4. Business has enough power, and additional social involvement would further increase its power and influence.
5. Business people lack the social skills to deal with the problems of society. Their training and experience with the economic matters and their skills may not be pertinent to social problems.
6. There is a lack of accountability of business to society. Unless accountability can be established, business should not get involved.
7. There is no complete support for involvement in social actions. Consequently, disagreements among groups with different view points will cause friction.

1.15 SOCIAL AUDIT

The social audit has been defined as "a commitment to systematic assessment of and reporting on some meaningful, definable domain of the company's activities that have social impacts".

One may distinguish between two types of audits. One is required by the government and involves, for example, pollution control, product performance requirements, and equal employment standards. The other kind of social audit concerns a great variety of voluntary social programs.

Review Questions

1. What are the objectives of a business? What are the essentials of a good business?
2. Define and distinguish the terms—administration and management.
3. What are the functions of management?
4. Explain the three basic skills required for a manager. What are the levels of management?
5. Explain the characteristics of the modern manager. What are the different roles he is expected to play while discharging his normal duties?
6. Discuss managerial objectives.
7. Differentiate between personal and business ethics.
8. What is the contribution of Henry Fayol to the management process? Are his administrative principles strictly enforceable in the current trends towards participative management style?
9. Describe in detail the systems approach to management.
10. Explain the contingency approach to management.
11. What are the elements of scientific management?
12. What is Hawthorne effect and why is it important to managers?
13. What factors constitute the internal environment of an organization?
14. Discuss the pros and cons of businesses assuming social responsibility.
15. What are the arguments for and against social involvement of business?

Caselets

MANAGING PEOPLE

Krishnan, a graduate from XLRI has joined his father's small business. After a week, his father called him and said, "Krishnan, you are just too nice to people. I know they taught you industrial relations at XLRI, but it just does not work here. When the Hawthorne studies were first reported, everyone in the academic field got excited about them. There is more to managing people than just being nice to them".

Question 1: If you were Krishnan, what would be your reaction to your father's comments?

PROBLEM OF BEING A SUPERVISOR

In Farm Products Limited, there was a supervisor who had risen to his position by way of hard work and sincerity. Before becoming a supervisor, he had been a very active and dynamic unionist. After becoming supervisor, he was forced to drift away from union activities. The union leaders did not like the clerk's promotion to a supervisory post. One day he assigned some work to the peon of the department but the peon refused to do the same. There was an exchange of heated arguments; lot of people gathered around and at a certain point of time, the supervisor, offensively gesticulated towards the peon. The basic issue remained aside and everyone started accusing the supervisor for his offensive gesticulation. The whole department refused to work unless the supervisor apologized for his behaviour and the trade union was also brought into the picture.

Question 1: If you were the personnel manager, how would you resolve the problem?

CHAPTER 2 Planning

Planning is deciding in advance what to do, how to do, when to do and who is to do. Planning bridges the gap from where we are to where we want to go. It makes possible for things to occur which would not otherwise happen (Figure 2.1).

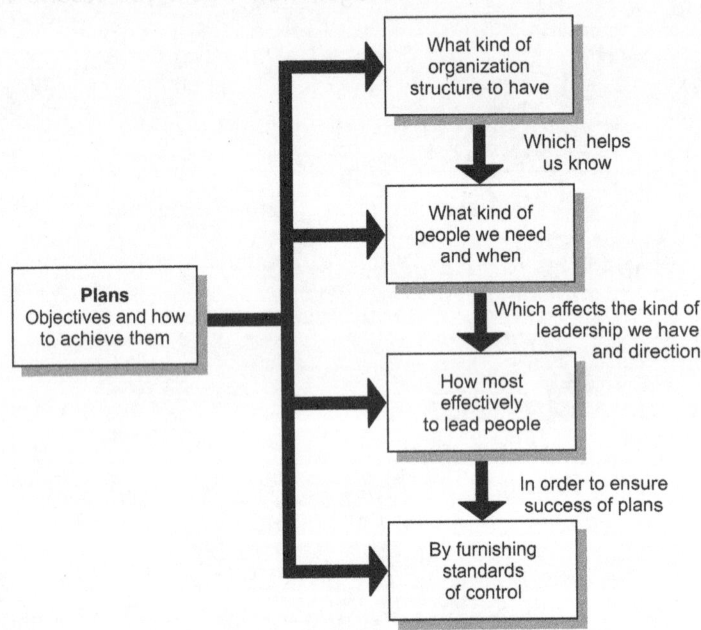

FIGURE 2.1 Planning Process.

2.1 CHARACTERISTICS OF PLANNING

1. Planning is closely associated with the goals of the organization. These goals might be implicit or explicit. However, well-defined goals lead to efficiency in planning.

2. Planning is primarily concerned with the forecasting of future situation in which an organization has to function. Accurate forecasting leads to correct decisions about future course of action.
3. Planning involves the selection of the best among several alternatives for achieving the organizational objectives, as all of them are not equally applicable and suitable to the organization.
4. Planning is comprehensive and is required in every course of action in the organization.
5. Planning is flexible as it is based on future conditions which are always dynamic. As such, an adjustment is needed between the various factors and planning.

2.2 NATURE OF PLANNING

The essential nature of planning can be highlighted in terms of the following four major aspects:

1. Contribution to purpose and objectives: The purpose of every plan and all derivative plans is to facilitate the accomplishment of enterprise purpose and objectives. This principle derives from the nature of organized enterprise, which exists for the accomplishment of group purpose through deliberate cooperation.

2. Primacy of planning: Managerial operations in organizing, staffing, leading and controlling are designed to support the accomplishment of enterprise objectives. Hence, planning logically precedes the execution of all other managerial functions. Planning and control are especially inseparable (Figure 2.2).

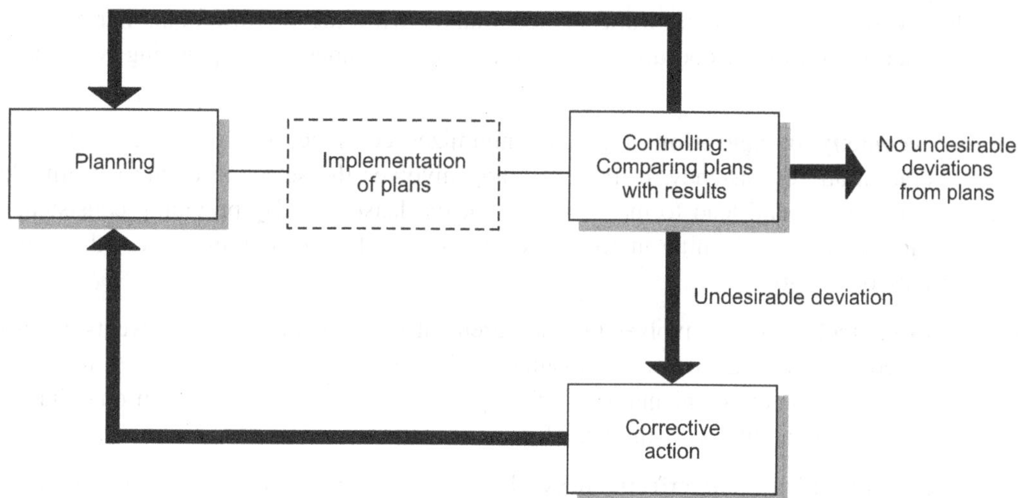

FIGURE 2.2 Relationship between Planning and Controlling.

Unplanned action cannot be controlled, for control involves keeping activities on course by correcting deviations from plans. Plans thus furnish the standards of control.

3. Pervasiveness of planning: Planning is a function of all managers, although the character and breadth of planning will vary with their authority and with the nature of policies and plans outlined by their superiors.

4. Efficiency of plans: The efficiency of a plan is measured by the amount it contributes to purpose and objectives as off-set by the costs and other consequences required to formulate and operate it.

2.3 IMPORTANCE OF PLANNING

For any organization, planning is important in following respects.

1. To off-set uncertainty and change: Future is always full of uncertainties and changes. The organization has to function in these uncertainties and changing conditions. However, some of the uncertainties and changes can be predicted on the basis of forecast. Thus, planning foresees the future and makes provisions for it, thereby, giving an added strength to the organization for continuous growth and steady prosperity.

2. To focus attention on objectives: Planning depends upon the objectives of the organization. All the activities are performed to achieve these objectives. However, planning makes these objectives more concrete and tangible by focusing attention on these. Defining and delineating these objectives help in providing guidelines for the individuals in the organization.

3. To help in coordination: Well conceived overall plans unify interdepartmental activities and consequently restrict the area of freedom in the development of purely departmental plans. Thus, when various departments work in accordance with the overall plan, harmony is achieved. It can be said that if coordination is the essence of management, planning is the base for it.

4. To gain economy in operation: Planning minimizes costs because of the emphasis on efficient operation and consistency. In fact, planning involves the selection of most profitable course of action that would lead to the best result at the least cost. By providing consistency and balance in the efforts, planning introduces continuous and even flow of work without any friction or loss of energy.

5. To help in control: Control involves the measurement of accomplishment of events against plans and the correction of deviations to assume attainment of objectives according to plans. It is exercised in the context of planning which expresses the goals and targets in quantitative forms, which are comparable with the actual achievements.

6. To increase organizational effectiveness: Through planning and control, organizational effectiveness is measured in the context of the stated objectives. If reliable information is not available about future conditions, planning loses its importance. Sometimes, planning may lead to internal inflexibility and procedural rigidities, which may work against the best interest of the organization.

2.4 TYPES OF PLANS

Planning consists of several individual plans or component parts which are bound together in a consistent structured operation. Identifying these components illustrates the breadth of planning. Planning process generally results into several specific plans. Some of these are in the form of *standing plans* while some others are *single-use* plans. Examples of standing plans are objectives, policy, rules, procedures, etc. Budgets, targets, and quotas are the examples of single-use plan. The basic difference between standing and single-use plan lies in their use over a period of time; standard plans are used over a long period of time, while single-use plans are used for only specific periods.

2.4.1 OBJECTIVES

Every organization, being a deliberate and purposive creation, has some objective or set of objectives. In complex organizations, objectives are structured in a hierarchy in which the objectives of each unit contribute to the objectives of the next higher unit. A broad objective states the purpose of the entire organization. The process of setting objectives is directed by management, and is the first step in planning. They serve as reference points for the efforts of the organization and are prerequisites to determine effective policies, procedures, methods, strategies, etc. Well defined objectives make clear to every individual in the organization what they are expected to achieve.

2.4.2 POLICIES

Policies are general statements or understandings, which provide guidance in decision-making by subordinates. A policy might be in the form of an explicit declaration in writing, or, as more often is the case, has to be interpreted from the behaviour of the organization members, particularly people at the top. Policies are the part of a plan in the sense that they also aid in mapping out a course of action.

2.4.3 STRATEGIES

Strategies are plans for bringing the organization from a given position to a desired position in future. It is the pattern of objectives, purposes and major policies and plans for achieving the goals. The purpose of competitive strategy is to encounter the forces of competitors so that competitions are faced properly.

2.4.4 PROCEDURES

A procedure includes how each of its tasks will take place, when it will take place, and by whom it is to be performed. Time factor is important not only to expedite the controlling efforts applied to a procedure but also to help coordinate the operation of various procedures within an organization. Once the procedure is established, this can be used over again, for accomplishing a particular work. Procedures are more exacting and numerous at lower levels as compared to higher levels. This is largely because at lower levels more exact and useful control is required; mostly routine jobs are performed at this level, which require less discretion in decision-making. Procedures often cut across departmental lines. For example, a procedure for executing a sales order prescribed in an organization will involve production, sales, finance, and inventory departments. Thus, procedure will prescribe how a sales order will be executed i.e. what will be the different steps in chronological order for this purpose.

2.4.4.1 Policy and Procedures

A procedure simply provides guidelines to the action by prescribing how stepwise action can be taken. Policy, on the other hand, provides guidance for managerial thinking as well as action. As a result, it does not tell a manager how to do something; it merely channels his decision-making along a particular line by delimiting his span of consideration. Thus, a policy is more flexible as compared to a procedure. The difference between policy and procedure may be understood by an example. An organization may have a policy of granting its employees vacation. For implementing this policy, certain procedure may be followed so that work does not suffer: employees get vacation by applying through certain procedure.

2.4.4.2 Characteristics of a Good Procedure

The following factors should be observed while setting a procedure.

1. Based on facts: A procedure should be based on adequate facts of the particular situation and not guesses or wishes. For each case, due consideration must be given to the objectives, physical facilities, the personnel and the type of work. Thus, a procedure which is good for one organization may not be suitable for other organizations. The procedure should be such that its each step contributes positively to managerial actions.

2. Procedure as a system: Procedures to be effective must be recognized as a system of interrelated activities in a network. The problem of procedures cannot be solved unless their complex systematic structure is analyzed. The designing of a procedure requires the same approach as that of organizing because it must properly integrate the various activities which are affected by a procedure.

3. Well-balanced: Designing a procedure is essentially a matter of maintaining balance between stability and flexibility in the procedure. A procedure should possess stability in that it provides steadfastness of the established course with changes made only when fundamental modifications in the factors affecting the operation of the procedure occur. On the other hand, flexibility in a procedure is required in order to cope with a crisis or emergency, special demands, or adjustment to a temporary condition.

4. Updating procedures: There should be a continuous review of the working of the procedures so that their utility is ascertained. In many cases it happens that a new procedure is added without deleting or modifying the existing ones. Thus, after certain time, the organization has too many procedures without taking full advantages of these. The periodical review may specify the desirability of a procedure and unnecessary ones may be eliminated.

5. Minimum procedures: The basic principle of procedures is that they should be kept to the minimum possible. After all, every procedure costs something to the organization in terms of manager's time, paper handling, delay, and lack of responsiveness to change. Thus in changing environment, more procedures may create more problems.

2.4.5 Rules

A rule is a specific guide for action, established authoritatively, and utilized in order to inform employees of conditions under which designated actions are to be taken or activities are to be performed. A rule provides definite action to be taken or not taken with respect to a situation. The rule does not allow any deviation from stated course of action. For example, if an organization frames a rule 'smoking is prohibited' there is no discretion except to accept it. A procedure can be looked upon as a sequence of rules; a rule may or may not be a part of a procedure, but if somebody violates it, he may be penalized according to a certain set procedure. Thus, rule does not prescribe a time sequence for an action whereas procedure does so. The rules also perform the function of communicating the obligations of the officials in the organization. Usually, rules are given more deliberately than orders, and thus, the statement of obligations they explicate can be taken to be definite.

2.4.6 Methods

A method is a step of a procedure. It can be defined as a prescribed manner for performing a given task with adequate consideration to the objective, facilities available, and total expenditures of time, money, and effort. Thus, a method specifies how a step of a procedure is followed. A method is normally confined to one department and frequently to the efforts of one individual engaged in the specified work. Thus, a method is more limited as compared to a procedure. Analysis of methods shows that greater output is achieved when the task is carefully defined, performed in a definite manner, and with a definite period of time. Various techniques available for methods improvement are time and motion study, work simplification and work standardization.

2.4.7 Projects

A project, or programme, is a type of plan which can be thought of in terms of planned actions integrated into a unit and designed to bring about a stated objective. The project is a scheme for investing resources and such a scheme of investment may be quite large or small. A project means that the activity is definable in terms of specific objectives, it is infrequent and unique, it is complex and interdependent on various tasks accomplishment and is critical to the organization. The overall policy of the organization provides guidelines about project selection and implementation. Whether a project should be decided on the basis of its contribution to the organizational profits or it should be selected on the basis of how it is going to affect organizational image is a matter of policy decision. Like a policy, procedures too affect the project selection and implementation. The organization may provide a procedure manual setting forth in detail, the capital expenditure, budgeting and techniques. Routing a proposal through several persons provides a mechanism for obtaining the view and judgments of others. This also facilitates the coordination of interrelated activities.

2.4.8 BUDGETS

Budgets express organizational and departmental objectives in financial and non-financial quantities. They anticipate operating results over some future period of time and provide a basis for measuring performance as plans are translated into accomplishments. The budgets may be prepared for various groups of activities. Some important budgets are production, purchasing, materials, sales, advertising, personnel, cost, and capital outlay.

2.5 STEPS IN PLANNING

It is not possible to prescribe a certain fixed process of planning for all organizations or for all types of plans. However, the major steps in planning are discussed below and depicted in Figure 2.3.

1. Perception of opportunities: Any organizational activity requires the help of environment, namely, social factors. Thus, before going through actual planning, one must be aware that opportunities exist for its performance. It is a preceding process of actual planning and, it is not strictly a part of the planning process. However, this awareness is very important for subsequent planning process. As such, it is a real starting point of planning.

2. Establishing objectives: The first step in planning process is the determination of organization objectives. These objectives set the pattern for the proposed course of action, and the purpose of the future action is to arrive at these objectives. The organizational objectives must be spelled out in key areas of operations and should be set according to various departments and sections. The objectives should be clearly specified and measurable as far as possible.

3. Establishing planning premises: Premises are the various factors that affect planning. These are political factors, ethical standards, government controls, fiscal policy, price, demand, and availability of various factors of production. The information is collected in respect of these. Their analysis leads to make certain forecasts and the limitations are determined within which proposed course of action is to be undertaken.

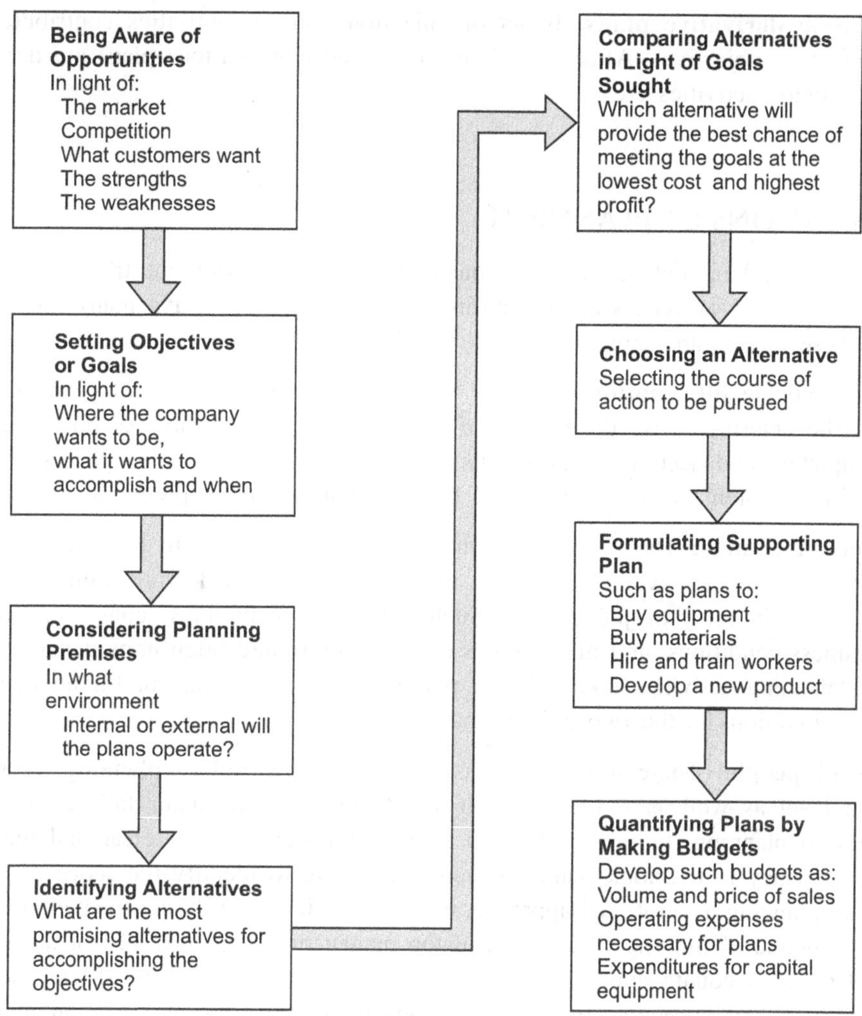

FIGURE 2.3 Steps in Planning.

4. Determining alternative courses of action: The various available alternatives should be examined in the light of planning premises, which helps to shortlist the number of alternatives that can be evaluated for selection.

5. Evaluating alternative courses: The various alternatives are evaluated in the light of objectives and premises. This step presents a difficult problem, because a particular alternative may be best from one point of view but not from the other.

6. Selecting the best course: After evaluating the various alternatives, the most suitable one is selected. Sometimes, the evaluation shows that more than one alternative is equally good. In such a case, a manager chooses a combination of these alternatives and put them in action.

7. Formulating derivative plans: In an organization, various activities contribute to the achievement of its objectives. After formulating the basic plan, various plans are derived for departments, units, activities etc.

2.6 LIMITATIONS OF PLANNING

Planning, as a fundamental function of management, is essential but there are practical limitations to its use. Awareness of the limiting factors help in removing many difficulties in planning. These factors are explained as follows.

1. Lack of accurate information: Planning is concerned with future activity and hence, its quality will be determined by the quality of forecast of future events. As no manager can predict completely and accurately the events of future, the planning may pose problems in operation. This problem is further increased by inaccurate planning premises.

2. Problems of change: The problem of change is often complex in long-range planning. Present conditions tend to weigh heavily in planning and overshadowing future needs, may sometimes result in error of judgements. Such factors as technology, consumer tastes and desires, business conditions, and many others change rapidly and often unpredictably. In such conditions, planning activities taken in one period may not be relevant for another period because the conditions in the two periods may be quite different.

3. Failure of people: There are many reasons why people fail in planning, both at the formulation level as well as implementation level. Some of the major failures are lack of commitment to planning, failure to develop sound strategies, lack of clear and meaningful objectives, tendency to overlook planning premises, failure to identify the scope of the plan, failure to see planning as a rational approach, excessive reliance on the past experience, failure to use the principle of limiting factor, lack of top management support, lack of delegation of authority, lack of adequate control techniques, and resistance to change. These factors are responsible for either inadequate planning or wrong planning in the organizations concerned.

4. Internal inflexibilities: The first internal inflexibility is in the form of human psychology as most of the people have regard for the present rather than for future. Thus, resistance to change is a basic factor which works against planning because planning often depends on the changes. The second type of internal inflexibility emerges because of organizational policies and procedures. Once these are established, they are difficult to change. Such problems are more common in bureaucratic organizations where rules and procedures are matters of prime concern. The third type of internal inflexibility comes because of long-term capital investment. Long-term planning is not a process of making future decisions, but a means of reflecting the future in today's decisions. If the organization has made a long-term investment, it is committed by that and future actions have to be taken in the light of the investment. Thus, managerial planning is limited to that extent.

5. External inflexibilities: Managers are confronted with many external inflexibilities and they do not have control over these. These factors may be social, technological, legal, labour union, geographical, and economic. The managers have to formulate their plans keeping in view the demand of these factors. Thus, their scope of action is limited making planning ineffective in many cases.

6. Rigidity in planning: Planning stifles employee initiative and forces managers into rigid or strait-jacket mode of work execution. In fact, rigidity may make managerial work more difficult than it need be. This may cause delay in work performance, and reduce employee initiative and adaptability with changing environment. Though this factor of rigidity is a limiting factor, it is really difficult to operate without planning in large organizations.

7. Time and cost factors: Time is a limiting factor for every manager in the organization, and if they are busy in preparing elaborate reports and instructions beyond certain level, they are risking their effectiveness. Excessive time spent on securing information and trying to fit all of it into a compact plan is dysfunctional in the organization. Costs increase if planning becomes more detailed, because more information is gathered. Such costs can better be applied to the actual performance of the work. Thus, planning cannot be undertaken beyond a certain limit, but it must justify its costs.

2.7 PLANNING PREMISES

Planning premises constitute the framework within which planning is done. They are also defined as the anticipated environment in which plans are expected to operate. They include assumptions or forecast of the future and known conditions that will affect the operation of plans.

2.7.1 IMPORTANCE OF FORECASTING

Forecasting plays an important part in effective planning. A systematic attempt to probe the future by inference from known facts helps integrate all planning so that unified overall plans can be developed into which divisional and departmental plans can be meshed. Forecasting offers the following advantages.

1. It helps in effective planning by providing scientific and reliable basis for anticipating future operations such as sales, production and so on.
2. It aims at reducing the area of uncertainty that surrounds management decision-making, the respective costs, profits etc.
3. Making and reviewing of forecast on a continuous basis will compel the managers to think ahead and to search for the best possible decision.
4. It is necessary for efficient managerial control as it can disclose the areas where control is lacking.

2.7.2 EFFECTIVE PREMISING

Effective premising will minimize the difficulty in identifying the factors in future environment that will affect the manager's plans. It is a process dealing with:

- selection of the premises which bear materially on the programmes.
- development of alternative premises for contingency planning.
- verification of the consistency of premises.
- communication of the premises.

2.7.3 FORECASTING METHODS

Qualitative techniques tend to apply to the long-term time scale and to cover the broad identification of future needs as a basis for selecting the best options open to the company. Quantitative techniques tend to be used as a means of quantifying future demand. Some of the common forecasting techniques are listed below. The list is only illustrative.

2.7.3.1 Qualitative Techniques

Qualitative technique comprises intuitive methods, opinion polls, brainstorming, scenario writing, trend exploration, delphi method, morphological techniques, and contextual mapping.

2.7.3.2 Quantitative Techniques

Quantitative technique comprises causal techniques, regression models, econometric models, input-output analysis, time series, curve fitting, and exponential smoothing.

2.8 CORPORATE PLANNING

Corporate planning is a process of determining the major objectives of an organization and the policies and strategies that will govern the acquisition and use of resources to achieve those objectives. Corporate planning is essentially based on strategic planning and at the same time takes care of operational planning and project planning. Corporate planning is concerned with changes in the overall shape of an organization and these changes usually take many years to be fruitful, which implies that corporate plans are necessarily long-range. However, corporate planning and long-range plans can be prepared for anything like building a submarine or modernizing the manufacturing plant of a company but they can not be called corporate plans.

2.8.1 CHARACTERISTICS

1. Corporate plan deals with formulation of objectives, plans, policies and strategies and making decisions on vital matters affecting the survival of the organization.
2. It deals with the future impact of current decisions.

3. It involves systematic identification of opportunities and threats arising out of the changing environment and matching them with strengths and weaknesses of the organization.
4. It provides an integrated framework within which the functional and departmental plans are formulated.

2.8.2 Corporate Objectives

The objectives of corporate planning are as follows:

1. Allocation of scarce resources like capital, materials and technological know-how among product/market alternatives.
2. Preparing the company to adapt to environmental opportunities and threats.
3. Coordinating strategic activities so as to reflect the firms own internal strengths and weaknesses in order to achieve efficient operation.
4. Preparing the company for Adaptation and integration which are complementary to each other. Adaptation implies a focus on where the firm is to go, where as integration focuses on how to get there in the most efficient manner.
5. To learn from the outcomes of past strategic decision so as to make better decisions in future. It also serves as a self-improvement system by laying down a basis for monitoring progress towards goals.

2.8.3 Importance of Corporate Planning

1. Corporate planning encourages the habit of forward thinking on the part of manager.
2. It helps in attaining overall coordination among the various levels of management.
3. It creates a greater awareness of the business environment and a sense of making a critical review of the business operations.
4. It enables the organization to anticipate technological changes and prepare for the same.
5. It can lead to improvement in overall performance of the organization.

2.8.4 Process of Corporate Planning

The process of corporate planning comprises the following steps:

1. Scanning the environment: This involves scanning of environmental factors such as economic, social, cultural, political, legal and technical. It is necessary to know how environmental changes affect the functioning of the enterprise and determine the threats and opportunities.

2. Making corporate appraisals: This helps to identify the strength and weaknesses of the enterprise in terms of the sources, products, profitability etc.

3. Determining of mission and objectives: It starts with spelling out the business mission or the purpose that might be pursued in future. A clear statement of mission would help to identify the function, character and the philosophy of the organization.

4. Making strategies: This involves choosing an appropriate strategy to attain the specified mission and objectives. This is done after evaluating alternative strategic approaches in terms of their consistency with objective, resource position, efficiency and risks.

5. Developing of action plans: After strategy making, corporate planning should be broken into policies, programmes, budgets etc. For effective implementation, the strategic plans should be broken into different components that are called operational or tactical plans. It involves, (a) identification of jobs to be accomplished, (b) determining the sequence of jobs and activities, (c) drawing a schedule of operations, and (d) laying down procedures and method of work.

6. Implementing the strategy: For implementation, corporate (or master) strategy should be translated into medium-range functional and short-range operational plans. An effective implementation strategy requires designing of suitable structure of the organization, effective management system and proper organizational culture to ensure employee motivation.

2.8.5 How Strategic and Operational Plans Differ

Strategic and operational plans differ in terms of the following:

1. Time horizon: Strategic plans take into consideration several years or even decades. For operational plans, a year is often the relevant time period.

2. Scope: Strategic plans affect a wide range of organizational activities, whereas operational plans have a narrow and more limited scope. The number of relationships involved is the key difference.

3. Degree of detail: Strategic goals are stated in terms that look simplistic and generic. On the other hand, operational plans, as derivatives of strategic plans are stated in relatively finer detail.

2.8.6 Strategies at Different Levels

1. Corporate strategy: At the corporate level, strategic decisions relate to organization-wide policies as in the case of multi-divisional companies having wide ranging business operations. Major policy decisions involving acquisition, diversification and structural re-designing belong to the category of corporate strategy.

2. Business level strategy: It is the strategy to achieve the specific objectives of the strategic business unit (SBU) so as to help achieve the overall corporate objectives. A SBU is an operating division of a firm, which serves a distinct product/market segment, or a well defined set of customers or a geographic area. The SBU is given the authority to make its own strategic decisions within corporate guidelines as long as it meets the corporate objectives. The scope of business strategy is limited as compared to corporate strategy. For example, in the case of multiproduct corporation, decision taken at the top-level management regarding diversification or acquisition of other companies are corporate decisions, but decisions taken at plants or divisional levels regarding introduction of a product or development of a new market are business decisions. In short, corporate strategy defines the business in which the company will compete and deploy its resources, whereas a business strategy determines how a company will compete in a given business and position itself among competitors.

3. Functional level strategy: The ultimate success of the SBU level strategy will depend, among other things, on the effectiveness with which it is translated into functional areas like marketing, finance, production, personnel research and development etc. For example, if the SBU level objectives are to be achieved by introducing a new product, the R&D, production, finance and marketing departments will have to be geared to develop functional level strategies. Thus, it is obvious that functional level strategies are guided by the SBU level strategy.

2.9 STRATEGIC PLANNING

Strategic planning is the process of deciding on the objectives of the organization, the changes therein, and the resources used to attain these and on the policies that will govern the acquisition, use and deployment of the resources.

2.9.1 Features of Strategic Planning

1. Strategic planning emphasizes the basic mission and goal of the organization.
2. It determines the basic policy and programmes of the organization. It provides a frame-work for operational planning on day-to-day decision-making.
3. The time frame is larger than other types of planning.
4. It provides for coherence in organization policy and decision on activity overtime.
5. It deals with uncertain environment by forecasting opportunities and threats therein.
6. It is comprehensive and is a unified plan for the deployment of scarce resources.

2.9.2 Limitations of Strategic Planning

1. Strategic planning requires a considerable investment in time, money and human resources. Sometimes, organizations defer important decisions because of shortage of resources. This might lead to losing important business opportunity.
2. Small organization cannot afford the cost of carrying out formal strategic planning.
3. Strategic planning requires trained persons to make use of opportunities. If the organization is lacking in internal personnel capabilities strategic planning will not be effective. If outside experts are employed, strategic planning would prove very costly.
4. Strategic planning may restrict the organization to comparatively risk-free options. This will defeat the purpose of strategic planning.

2.10 VISION, MISSION AND PURPOSE

Vision is a vividly descriptive image of what a company wants to be or wants to be known for. To the leader, vision is a personal perspective on a condition that he thinks is the best for his followers. To his followers, vision is an articulation of where their leader is taking them. Vision is an inspired picture of a future that can be created, offering clarity amidst confusion, hope amidst despair and unity of purpose amidst diversity. It is true that a few management principles have been as misused as vision has been in post-liberalization India. Viewed by some companies as a panacea, and by others as a token gesture, vision became popular as a statement of intention. An organization vision offers a compelling method for forging employees into an empowered, highly motivated team. It is the corner-stone of the strategic architecture of a truly successful organization. The best vision portrays the future, but does not necessarily dictate how to get there.

2.10.1 Conceiving Vision

The most effective vision should link the company's core values to a perception of how you want your future to look like. For, without them, the vision will not be rooted in the reality of the company but simply be a product of imagination of its creators, putting it out of reach, both in operational and strategic terms. The next step is to identify the core purpose of the organization. Purpose must be built so as to ensure that it never contravenes the spirit of your vision so as to ensure that it never contravenes the spirit of your purpose. Not to be confused with your current product or target segments, your core purpose should be aimed at adding value to your customer's through whatever product or service is relevant. Once this preparatory phase is completed the actual process of vision-building begins. There is no alternative to involving every one in the vision-building process. Participation, however, should come in the form of unstructured or structured inputs rather than direct involvement in the formulation of the final vision statement. Only a vision that has been built with the participation of people will incorporate the organizational culture and values, which are inextricably linked to people. With that condition laid down, different companies arrive at their visions through different routes.

2.10.2 Shared Vision

No vision is just like an island. Only by linking it to an entire strategic chain can it be made useful for the company. In other words, the vision must become the starting point of the process that culminates in setting specific quantifiable objectives for every division or business unit, every section, every department, every team, and every employee. From the vision, therefore, must flow the mission, or strategic planning. Fundamentally, if vision answers the question of what the company wants to be, or do, the mission must translate that into particular businesses, and the goals into quantifiable targets through which the vision will be reached. While the vision is meant to endure, company could find themselves compelled to exit their old businesses and enter into new ones, so that they may keep pace with changes in technology and customer preferences, in order to fulfill their vision. But, only by specifying the business activities can a company proceed from the vision and mission to the next step, namely, strategizing. Vision is not to be confused with strategy because it does not show the road map to the destination that it sketches out. For these goals to be realized, the vision must be injected into the views of the organization, being shared, owned, and lived by every single person in the company. That is why visionary CEOs take as much interest in communicating the vision down the length and breadth of their companies as in creating it. The media for this communication are official newsletters, speeches, and magazines and critically, the day-to-day decisions-making. Visionary companies accomplish this task by getting the first set of orders of the vision to be preached around the company. Companies that really believe in their vision, lose no opportunity to broadcast it to their people, through devices ranging from prominently placed board in the reception foyers to windshield stickers. However, it is the second process i.e. letting the decision to speak, that really embeds the vision in everyone's action. The process of creating the vision must be followed by its institutionalization. Only then will the vision deliver what it promises.

2.10.3 Why Need a Vision

Vision is crucial for adding meaning to the activities of the people. Without vision people will fall into the activity trap. In times of change, a vision becomes even more vital. Vision is the hallmark of an enlightened forward–looking organization. Enlightened people in the organization need a passion that they can follow with missionary zeal. Difficult decisions taken with the vision as their prime motive such as exiting businesses, selling plants, or cutting costs will be backed by the entire team.

2.10.4 What Can Go wrong with Vision

In its very conception often lie the pitfalls of vision. Convinced of its value as a compass that will show the way unwaveringly, companies run the risk of confusing it for a magic wand instead of wielding it as a strategic tool that it really is. Quicksand also surrounds the company that becomes the slave of its vision. Besides, the company's vision can become the extension of CEO's ego, at which point it can be used to justify the bad acquisition and diversification. Having once worked out what they want to be, some companies overcommit themselves to their vision, ignoring the changes around them.

Review Questions

1. Discuss why planning is an important function of management. How does planning contribute towards effective operations management?
2. Explain some of the reasons for planning. Are there 'good plans' and 'bad plans'. Describe some of the characteristics of good plans?
3. What are the problems encountered in the process of planning? Which of these problems generally contribute heavily towards failure of some plans?
4. Discuss the nature and importance of planning.
5. What are the characteristics of a good procedures and objectives?
6. Explain in detail as to what you mean by policies, rules and procedures?
7. What is premising?
8. Write a brief note on the objectives and importance of corporate planning.
9. Discuss the process of corporate planning.
10. Differentiate strategic planning from other types of planning. How does contingency planning affect each type of plans?

Caselets

PLANNING IN ABC COMPUTERS

ABC Computers was founded in 1975 and it enjoyed a fast early growth. However, success did not last long because of the introduction of personal computer and stiff competition in the market. Several executives were of the opinion that the company needed a more professional approach. The pros and cons were weighed and a CEO with a proven track record from an MNC was appointed to give ABC Computers the much needed direction.

The new CEO employed cost-cutting measures to improve the company's profitability. He also resorted to other measures like minimizing duplicaton of efforts, improving R&D, and promoting a healthy interpersonal relationship amongst departments. These and other steps taken resulted in a tremendous increase in the company's earnings.

Question 1. Explain the relationship between planning and controlling.

Question 2. What other types of plans can be used for controlling ABC Computers?

CHAPTER 3

Organizing

Organizing refers to the formal grouping of people and activities to facilitate achievement of the firm's objectives. Figure 3.1 indicates the relationship of objectives and the organizational hierarchy.

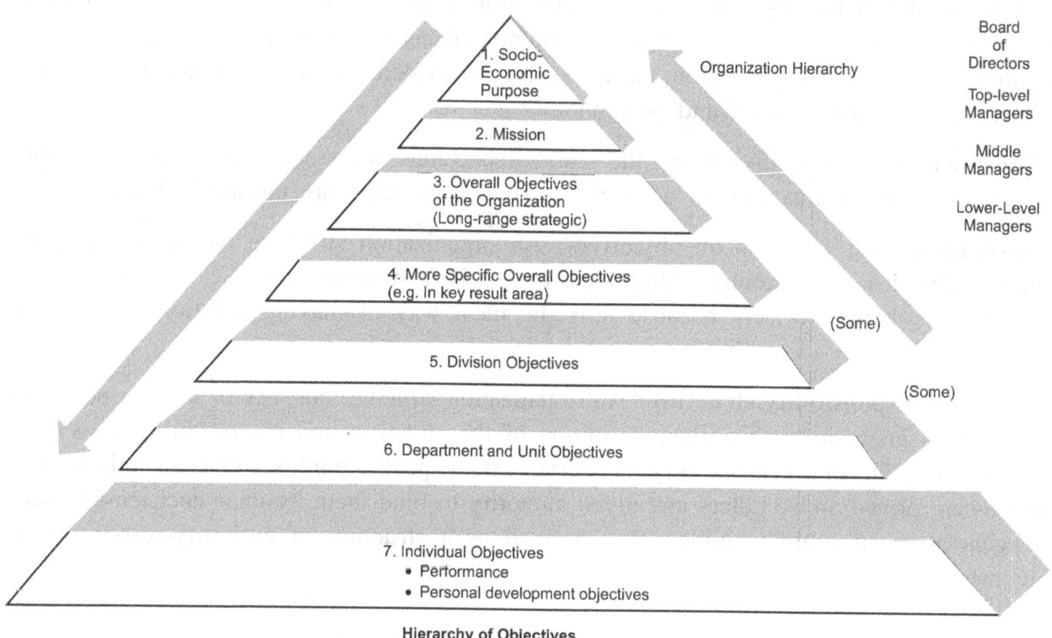

FIGURE 3.1 Relationship of Objectives and Organizational Levels.

3.1 ORGANIZATION THEORY

Organization theory is the study of structure, functioning and performance of organizations and the behaviour of groups and individuals within them. Organization theory is defined as a set of interrelated constructs, definitions and propositions that present a systematic view of behaviour of individuals, groups and subgroups interacting in some relatively patterned sequence of activity, the interest of which is goal-directed.

3.1.1 Approaches

There are two approaches to understanding organization. In the first sense, organization is understood as a dynamic process and a managerial activity which is necessary for bringing people together and unifying them in the pursuit of common objectives. This may well be called the process of organizing. When used in the other sense, organization refers to the structure of relationships among positions and jobs through which goals are sought to be attained. Some view it as a social system, and to others, an organization is a system with inputs and processes through which the inputs are converted into outputs.

3.1.2 Common Features

There are some common features for all organization structures.

1. Division of labour: Organization structure comes into existence when the total work considered necessary for the realization of common objectives is divided into activities and functions. In a business organization, the work may be divided, say, according to functions like production, marketing, finance and personnel.

2. Coordination: Having divided up the work, it becomes necessary to link up or integrate the various divisions, functions or activities so that all of them are unified in harmony.

3. **Accomplishment of goals or objectives:** An organization structure has no meaning or purpose unless it is built around certain clear-cut goals or objectives. In fact, an organization structure is built up precisely because it is the ideal way of making a rational pursuit of objectives.

4. Authority-responsibility structure: An organization structure consists of various positions arranged in a hierarchy with a clear definition of the authority and responsibility associated with each of these. An organization cannot serve certain specific purposes or goals unless some positions are placed above others and given authority to bind them by their decisions. Hence, an organization structure is quite often defined as a structure of authority-responsibility relationships.

3.1.3 Process of Organizing

The process of organizing consists of the following steps, as illustrated in Figure 3.2.

1. Determination of objectives: Organizations are built around objectives. For example, a business firm must decide whether it will publish books, manufacture cloth, sell machinery or

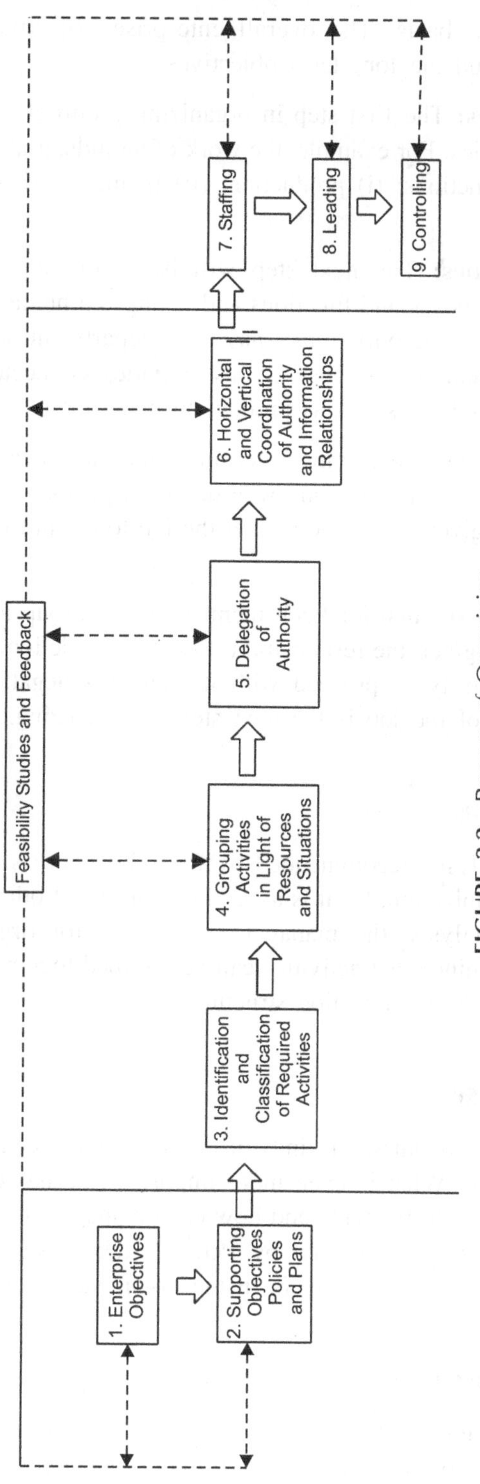

FIGURE 3.2 Process of Organizing.

run vehicles on commercial basis. The overall enterprise objectives will depend on the immediate, the short-term and the long-term objectives.

2. Enumeration of activities: The first step in organizing group effort is the division of the total job into essential activities. For example, the work of an industrial concern may be divided into the following major functions: (i) production, (ii) financing, (iii) purchasing, (iv) sales, and (v) personnel.

3. Classification of activities: The next step will be to classify activities according to similarities, and common purposes and functions and taking the human and material resources into account. For each class of activity, there may be a department and for each sub-class, a section of the department, and so on. The various activities connected with production, for example, may be grouped and classified as production department activities.

4. Fitting individuals to functions: Having determined the various activities of the job to be done, the next step will be to fix suitable and well qualified persons into these activities. Each person in the group will be given a specific part of the job to do and will be made responsible for it.

5. **Assignment of authority for action:** Each member of the group available for a particular part of the job, having been given the responsibility for its completion, will be able to proceed only when he has the authority to proceed with it. Hence, delegation of authority to help complete the assigned part of the job is the next step in organizing.

3.1.4 Activity Analysis

The purpose of activity analysis, recommended by Peter Drucker, is to discover the primary activity of the proposed organization, for it is around this only that other activities will be built. In making this type of analysis, the manager responsible for organization building and development will also determine what activities can be grouped together and how each activity needs to be emphasized in the organization structure.

3.1.5 Decision Analysis

At this stage the manager finds out what kinds of decisions will need to be made to carry on the work of the organization. What is even more important, he has to see where or at what level these decisions will have to be made and how each manager should be involved in them. This type of analysis, again recommended by Peter Drucker, is particularly important for deciding upon the number of levels or layers in the organization structure.

3.1.6 Formal and Informal Organization

The formal organization refers to the structure of jobs and positions with clearly defined functions and relationship as prescribed by the top management and bound by rules, systems and procedures. Informal organization refers to the relationships between people in an organization based not on procedures and regulations but on personal attitudes, whims, prejudices, likes, dislikes, etc. Since the informal organization has its basis in the emotions and attitudes of people, management cannot be effective and expeditious unless it recognizes and makes use of the informal organization for realizing organizational objectives.

3.1.7 Importance of Organization

The importance of a sound organization structure can hardly be overemphasized. An organization is not merely a chart or a lifeless structure. It comprises people and is the agency through which management performs the important functions of direction, coordination and control. In this sense, it is the foundation of management as well as its chief tool. It facilitates administration, makes growth and diversification possible, provides for the optimum use of technological improvements, and stimulates creative thinking.

3.2 PRINCIPLES OF ORGANIZING

The success or failure of an organization would be revealed by its results. If it is able to achieve the desired objects, it is sound and efficient; if it fails to do so, there is something wrong somewhere in the organizational structure. However, the success of a business organization can perhaps be ensured better if the following basic principles are observed.

1. Unity of objective: Every part of the organization and the organization as a whole should be geared to the basic objective determined for the enterprise.

2. Efficiency: The organization should be able to attain the predetermined goals and objectives at the minimum cost. If it does so, it will satisfy the test of efficiency. From the point of view of an individual, a good organization should provide the maximum work satisfaction. Similarly, from the social point of view, an organization will be efficient when it contributes the maximum towards the welfare of the society.

3. Span of management: It is widely recognized that a manager can directly supervise only a limited number of executives. It is necessary to have a proper number of executives, answerable to the top manager. Most of the authorities prescribe a maximum of six for this (Figure 3.3).

4. Division of work: A good organization should consist of departments established to reflect the most efficient breakdown of enterprise activities. Proper departmentalization is an important principle of sound organization.

5. Functional definition: The duties and the authority relationships in a good organization must be properly and clearly defined, so that there is no confusion or overlapping.

6. Scalar Principle (Chain of command): The chain of command or the line of authority must be clearly defined for building sound organization. Every subordinate must know who is superior and to whom policy matters beyond his own authority must be referred for decision.

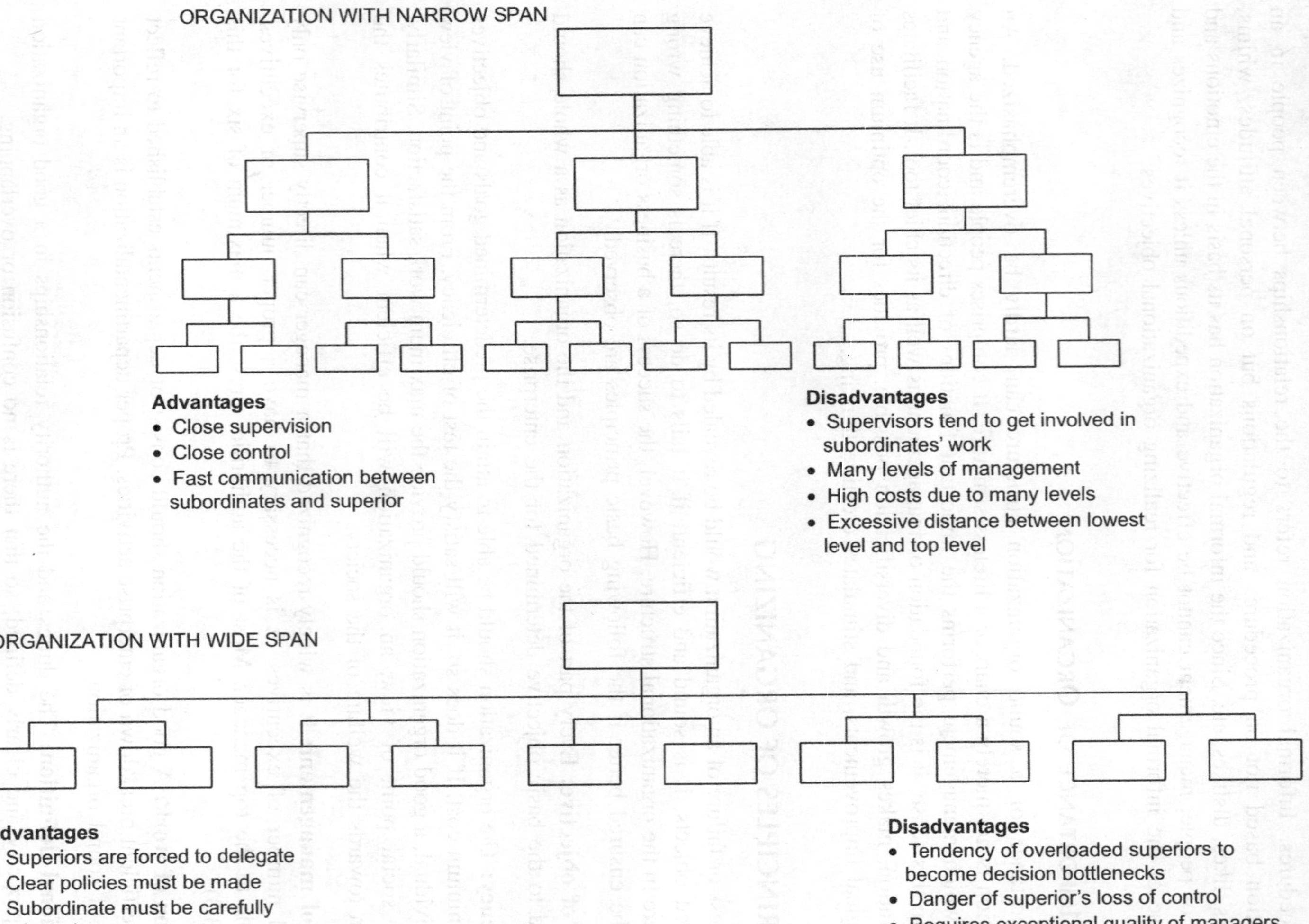

FIGURE 3.3 Span of Management.

7. Exception principle: A good organization is so arranged that only exceptionally complex problems are referred to the higher levels of management and the routine matters are dealt with by executives at lower levels. This is called exception principle.

8. Unity of command: In a good organization, each subordinate should have one superior whose command he has to obey. This will avoid conflict of commands and help in fixing responsibility.

9. Unity of direction: There must be only one plan for a group of activities directed towards the same end. If each person in a department begins to work under a different plan or program of action, nothing but confusion will follow.

10. Responsibility: In a good organization, the superior is responsible for the activities of his subordinates and the subordinates must be held responsible to their superiors for the performance of the tasks assigned to them.

11. Authority and responsibility: The authority and responsibility must be coexisting in an organization. If it is not so, the subordinates cannot discharge their responsibility for want of necessary power to proceed with the task assigned.

12. Balance: Some matters may be left to be disposed of by the subordinates at the lower or the lowest level while some other (say, control over capital expenditure) must be centralized and a balance between centralization and decentralization should thus be achieved.

13. Flexibility: The organization must avoid complicated procedures, red-tapism and excessive complication of control so that it can adapt itself easily and economically to business and technical changes.

14. Continuity: The organization must be so arranged as to provide for the continuity of the enterprise. For this, there must be proper provision for executive development or training.

15. Facilitation of leadership: The organization structure should be so devised that there is enough opportunity for the management to give effective lead to the enterprise.

3.3 TYPES OF ORGANIZATIONS

The problem in organizing is to select and combine the efforts of personnel so as to produce the desired result. The following are the broad patterns of organizing the personnel.

- Military or Line system
- Functional system
- Line and staff system
- Matrix system
- Hybrid design

3.3.1 MILITARY OR LINE ORGANIZATION

Under this system (Figure 3.4), authority flows from the person at the top to the lowest person, vertically. In pure organization, the activities at any one level are the same, with each person performing the same type of work, and the divisions exist solely for control and direction. In the departmental line organization, the general manager may be put in charge of the whole organization. The business unit may be divided into departments headed by departmental heads. A departmental head may receive orders from the general manager and pass them on to his immediate subordinates. The subordinates may similarly communicate the order to the workers. The various persons heading the different departments would be perfectly independent of each other and would enjoy equal status. In an industrial concern, for instance, a foreman neither receives any instructions from, nor issues commands to, another foreman. He has to perform all the functions connected with production, including planning of work, ensuring proper condition of the equipments, training of workers and instructing them in their work. Further promotion of the workers would depend upon the reports made about them by the foreman concerned. The workers do not have the authority to approach higher officers except through their immediate boss. In case, the manager of one department wishes to issue guidance or directions to a subordinate in another department, he will go up the line and convey the message to the top manager, who will then pass it down the line in the other department.

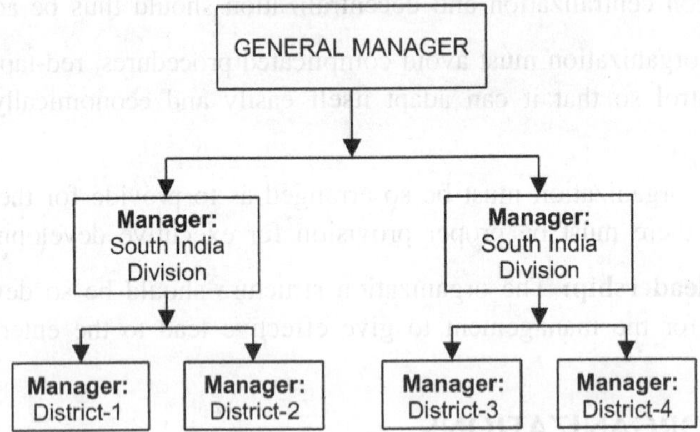

FIGURE 3.4 Military or Line Type of Organization.

3.3.1.1 Merits

1. Simplicity: It is the easiest to establish and simplest to explain to the employees.

2. Unified control: It makes for unity of control thus conforming to the scalar principle of organization.

3. Strong discipline: It ensures excellent discipline. This is because of unified control: The subordinates have no doubt regarding the person from whom they receive instructions. They are also aware of the necessity of satisfying the superior in their own interests.

4. Fixed responsibility: Everybody in this type of organization knows to whom he is responsible, and who are responsible to him.

5. Prompt decision: The unification of authority and responsibility ensures quick and prompt decisions.

6. Flexibility: Since each executive has sole responsibility of his position and sphere of work, he can easily adjust the organization to changes in the business situation.

3.3.1.2 Demerits

1. Overloading: The chief disadvantage of the system is that too much is expected of the person in authority. Since all work is done according to the wishes of one person alone, the efficiency of the whole department will come to depend upon the qualitites of management displayed by the head of that department.

2. Lack of specialization: It suffers from lack of specialized skill of experts. For example, it is not possible for a foreman alone to give full guidance on all matters relating to use of materials, use of machines, methods, personnel practice etc.

3. Inadequacy of communication: There is usually no communication from the lower ranks. Moreover, their suggestions cannot be utilized because generally the higher officers look down upon the views of their subordinates.

4. Scope for favouritism: If an officer is partial he may judge people according to his own notions, and therefore, it is possible that efficient people may be left behind and inefficient people may get higher and better posts.

5. Suitability: The system can be followed successfully only: (i) in small businesses with a small number of subordinates, (ii) in routine type of concerns, (iii) in industries where continuous processes are followed, and (iv) in industries where automatic machinery is installed, so that the foreman is not called upon to exercise his judgement frequently.

3.3.2 FUNCTIONAL ORGANIZATION

Most of the business houses have separate departments to look after production, sales and the general office. Each one of these departments (Figure 3.5) would serve the rest of the organization. However, vigil should be exercised to see: (i) that the entire work has been divided into various departments, (ii) there is no duplication, and (iii) the work allotted to one department consists of interrelated jobs.

All related and similar work is placed in one department or division under one executive. Thus, the marketing manager will be responsible for all marketing work of the company, of all the plants and for all product lines.

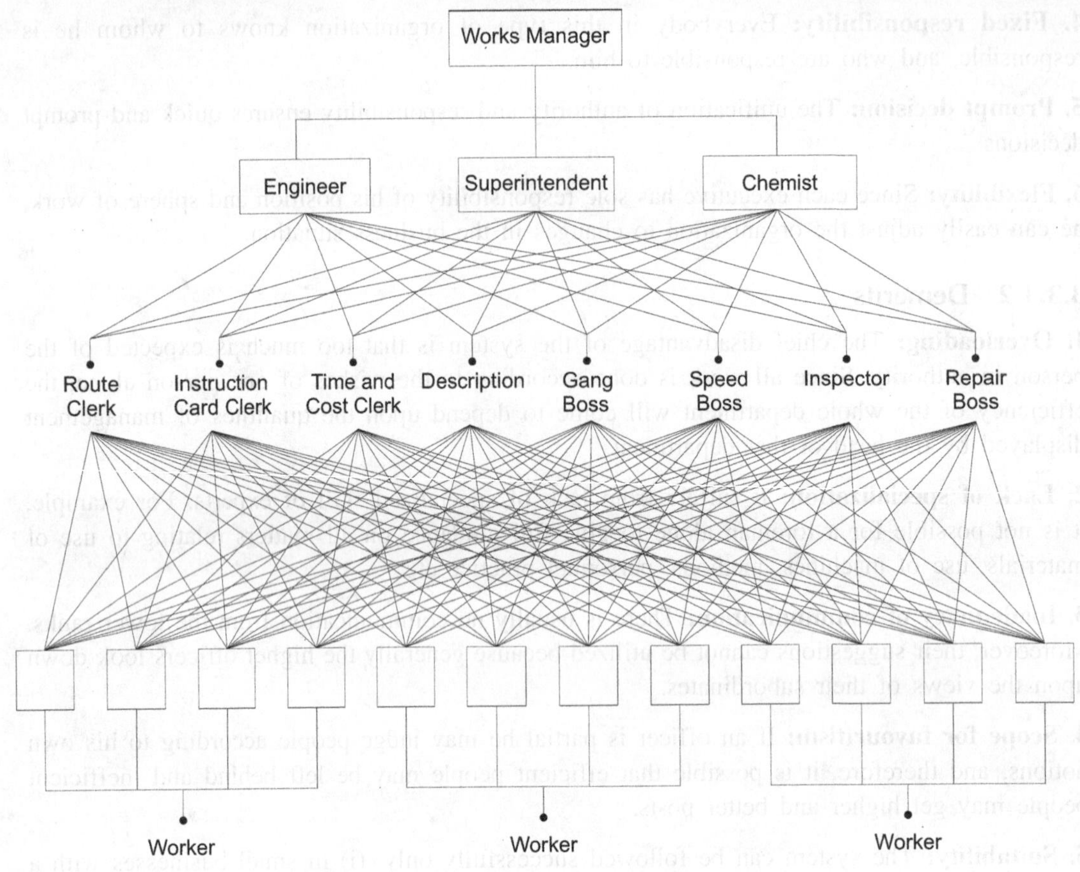

FIGURE 3.5 Functional Type of Organization.

3.3.2.1 Merits

1. It ensures a greater division of labour and enables the concern to take advantage of specialization of functions.
2. It makes for a higher degree of efficiency as the workers and others in the organization have to perform a limited number of operations.
3. It ensures the separation of mental and manual functions.
4. It facilitates mass production through specialization and standardization.

3.3.2.2 Demerits

1. It is unstable because it weakens the disciplinary controls, by making the workers work under several different bosses.
2. It is too complicated in operation because it entails the division of functions into a number of sub-functions. This also leads to lack of coordination among the workers.
3. It makes difficult for the management to fix responsibility for unsatisfactory results.
4. It may also lead to conflict among foremen of equal rank.

3.3.3 Line and Staff Organization

Line and staff organization (Figure 3.6) refers to a pattern in which staff specialists advise line managers in performing their duties. When the work of an executive increases, its performance requires the services of specialists. The staff positions are of purely advisory in nature. They have the right to recommend, but have no authority to enforce their preference on other departments. In reality, it is difficult to determine which departments are line or staff. The problem can usually be solved by classifying activities within an organization in two ways:

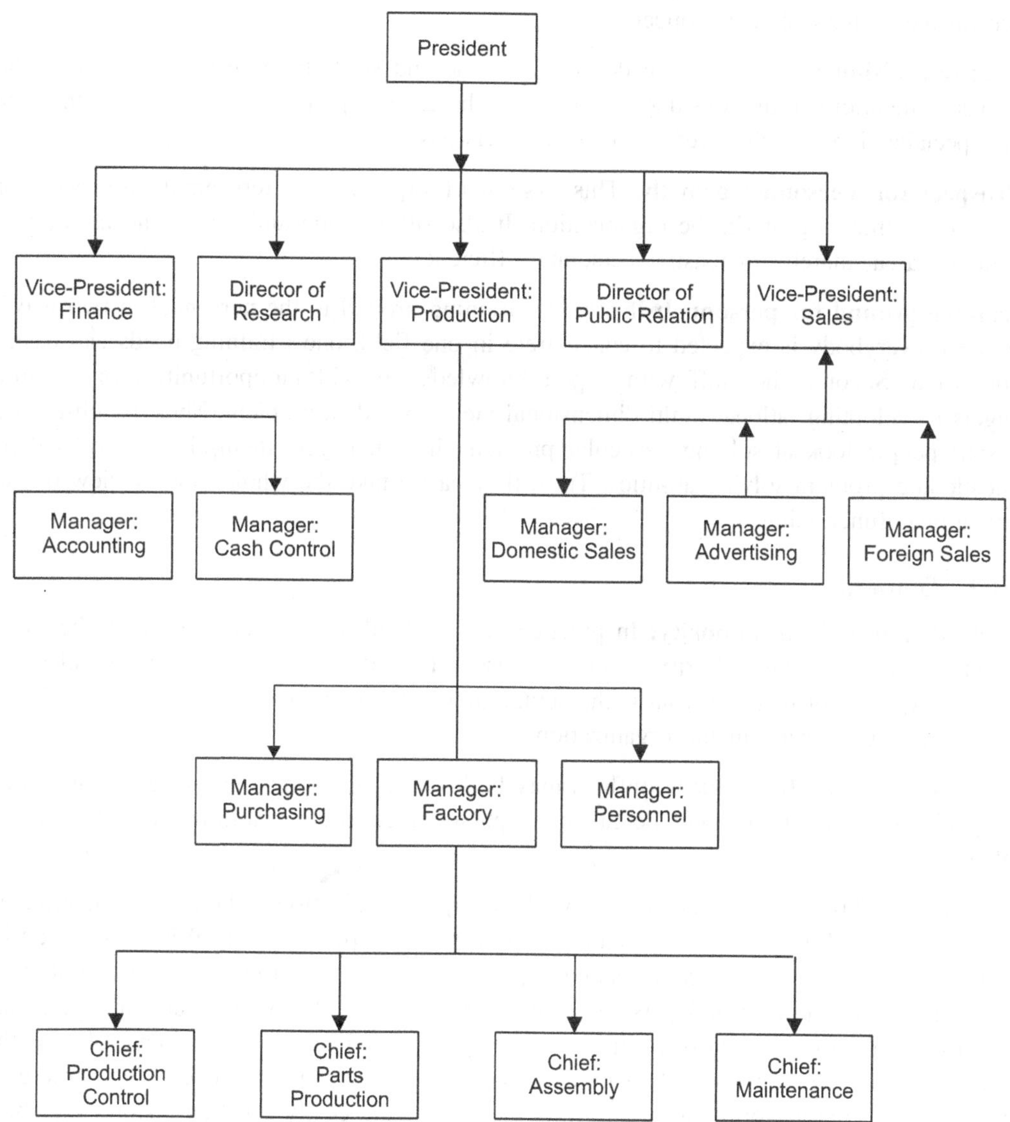

FIGURE 3.6 Line and Staff Type of Organization.

(i) that which is substantive(direct) in its contribution to the organization's overall objectives, and (ii) that which is objective (indirect) in its contribution. The departments performing former group of activities are in line ones, and those performing latter group of activities are staff ones.

3.3.3.1 Merits

1. Planned specialization: The line and staff structure is based upon the principle of specialization. The line managers are responsible for operations contributing directly to the achievement of organizational objectives, whereas staff people are there to provide expert advice on the matters of their concerns.

2. Quality decisions: The quality of decisions in line and staff structure is high because the decisions come after careful consideration and thought. Each expert gives his advice in the area of his specialization, which is reflected in the decisions.

3. Prospect for personnel growth: This system of organizing offers ample prospect for efficient personnel to grow in the organization. It also offers opportunity for concentrating in a particular area, thereby increasing personnel efficiency.

4. Training ground for personnel: It provides training ground to the personnel in two ways. First, since everybody is expected to concentrate in one field, one's training needs can easily be identified. Second, the staff with expert knowledge provides opportunities to the line managers for adopting rational multi-dimensional view towards a problem. Thus, by observing how staff people look at solving particular problem, line managers themselves sharpen their diagnostic and problem-solving abilities. Thus, they easily take the wholesome of view of the organizational functioning.

3.3.3.2 Demerits

1. Lack of well-defined authority: In practice, it is difficult to differentiate clearly between line and staff because the authority is often diffused. Thus the managers may not be clear as to what is expected of them or what is the actual area of the operation of their authority. Thus confusion may be created in the organization.

2. Line and staff conflicts: Such conflicts may be because of various reasons and sometimes the organizational conflicts may be taken as personal conflicts resulting in interpersonal problems.

3. Suitability: This structure can be followed in large organizations where specialization of activities is required because it offers ample opportunity for specialization. When employed in the large organizations, its success depends upon the degree of harmony that is maintained among various departments and personnel, the clarity in line of authority, and interpersonal contact of executives particularly in line and staff positions. In the natural course of growth, an expanding organization may adopt this structure to enhance the efficiency. This structure, however, is not suitable for small organizations as it is quite costly for them. Moreover, they cannot take the full advantage of experts because of lack of adequate activities for them.

3.3.4 MATRIX ORGANIZATION

The matrix design (Figure 3.7) is created by superimposing a set of project structures on top of a functional structure. Members of each project team are selected or assigned from the functional department. The matrix design features a multiple command structure in which an individual may have any number of superiors, including one functional superior and one or more project manager. The matrix structure has been found to be successful under three major situations. First, when there is strong environmental pressure, such as intense competition, which calls for stronger marketing efforts, while the diversity of firm's products call for individualized marketing programme. Second, when there is a need to share and integrate vast amounts of information within the company. Third, when there are limited resources to be shared.

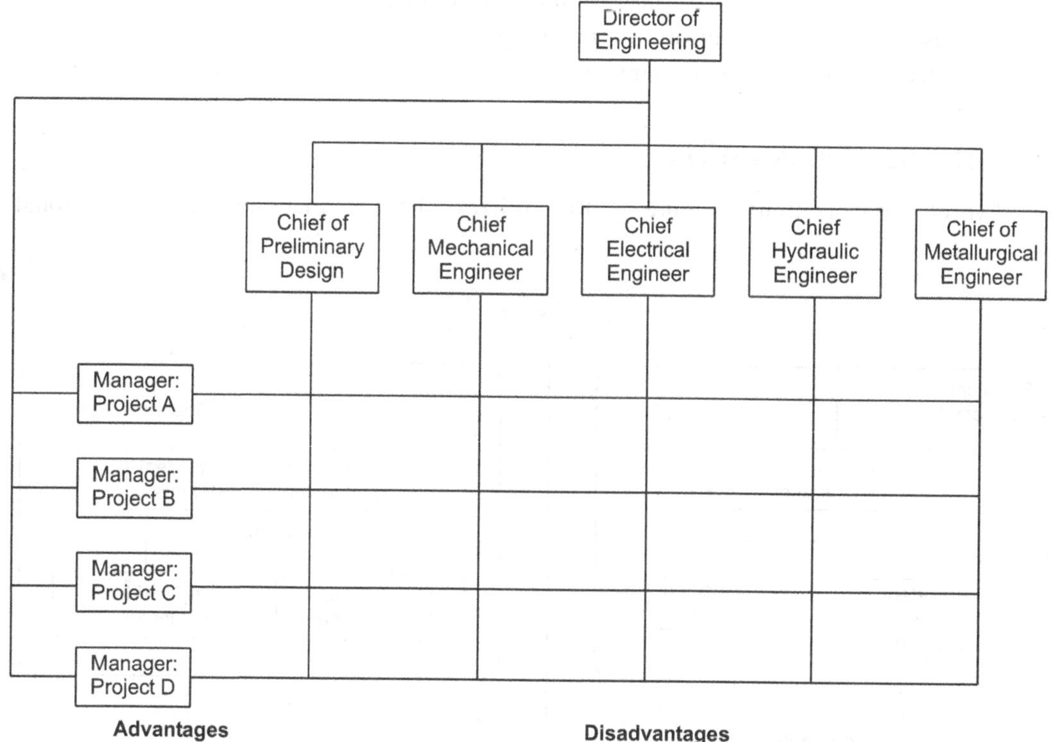

FIGURE 3.7 Matrix Type of Organization.

3.3.4.1 Merits

1. Involves and challenges matrix team members.
2. Provides enlarged tasks for people.
3. Develops employee skills.
4. Encourages people to identify with end products.

5. Fosters flexibility throughout the organization.
6. Motivates interdisciplinary cooperation.
7. Provides for integration of organizational information.
8. Fosters the development of managerial skills.
9. Frees top management for effective planning.

3.3.4.2 Demerits

1. Demands high level of interpersonal skills.
2. Leaves negative impact on morale when personnel are reshuffled.
3. Fosters confusion and frustration from its multiple-command structure.
4. Leads to power struggles between functional and project managers.
5. Causes to lose sight of broader organizational goals.
6. Causes duplication of efforts by project groups.
7. Costly to implement and maintain.

3.3.5 Hybrid Organization

The hybrid organization (Figure 3.8) utilizes both functional and divisional

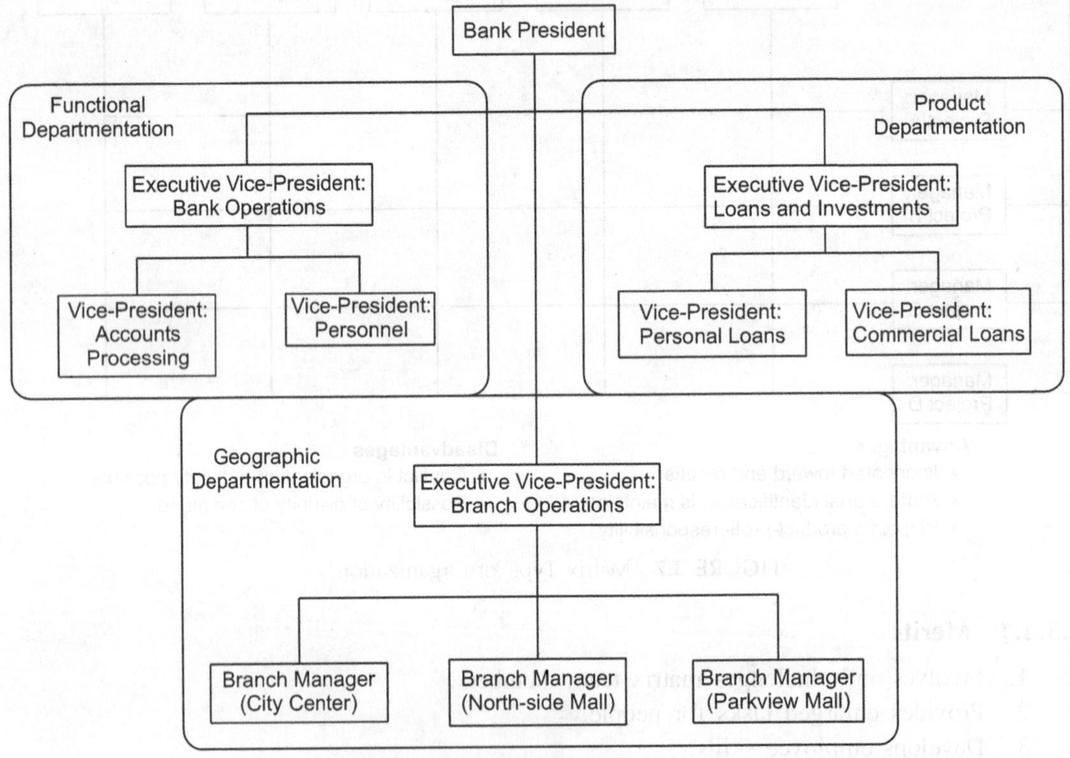

FIGURE 3.8 Hybrid Design.

departmentalization, as needed by the unique characteristics of the overall organization. Some departments are arranged along functional lines so that those workers who perform similar tasks can be grouped together. Other departments are subdivided and assigned to various product divisions. The advantage is that the whole organization enjoys the unique benefits of both functional and divisional structures. The design also helps in proper alignment of corporate and divisional goals. It fosters flexibility within divisions and efficiency within functional departments. The serious drawback is excessive duplication of activities between functions and divisions. The design has a tendency to create conflict between headquarter and divisional functions.

3.4 DEPARTMENTATION

Departmentation can broadly be of two types: (i) functional departmentation, and (ii) divisional departmentation. Divisional departmentation can further be divided on the basis of: (a) product, (b) customer, and (c) location.

3.4.1 FUNCTIONAL DEPARTMENTATION

This involves grouping of people on the basis of their overall function. Most large corporations make heavy use of functional departments (Figure 3.9).

Advantages

- Provides specialization
- Allows task assignments consistent with technical training
- Allows economies of scale
- Allows excellent coordination within functions
- Suited to a suitable environment
- Facilitates top management in direction and control

Disadvantages

- Poor communication across functional departments
- Slow response times to external changes
- Concentration of decisions at the top causing delay
- Difficulty in pinpointing responsibility
- Narrow perspectives within functions
- Fails to encourage creativity

3.4.2 DIVISIONAL DEPARTMENTATION

1. Product departmentation: Divisional departmentation comes into play when there is a need for decentralization or semiautonomy due to the organization's thrust upon product and/or market expansion. In this case, the top management provides the division with all the resources necessary to produce, sell or supply the product in the market under its control. A division can be departmentalized as follows.

It is the technique of creating a division or department for each product or product line. The functional departments are usually subordinate to the product divisions (Figure 3.10).

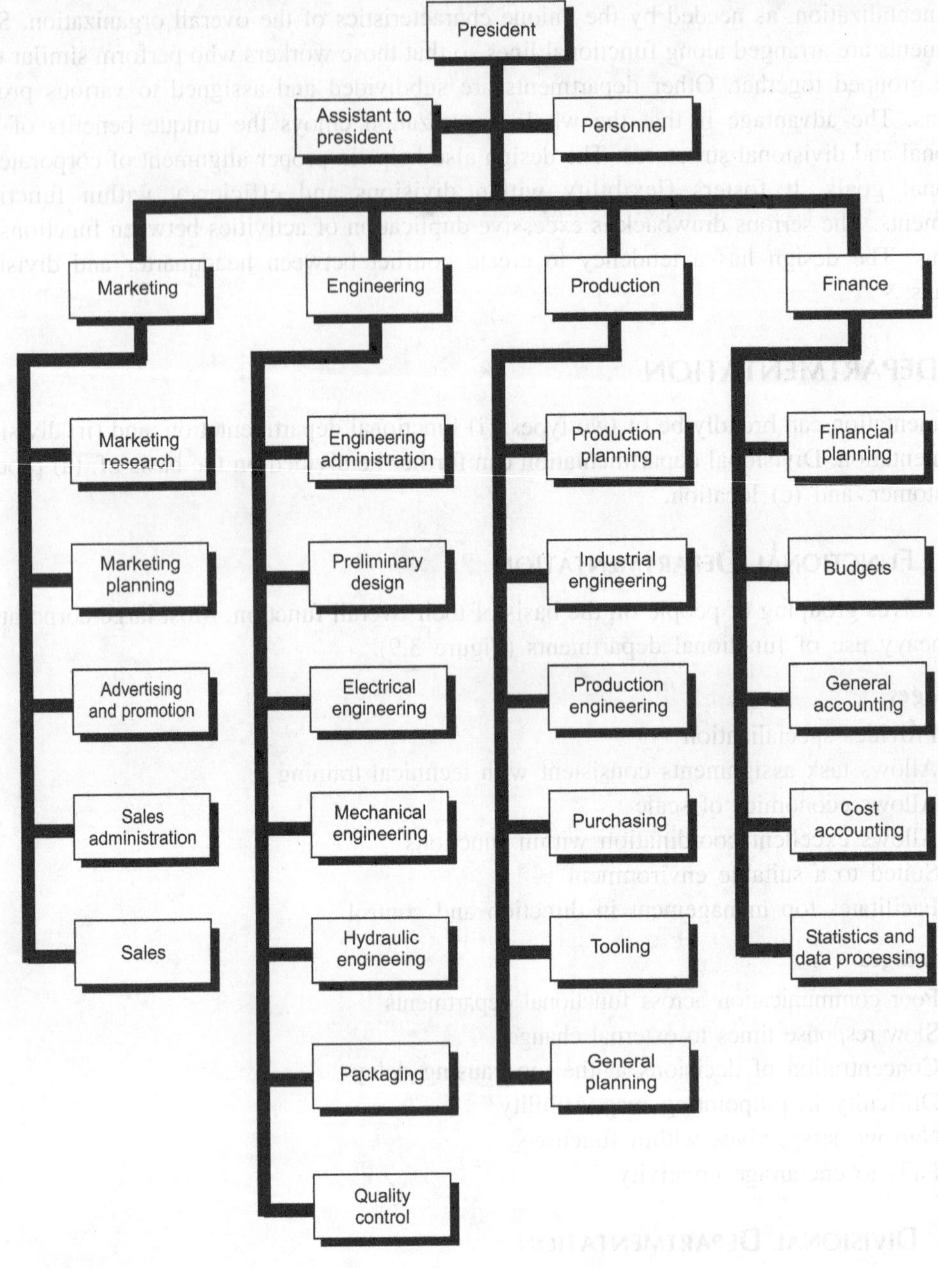

Advantages
- Is logical reflection of functions
- Maintains power and prestige of major functions
- Follows principles of occupational specialization
- Simplifies training
- Furnishes means of tight control at top

Disadvantages
- Deemphasis of overall company objectives
- Overspecialises and narrow viewpoints of key personnel
- Reduces coordination between functions
- Slow adaptation to changes in environment
- Limits development of general managers

FIGURE 3.9 Functional Type of Departmentation.

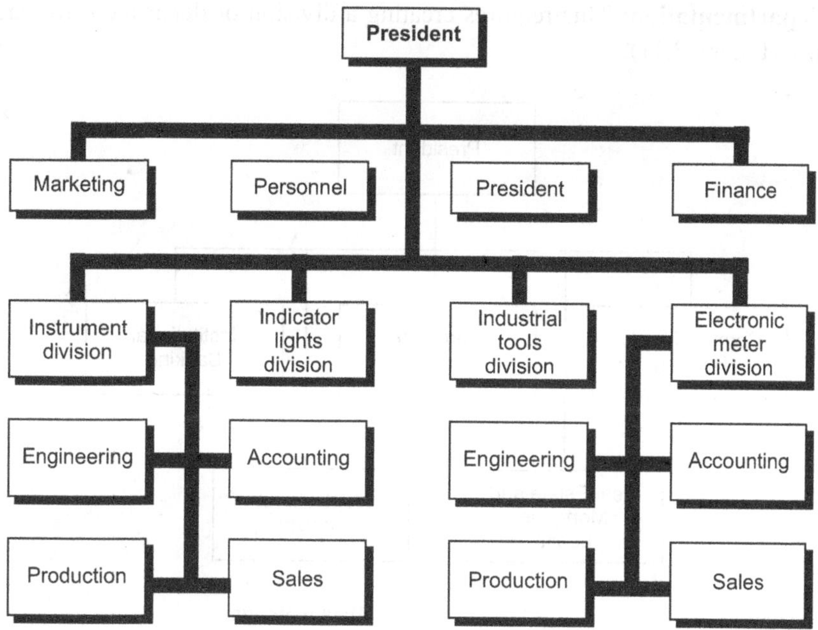

FIGURE 3.10 Product Type of Departmentation.

Advantages

- Provides high product visibility
- Suited for rapid change
- Allows parallel processing of multiple tasks
- Clearly defines responsibility
- Permits full time concentration on tasks
- Fosters the training of general managers

Disadvantages

- Promotes neglect of long-term priorities
- Causes conflict between divisional tasks and corporate priorities
- Fails to encourage the coordination of activities
- Allows in-depth competencies to decline

2. Customer departmentation: This requires creating a division or department for each of its customer groups (Figure 3.11).

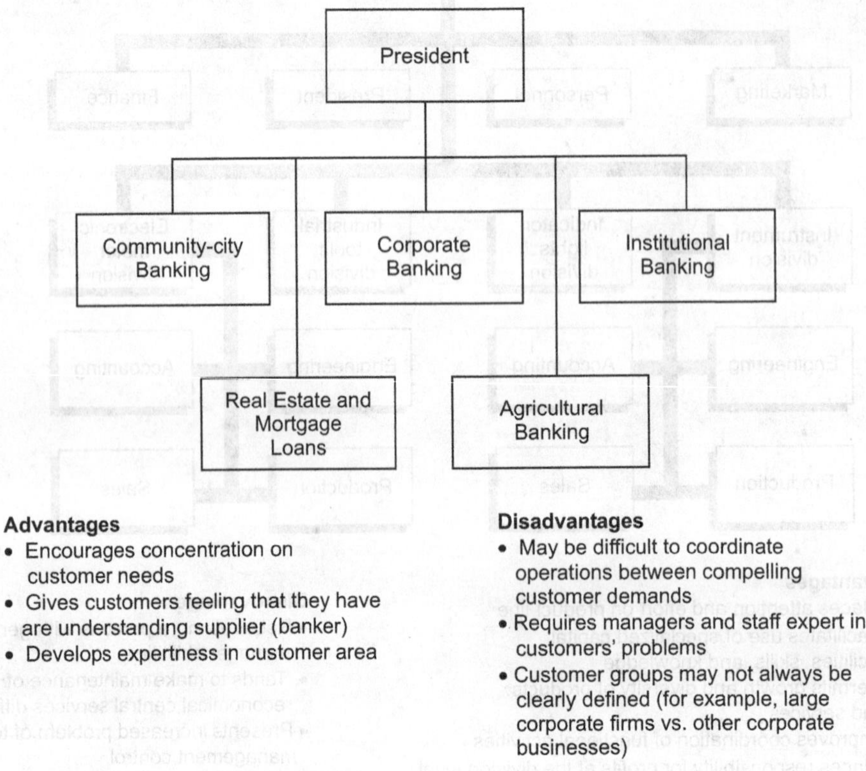

FIGURE 3.11 Customer Type of Departmentation.

Advantages

Fosters an intense focus on the unique needs of the customer

- Promotes strong public image
- Adaptive to environmental changes
- Facilitates parallel processing of multiple tasks
- Facilitates a strong marketing philosophy
- Provides a clear placement of responsibilities.

Disadvantages

Create conflicts between divisional tasks and corporate priorities

- Does not promote coordination
- Wastes resources through duplication of effort
- Tends to lessen top management control

3. Geographical departmentation: Geographic departmentation (Figure 3.12) requires the creation of divisions and/or departments to fulfill the territorial needs of an organization.

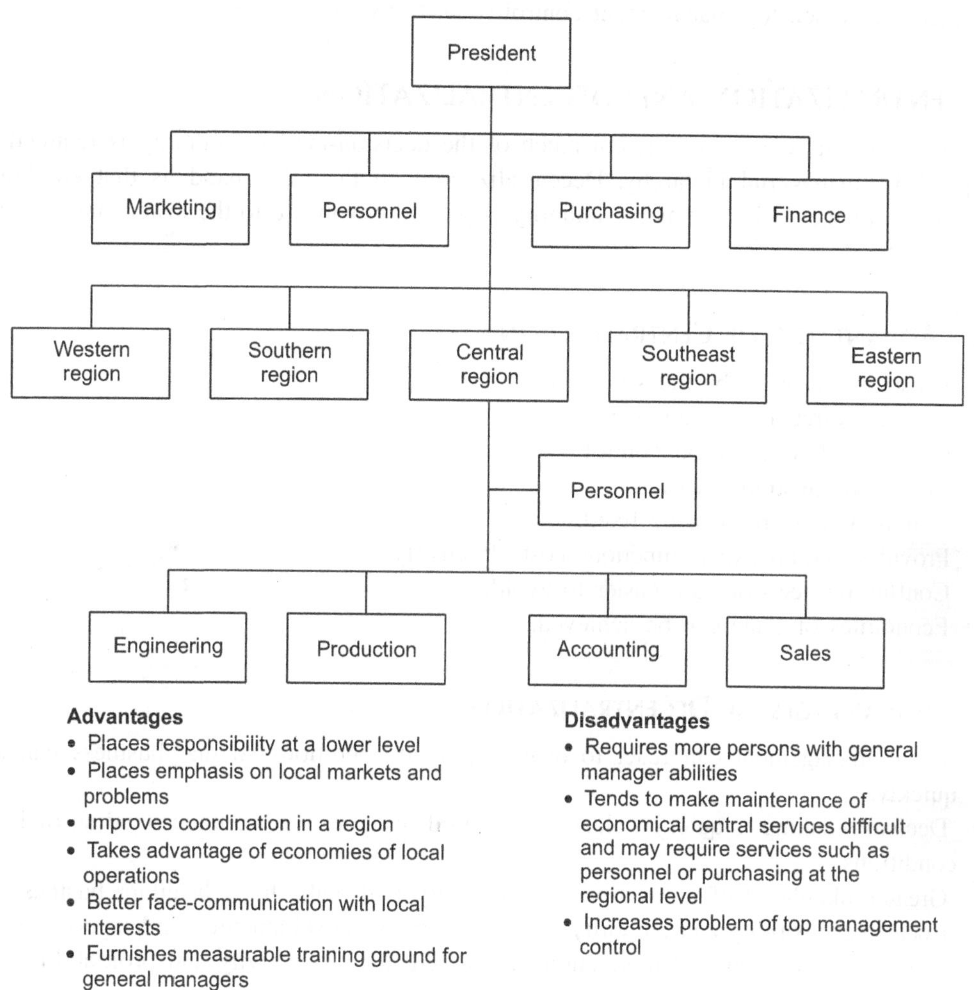

Figure 3.12 Geographical Type of Departmentation.

Advantages

Promotes concern for regional customer needs

- Fast response to the environment
- Promotes flexibility, focus on regional goals
- Fosters coordination across functional departments
- Aids in the development of general management

Disadvantages

- Fails to produce specialization
- Encourages competition for resources
- Tends to lessen top management control

3.5 CENTRALIZATION AND DECENTRALIZATION

Centralization is that condition wherein much of the decision-making authority is retained at the top of the managerial hierarchy. Decentralization, on the other hand, is that condition wherein much of the decision-making authority is pushed downward to the lower management levels.

3.5.1 Advantages of Centralization

- Broad overview of business is easier to achieve.
- Strategic direction setting is easier.
- Gives absolute and clear control.
- Makes administration easier.
- Common standards can be fixed.
- Provides certain expert functions cost effectively.
- Conflicting decisions are easier to avoid.
- Economies of scale can be achieved.

3.5.2 Advantages of Decentralization

- Local management can react to changing local conditions so that business can act quickly.
- Decision-making is quicker, clearer and based on more precise understanding of local conditions.
- Greater likelihood of innovation and creativity will make for a healthier business.
- Local responsibility and authority result in effective development of managerial skills.
- Higher involvement and motivation lead to greater productivity and profitability.
- Burden of administration and paper work are reduced.
- Functional departments will be leaner and easier to control.

3.6 AUTHORITY AND RESPONSIBILITY

The standard definition of authority is "legal, or rightful power that gives a right to command or to act". The process of organizing encompasses grouping of activities for purposes of management and specification of authority relationships between superiors and subordinates and horizontally between managers. Consequently, there are authority and responsibility relationships in all undertakings where the superior-subordinate link exists. Responsibility may be defined as the obligation of a subordinate to whom a duty has been assigned, to perform the duty.

3.6.1 Source of Authority

There are two theories: (i) the formal *authority* theory and (ii) the *acceptance* theory. The origin of authority may be traced to the elements of basic group behaviour. The concept of authority as being a power, transmitted from basic social institutions to individual managers, has been called formal authority. The notion that the real source of managerial authority is the subordinates' acceptance of the power that the managers hold over them, is held by the acceptance theory.

3.6.2 Responsibility

Responsibility arises from the superior-subordinate relationship. While authority flows from the superior to the subordinate manager, when duties are assigned, responsibility is the obligation simultaneously exacted from the subordinate for the accomplishment of these duties. A problem in responsibility sometimes arises when informal leadership appears. The informal relationship may have the effect of reducing the influence and power of the manager.

3.6.3 Responsibility and Delegation

Responsibility cannot be delegated. Responsibility, being an obligation to perform, is owed to one's superior, and no subordinate can reduce his responsibility by delegating a person the authority to perform a duty. 'Accountability' indicates liability for the proper discharge of duties by the subordinate. The grouping of duties into subdivisions of the enterprise involves delegating authority, that may be specific or general, written or unwritten, but they must be accompanied by some kind of assignment of duties. The fear that specific delegations will result in inflexibility is best dispelled by developing a tradition of flexibility. Delegated authority is frequently recovered when the need arises to modify enterprise objectives, policies and programmes, organization structure, department objectives, and the assignments of personnels.

3.6.4 Principles of Delegation

The following principles are guides to delegation of authority:

1. Principle of functional definition: This principle, though simple in concept, is often difficult to apply. To define a job and delegate authority to do it requires patience, intelligence, and clarity of objectives and plans.

2. Scalar principle: This refers to the chain of direct authority relationships from superior to subordinate throughout the organization.

3. Authority-level principle: The above two principles, when combined, gives rise to the authority-level principle. Each manager at each level should make whatever decisions he can in the light of his authority, and only those matters that keep (limit) him from deciding should be referred to his superior.

4. Principle of unity of command: This is useful in the clarification of authority-responsibility relationships. Each subordinate should report to only one superior.

5. Principle of parity: Since authority is the power to carry out assignments and responsibility is the obligation to accomplish them, it logically follows that the authority needed to do this should be commensurate to the responsibility.

3.7 MISTAKES IN ORGANIZATION

1. Failure to plan properly: Organizations fail to plan properly toward a future materially different from the past or present. Another failure in planning involves organizing around people. Organization structures must normally be modified to take people into account; to take full advantage of employee strengths and weaknesses.

2. Failure to clarify relationships: This accounts for friction, politics, and inefficiencies. Lack of clarity means lack of knowledge about the role employees are to play in an enterprise team.

3. Failure to delegate authority

4. Failure to balance delegation

5. Confusion of lines of authority and of information: Enterprises often force lines of information to follow authority lines. Unless information is confidential, there is no reason why lines of information should follow lines of authority. Information gathering should be separated from decision-making.

6. Authority without responsibility

7. Responsibility without authority

8. Careless application of staff device: Staff personnel exercising line authority, which has not been delegated to them.

9. Misuse of functional authority: While the specialist and the specialized department are essential for business efficiency, they are meant to assist and facilitate the central activities of the business. Functional authority, creating conflict and confusion, as it may, should be used sparingly.

10. Multiple subordination: This results not only from delegations of functional authority, but also from faulty organization and from instances of plural executives. Multiple subordination causes confusion, undermines the authenticity and effectiveness of authority, and threatens organizational stability.

11. Misuse of service departments: These departments are often looked upon as not much concerned with the accomplishment of major enterprise objectives, when they are in fact as much concerned as any other operational department.

12. Overorganizing: Overorganizing usually results from failure to put into practice the concept that the activity-authority structure of the enterprise is merely a framework for efficient performance of people.

Review Questions

1. Explain the organization theory.
2. What are some of the features common to all organizations?
3. Explain the principles of organizing.
4. What do you mean by span of management?
5. Describe some of the guidelines that can be followed to make organizations more effective.
6. Differentiate between authority and responsibility. Can one be exercised without the other?
7. Is delegation of authority desirable? What advantages accrue from delegation of authority?
8. Discuss the centralization – decentralization issue with its pros and cons.
9. What are the benefits of a good organization? Give examples.
10. What are the various types of organizations? Explain each type with its merits and demerits.
11. Explain in detail the various steps involved in the formation of organizational structure.
12. Explain the various forms of departmentation?

Caselets

AUTHORITY AND RESPONSIBILITY

Ramlal, Sales Manager of XYZ Company, Southern Region, did not find the performance of Harish, one of the sales representatives, up to the mark. Many a time, Ramlal personally discussed with Harish, the ways and means of improving performance. During his last meeting, Ramlal gave a warning to Harish that if his sales were not up to the quota for the month he would be fired. Harish failed to meet the quota. Ramlal could not bear this and decided to go for further action. He wrote to Harish informing him of his dismissal. Three days later, Ramlal received a call from the General Sales Manager asking him to put Harish back on the pay roll immediately as he was the nephew of the Mazdoor Union President. Ramlal had no other choice except to agree.

Question 1. What are the authority–power–responsibility–accountability–relationship.

Question 2. What can be the impact of the relationship on the functioning of the company.

DELEGATION OF AUTHORITY

In 1990, Natesan started a music cassette recording company on a very small scale. In about 5 years, his company sales equalled the combined sales of the then three leading companies in India. This was mainly due to Natesan's business acumen, extraordinary managerial skill, imaginative sales promotion programs, and above all his ear for good music and lower overhead expenses. With confidence, Natesan entered into other manufacturing activities. However, he found it difficult to delegate authority and continued to make all final decisions on every aspect of manufacturing and finance. Senior executive were frustrated due to Natesan's unwillingness to delegate authority.

Question 1. What are the possible reasons for Natesan's reluctance to delegate authority?

Question 2. How you would have convinced Natesan about the utility of delegating authority?

CHAPTER 4

Staffing

The managerial function of staffing involves effective recruitment, selection, placement, approval, and development of people to occupy the roles in the organization structure. Staffing is closely related, therefore, to organizing i.e. to the setting up of intentional structure of roles and positions.

4.1 PERSONNEL MANAGEMENT

Personnel management or human resource management (HRM) is an integral but distinctive part of management, concerned with people at work and their relationships within the enterprise. Development of human resources is essential for any organization that would like to be dynamic and growth-oriented. Unlike other resources, human resources have rather unlimited potential capabilities. The potential can be used only by creating a climate that can continuously identify, bring to surface, nurture, and use the capabilities of people.

4.2 SYSTEMS APPROACH TO STAFFING

The key staffing activities are described below (Figure 4.1).

1. Enterprise plans are the basis of staffing: At the base of staffing are enterprise plans, which are formulated during the planning process. In planning, opportunities for enterprises are identified and objectives are set based on forecast and strategy.

2. Organization plans provide a key to staffing needs: In order to carry out the plans, organizational arrangements must be made. To carry out every phase of any program successfully, the organization structure must be filled and maintained with competent managers.

3. Requirement of managers are determined: The number of managers needed in an enterprise depends not only upon its size but also upon the complexity of the organization structure, its plans for expansion, and the rate of turnover among managerial personnel. The

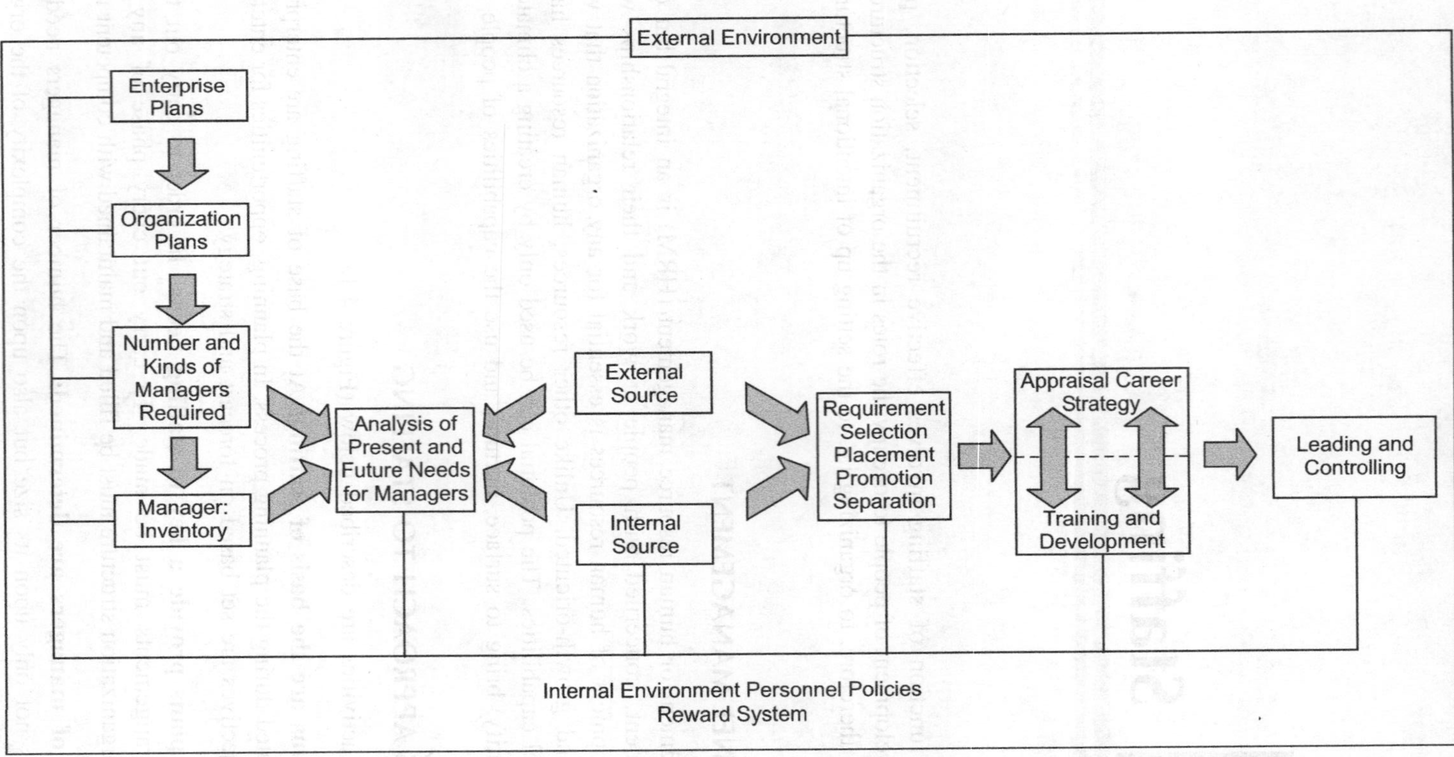

FIGURE 4.1 Systems Approach to Staffing.

ratio between the number of managers and the number of employees does not follow any law of proportion.

4. Management inventory is developed: It is common for any business to keep an inventory of raw materials and goods to enable it to carry on its operations. However, it is far less common for enterprises to keep an inventory of available human resource, particularly managers, despite the fact that the optimum number of competent managers is a vital requirement to ensure success.

5. Recruitment, selection, placement and promotion is ensured: After the need for managerial personnel has been determined, a number of candidates may have to be recruited. This involves attracting qualified managerial candidates to fill organizational roles. From these candidates, potential managers are selected. Then promotion is given from the results. Both internal and external sources are used. A systems approach to selection process is shown in Figure 4.2.

6. Managers are appraised: Appraisal serves as a basis for identifying personnel within the enterprise who deserve promotion. Appraisal is a necessity in organizational life. Superiors need to know about the quality of performance of their subordinates and for which appraisal is made appropriately.

7. Provision of training and development is ensured: Managerial appraisal should also be used as the basis for identifying training and development needs.

8. Leading and controlling functions carried out: Well-selected and well-trained managers provide good leadership and create an environment in which people are motivated and communicate effectively. Likewise, controlling is enhanced by effective staffing. Higher the quality of selected managers and their subordinates, the lower the need for correcting undesirable deviations from performance standards.

4.3 ESTABLISHING ORGANIZATION STRUCTURE

The first step in establishing the organization's structure is the development of structural guidelines. The structure should be appropriate for and compatible with the external environment, consistent with and supportive of organization's critical goals and strategies, appropriate for organization's technology and accommodating the differences of the people in the organization. The next step is job designing. Job designing is the determination of a particular individual's work-related responsibilities. Oncc jobs have been analyzed and tasks assigned, the next step is to group the jobs in some logical arrangement. This step is called departmentation. Job content refers to the job or work itself. Since the motivational (intrinsic) factors emerge from the work-worker relationship, they are included under job content. On the other hand, job context includes the maintenance factors (extrinsic) because these factors are exogenous to the work and the employee.

The two are closely related in most work situations. But observe that motivational factors, or job content, are always timely and reinforce behaviour as it occurs. They must be present if motivation efforts are to reach their zenith. In contrast, maintenance factors tend to be of

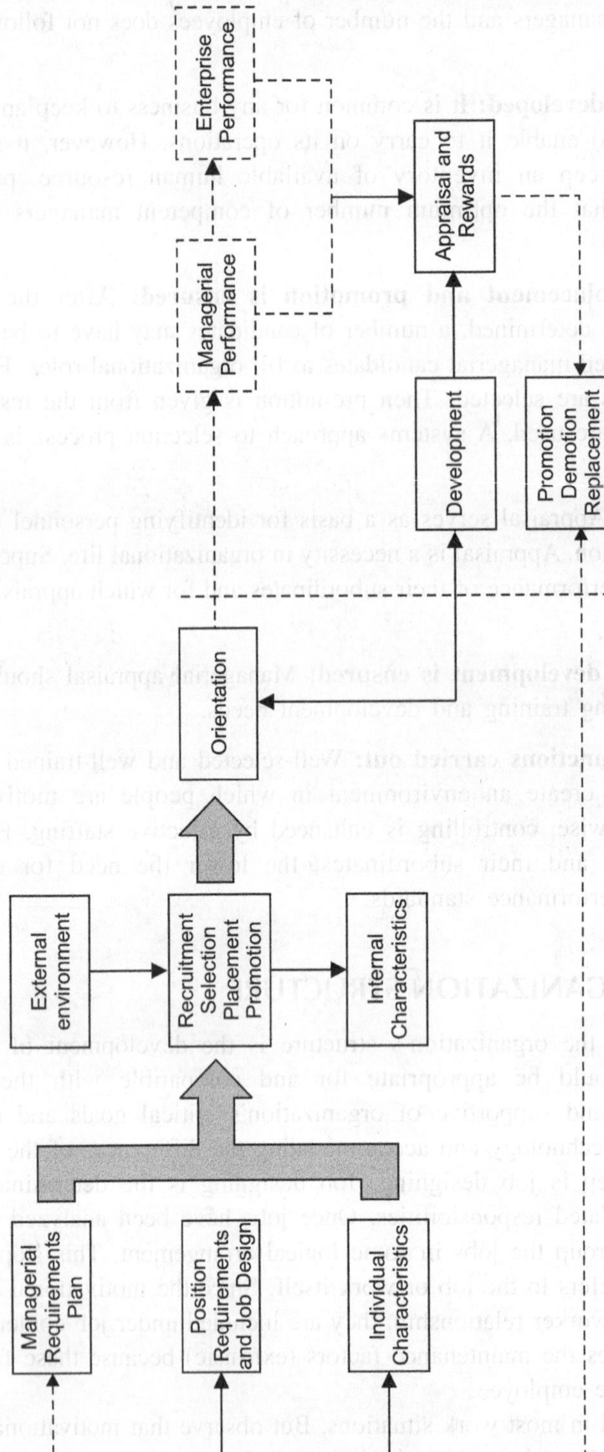

FIGURE 4.2 Systems Approach to Selection

relatively short duration; they lose some of their impact and importance with time. Herzberg observed that achievement feasibility and achievement itself lead to motivation; it is not the reverse i.e. motivation leading to achievement. The hygiene factors correspond to Maslow's first three need levels while the motivation factors with esteem and self-actualization. Job specifications are statements which describe something about the jobs of a company. They may describe the job itself. They may describe that kind of a person who should fill the given job. The difference between the two may be seen in connection with a middle management position. In practice, the term job specification is often used to include varying amounts of both job and information. Practice is not uniform regarding how much detail is included in a specification. And in many cases, it might be wise to translate job requirements into statements of human characteristics such as finger dexterity, physical strength, hand-eye coordination, and emotional poise.

4.4 RECRUITMENT AND SELECTION

The different procedural steps involved in the selection process are:

1. Job description
2. Application forms
3. Employment tests
4. Interviewing
5. Physical examination and
6. Induction or orientation

4.4.1 Job Description

A job description is a combination of short statements that describe both the work to be performed and the essential requirements of the particular jobs.

The job description includes:

- Job title
- Department in which the job exists
- Work to be performed by the new employee
- Job responsibilities
- Job knowledge
- Mental concentration required
- Dexterity and accuracy required
- Machines, tools and processes to be handled
- Relation with other jobs
- Qualification and experience required
- Amount of supervision to be provided
- Physical activities
- Working conditions

4.4.2 Application Forms

An application blank or form is the most universal mechanism used to screen the applicants to be called for interview and other tests for selection purposes.

4.4.3 Employment Tests

Very often considerable training and money is expended upon an employee when it is discovered that he is unsuited to do the job for which he was employed. For this reason, and in order to avoid the recurrence of such a situation, employment tests are, sometimes, considered an essential part of the selection programme. An employment test measures selected psychological factors such as ability to reason, capacity for learning, temperament, specific aptitudes, physical or motor abilities etc.

4.4.3.1 Characteristics of Employment Tests

The characteristics of an employment test are as follows:

- A test should be designed on the basis of a sound job analysis programme.
- The test should be reliable. An applicant if tested even second or third time under the same condition should achieve the same score.
- The test should be valid (i.e.), highly specific to the objective it intends to measure and to the particular business situation.

4.4.3.2 Types of Employment Tests

Various types of employment tests include:

- Achievement tests
- Aptitude tests
- Intelligence tests
- Interest tests
- Dexterity (motor) tests
- Personality tests

4.4.4 Interviewing

An interview is a conversation directed to a definite purpose between an applicant and the interviewer and much of the interaction between these two is carried on by gestures, postures, facial expressions and other communicative behaviour. It is in the interview that both the prospective employee and employer get the chance to learn and know about each other.

4.4.4.1 Purpose of Interview

- To find the most suitable candidate for the job
- To view and appraise the applicant in totality

- To study the applicant's motivational and emotional patterns
- To measure the applicant against the specific requirements for the job
- To explore the applicant's innate abilities
- To study the impact of the applicant's personality upon others

4.4.4.2 Types of Interviews

Interviews are basically of two types: (i) guided, and (ii) unguided. In guided, directed or patterned interview, a list of questions is prepared based on an analysis of the job specifications. This type of interview measures the personality traits such as self-reliance, emotional stability, ability to get along with others, willingness to shoulder responsibility etc.

Unguided or unpatterned interview, as its name implies, is not directed by the interviewer; instead the applicant talks about what he chooses. Unguided interview is more often used in situations other than employment, e.g. counselling, handling grievances etc.

4.4.5 PHYSICAL EXAMINATION

Physical examination or medical check-up has to be carried out for the freshly recruited people. In many organizations, medical check-up is a must and it denotes the physical well being of an employee. Physical examination has at least three objectives:

1. It serves to ascertain the applicant's capability to meet the job requirements.
2. It serves to protect the organization against the unwarranted claims under Workman's Compensation Act or against law suits for damages.
3. It helps to prevent communicable diseases entering the organization.

The physical examination should be done by a qualified expert appointed by the organization to certify whether the candidate is physically fit to meet the requirements of the job.

4.4.6 INDUCTION OR ORIENTATION TRAINING

Induction or orientation training is concerned with the process of welcoming the new employees or orienting a new employee to the organization and its procedures, rules, and regulations. When a newly appointed employee reports for works, he must be helped to get acquainted with the work environment and fellow-employees. An induction programme should aim at achieving the following objectives:

1. To strengthen the confidence of the new employees.
2. To ensure that new employees may not form false impressions about their place of work.
3. To promote a feeling of belongingness and loyalty to the organization.
4. To give the new employees the information they need such as regarding the facilities, rules and regulations.

The orientation training course should not be too lengthy. The range of information that can be covered under orientation training may include history of the company, products of the company, organizational structure, employee services, personnel policies and practices and safety measures.

4.5 INDUSTRIAL LAW

A number of industrial laws have been enacted from time to time to take care of the working class. Some of the important laws are listed below.

1. The Employment Exchanges (Compulsory Notification of Vacancies) Act, 1959
2. The Contract Labour (Regulation and Abolition) Act, 1970.
3. The Apprentices Act, 1961
4. The Payment of Wages Act, 1936
5. The Minimum Wages Act, 1948
6. The Payment of Gratuity Act, 1972
7. The Employees' Provident Funds and Miscellaneous Provisionns Act, 1952
8. The Employees' State Insurance Act, 1948
9. The Maternity Benefit Act, 1961

4.6 CONCEPT OF HUMAN RESOURCE DEVELOPMENT

Human resource development (HRD), in the organizational context, is a process by which the employees of an organization are helped in a continuous and planned way to:

1. Acquire or sharpen capabilities required to perform various functions associated with their present or expected future roles.
2. Develop their general capabilities as individuals and discover and exploit their own inner potentials for their own and/or organizational development purposes.
3. Develop an organizational culture in which supervisor-subordinate relationships, team work, and collaboration among subunits are strong and contribute to the professional well-being, motivation, and pride of employees.

4.6.1 NEED FOR HRD

Organizations can become dynamic and grow only through the efforts and competencies of their human resources. Personnel policies can keep the morale and motivation of employees high, but these efforts are not enough to make the organization dynamic and take it in new directions. Employee capabilities must continuously be acquired, sharpened, and used. For this purpose, an "enabling" organizational culture is essential. When employees use their initiative, take risks, experiment, innovate, and make things happen, the organization may be said to have an "enabling" culture.

4.6.2 Goals of HRD

The goals of human resources development system is to improve:

1. The capabilities of each employee as an individual.
2. The capabilities of each individual in relation to his or her present roles.
3. The capabilities of each employee in relation to his or her expected future role.
4. The relationship between each employee and his or her supervisor.
5. The team spirit and functioning in every organizational unit (department, group, etc).
6. Collaboration among different units of the organization.

4.6.3 Underlying Beliefs

The HRD mechanism is designed on the basis of the following beliefs:

1. Human resources are the most important assets in the organization.
2. Unlike other resources, human resources can be developed and increased to an unlimited extent.
3. A healthy climate, characterized by the values of openness, enthusiasm, trust, mutuality, and collaboration, is essential for developing human resources.
4. HRD can be planned and monitored in ways that are beneficial both to the individual and to the organization.
5. Employees feel committed to their work and organization if the organization perpetuates a feeling of "belongingness".
6. Employees are likely to have this feeling if the organization provides for their basic needs and for their higher needs through appropriate management styles and systems.
7. Employee commitments increase with the opportunity to discover and use one's capabilities and potential in one's work.
8. It is every manager's responsibility to ensure the development and utilization of the capabilities of subordinates, to create a healthy and motivating work climate, and to set examples for subordinates to follow.
9. The higher the level of the manager, the more attention should be paid to the HRD function in order to ensure its effectiveness.
10. The maintenance of a healthy working climate and the development of its human resources are the responsibilities of every organization (especially the corporate management).

4.6.4 HRD Subsystems

The HRD subsystems include:

- Performance Appraisal
- Potential Appraisal and Development

- Feedback and Performance Coaching
- Career Planning
- Training
- Organizational Development(OD)
- Employee Welfare
- Human Resources Information
- Quality of Work Life

4.6.4.1 Performance Appraisal

Performance appraisal is used as a mechanism for supervisors to:

1. Understand the difficulties of their subordinates and try to sort them out
2. Understand the strengths and weaknesses of their subordinates and help the subordinates to realize these
3. Help the subordinates to become aware of their positive contributions
4. Encourage subordinates to accept more responsibilities and challenges
5. Help subordinates to acquire new capabilities
6. Plan for effective utilization of the subordinates' talents

Process: In HRD organizations, every supervisor has the responsibility to insure the development of his or her subordinates in relation to the capabilities required to perform their jobs effectively. Generally, the supervisor schedules individual meetings with each employee to discuss the employee's performance, communicate the performance areas that need attention, and jointly establish areas to be worked upon or goals to be achieved by the next scheduled discussion. Such performance appraisal interviews may be scheduled every three months or once or twice a year. Goals and objectives that have been agreed upon in each meeting are reviewed in the next meeting. During this review, the supervisor attempts to understand the difficulties of the subordinate and to identify his or her developmental needs. Before each review, the employee is prepared for the discussion through self-assessment, identifying factors that have contributed to his or her performance and factors that have hindered it, as well as the types of support that he or she needs from the supervisor. The employee also prepares for the meeting by listing observations, problems, suggestions, and expectations. During the appraisal meeting, the supervisor and the subordinate share their observations and concerns. Each responds to the issues raised by the other. Such discussions help to develop mutual understanding, and the data generated are reported to the higher management and is used in making decisions about individual employee development as well as developmental needs of the work group or the entire organization. An overview of the appraisal process is given in Figure 4.3.

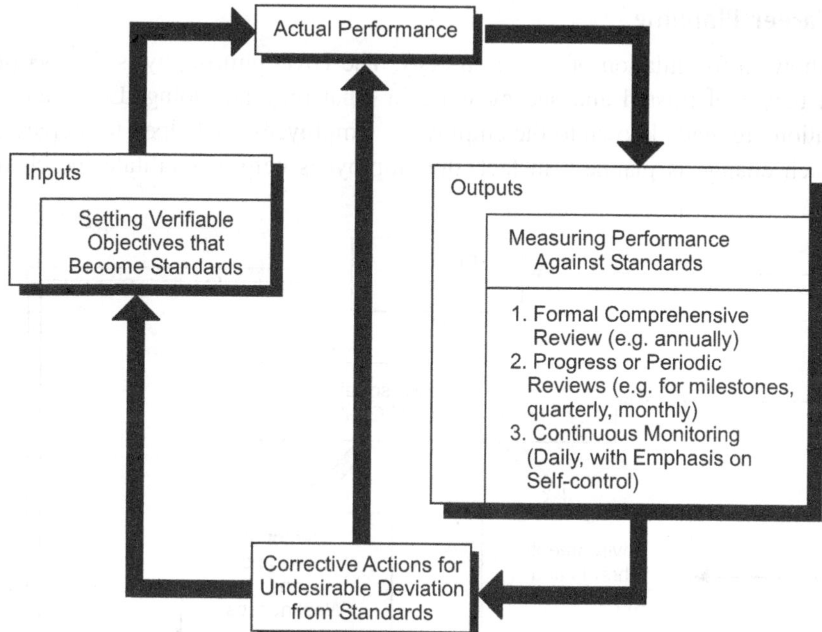

FIGURE 4.3 The Appraisal Process.

4.6.4.2 Potential Appraisal and Development

In organizations that subscribe to HRD, the potential (career-enhancement possibilities) of every employee is assessed periodically. Such assessment is used for developmental planning as well as for placement. It is assumed under this system that the company is growing continuously; it may be expanding in scale, diversifying its operations, introducing technological changes, or entering new markets. A dynamic and growing organization needs to continually review its structure and systems, creating new roles and assigning new responsibilities. Capabilities to perform new roles and responsibilities must continually be developed among employees. The identification of employee potential to ensure the availability of people to do different jobs helps to motivate employees in addition to serving organizational needs.

4.6.4.3 Feedback and Performance Coaching

Knowledge of one's strengths helps one to become more effective, to choose situations in which one's strengths are required, and to avoid situations in which one's weaknesses could create problems. This also increases the satisfaction of the individual. Often, people do not recognize their strengths. Supervisors in the HRD system have the responsibility for observing and providing feedback to subordinates about strengths and weaknesses, as well as for guiding them in improving their performance capabilities.

4.6.4.4 Career Planning

Figure 4.4 shows a formulation of career strategy. The HRD philosophy is that people perform better when they feel trusted and see meaning in what they are doing. Long-range plans for the organization are made known to the employees. Employees are helped to prepare for change whenever such change is planned; in fact, the employees help to facilitate the change. Major

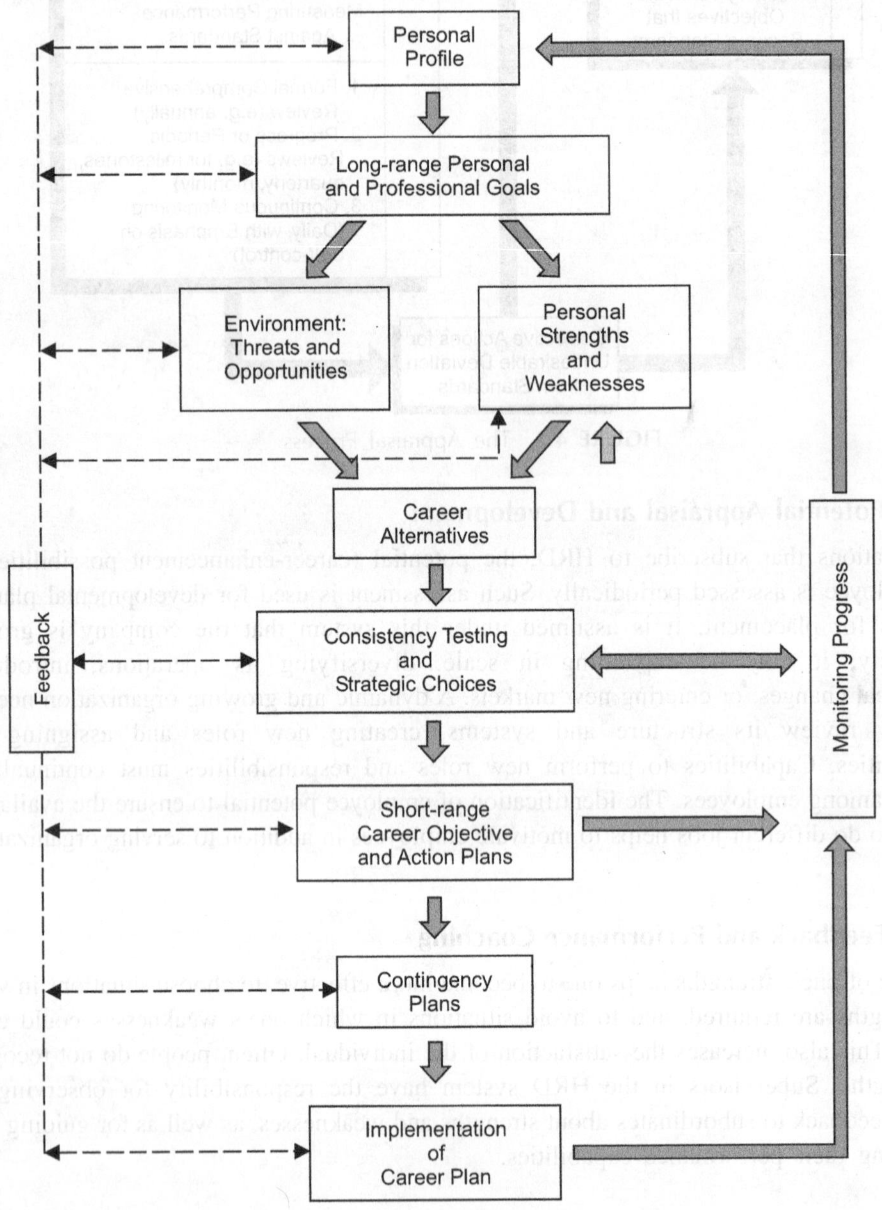

FIGURE 4.4 Formulation of Career Strategy.

changes are discussed at all levels to increase employee understanding and commitment. Most people want to know the possibilities for their own growth and career opportunities. Because managers and supervisors have information about the growth plans of the company, it is their responsibility to transmit information to their subordinates and to assist them in planning their careers within the organization. Of course, the plans may not become reality, but all are aware of the possibilities and are prepared for them.

4.6.4.5 Training

Training is linked with performance appraisal and career development. Employees generally are trained on the job or through special in-house training programmes. For some employees (including managers), outside training may be utilized to enhance, update, or develop specific skills. This is especially valuable if the outside training can provide expertise, equipment, or sharing of experiences that are not available within the organization. In-house training programmes are developed by in-house trainers or consultants hired for the task, and periodic assessments are made of the training needs within the organization. The effects of all programmes are monitored and added to the data concerning training needs. Managers and employees who attend in-house or outside training events are also expected to submit proposals concerning any changes they would like to suggest on the basis of their knowledge. The training received by employees is thus utilized by the organization.

4.6.4.6 Organizational Development (OD)

This function includes research to ascertain the psychological health of the organization (Figure 4.5). This is generally accomplished by means of periodic employee surveys. Efforts are made to improve organizational health through various means in order to maintain a

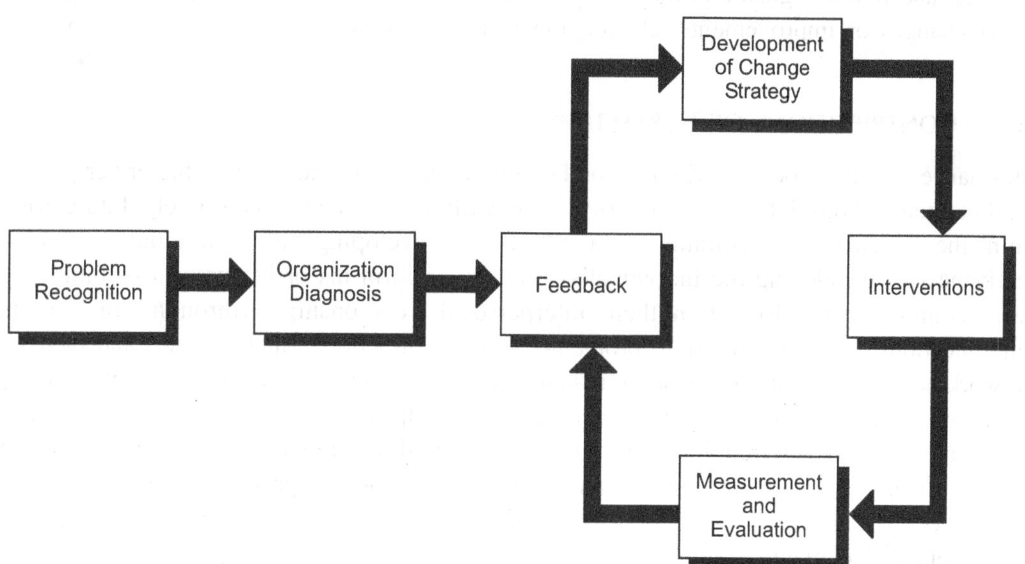

FIGURE 4.5 Model of the Organization Development Process.

psychological climate that is conducive to productivity. The OD system experts also help the department or unit in the company that has problems such as absenteeism, low production, interpersonal conflict, or resistance to change. These experts also revamp and develop various systems within the organization to improve their functioning.

4.6.4.7 Employee Welfare

Employees at lower levels in the organization usually perform relatively monotonous tasks and have fewer opportunities for promotion or change. In order to maintain their work commitment and motivation, the organization must provide some welfare benefits such as medical insurance, disability insurance, and holidays and vacations. HRD systems focus on employee welfare by continually examining employee needs and meeting them to the extent feasible.

4.6.4.8 Human Resources Information

All appropriate information about employees should be stored in a central human resources data bank. This includes all basic information about each employee, training programmes attended, performance records, potential appraisals, accomplishments, etc. This data is utilized whenever there is a need to identify employees for special projects, additional training, or higher-level jobs.

4.6.4.9 Quality of Work life

Quality of work life programmes generally focus on the environment within the organization and include basic physical concerns such as heating and airconditioning, lighting, and safety precautions; additional physical amenities such as food and beverage facilities, recreation, and aesthetics; and psychological and motivational factors such as flexible work hours, freedom to suggest changes or improvements, challenging work, and varying degrees of autonomy.

4.6.5 Contributions of Subsystems

Performance appraisal focuses primarily on helping the individual to develop his or her present role. Potential appraisal focuses primarily on identifying the employee's likely future roles within the organization. Training is a means of developing the individual's personal effectiveness or developing the individual's ability to perform his or her present or future job roles. Training can also strengthen interpersonal relationships (through training in communications, conflict resolution, problem-solving, transactional analysis etc.) and increase teamwork and collaboration (through management and leadership training, team building programmes etc). Feedback and performance coaching helps the development of the individual as well as interpersonal relationships. Organizational development is the mechanism for developing team collaboration and self-renewing skills. Efforts to promote employee welfare and ensure the quality of work life, along with rewards, promote a general climate of development and motivation among employees.

4.7 DESIGNING AN INTEGRATED HRD SYSTEM

Designing an integrated HRD system requires a thorough understanding of the principles and models of human resource development and a diagnosis of the organization culture, existing HRD practice in the organization, employee perceptions of these practices, and the developmental climate within the organization. The following principles related to focus, structure, and functioning should be considered when designing integrated HRD systems.

4.7.1 FOCUS

The primary purpose of HRD is to help the organization to increase its "enabling" capabilities. This can be done by ensuring development of human resources, organizational health, and diagnostic ability, and improvement of problem-solving capabilities, and employee productivity and commitment. The HRD system focusses on the following issues:

1. **Adaptation and change in organization culture:** Although HRD systems are designed to suit the organizational culture, the role of HRD may be to modify that culture to increase the effectiveness of the organization. HRD should take the organization toward progress, and this can be done only if its design anticipates change and evolution in the future.

2. **Contextual factors:** Various issues such as—what is to be included in the HRD systems, how is it to be subdivided, what designations and titles to be used etc. should be settled after consideration of the various contextual factors of the organization, like culture and tradition, size, technology, levels of existing skills, available support for the function, availability of outside help etc.

3. **Building linkages with other functions:** HRD systems should be designed to strengthen other functions in the company such as long-range corporate planning, budgeting and finance, marketing, production etc. These linkages are extremely important.

4. **Specialization and diffusion of the function:** Although HRD involves specialized functions, line people should be involved in various aspects of HRD. Action is the sole responsibility of the line people, and HRD should strengthen their roles.

4.7.2 STRUCTURE OF HRD SYSTEM

For structuring the HRD system, following activities are required to be done:

1. **Establishing the identity of HRD:** It is important that the distinct identify of HRD be recognized. The person in charge of HRD should have responsibility for this function exclusively and should not be expected to do it in addition to any other function as multiple responsibilities produce several kinds of conflict. This person should report directly to the chief executive of the organization.

2. **Ensuring respectability for the function:** In many companies, the personnel function does not have much credibility because it is not perceived as a major function within the organization. It is necessary that HRD be instituted at a very high level in the organization and

that the head of the HRD department be classified as a senior manager. Both the credibility and usefulness of HRD depend on this.

3. Balancing differentiation and integration: The HRD function often includes personnel administration, human resources development and training, and industrial relations. These three functions have distinct identities and requirements and should be differentiated within the HRD department. One person may be responsible for OD, yet another for training, another for potential appraisal and assessment, etc. At the same time, these roles should be integrated through a variety of mechanisms. For example, inputs from manpower planning should be available to line managers for career planning and HRD units for potential appraisal and development.

Data from recruitment should be fed into the human resources information system. Salary administration and placement should be handled separately; they should be linked to performance appraisals. Differentiation as well as integration mechanisms are essential if the HRD system is to function well.

4. Establishing linkage mechanisms: HRD has linkage with outside systems as well as with internal subsystems. It is wise to establish specific linkages to be used to manage the system. Standing committees for various parts and levels of the organization, task groups, and ad hoc committees for specific tasks are useful mechanisms.

5. Developing monitoring mechanisms: The HRD function is always evolving. It, therefore, requires systematic monitoring to review the progress and level of effectiveness of the system and to plan for its next step. A thorough annual review, and a reappraisal at every three years will be invaluable in reviewing and planning the system. It may be helpful to include persons from other functions in the organization in the HRD assessment effort.

4.7.3 FUNCTIONING OF HRD SYSTEM

The following elements play an important role in the functioning of the HRD system.

1. Building feedback and reinforcing mechanisms: The various subsystems within HRD should provide feedback to one another. Systematic feedback loops should be designed for this purpose. For example, performance and potential appraisals provide necessary information for training while OD programmes provide information for work redesign.

2. Balancing quantitative and qualitative decisions: Many aspects of HRD such as performance and potential appraisals, are difficult to quantify. Of course, attempts should be made to quantify many variables and to design computer storage of various types of information, but qualitative and insightful decisions are also necessary and desirable. For example, in considering people for promotions, quantitative data are necessary inputs, but other factors must also be taken into consideration. Thus, a balance between the mechanical and the human factors is necessary.

3. Balancing internal and external expertise: The HRD system requires the development of internal expertise and resources, specifically in content areas that are used frequently within the organization. For expertise that is required only occasionally, the use of external resources or consultants may be the most feasible. It is necessary to plan for an economical and workable balance between the two. It is preferable to use internal personnel to conduct training; however, an organization that uses only in-house expertise may not benefit from new thinking in the field. On the other hand, a company that relies solely on external HRD help does not develop the internal resources that are necessary for effective functioning.

4. Planning for the evolution of HRD: Various aspects of HRD can be introduced into the organization in stages, depending on its needs, size and level of sophistication. Some aspects may require a great deal of preparation. Each stage should be planned carefully with sequenced phases built one over the other. This may include:

(i) Geographical phasing: It means, introducing the system in a few parts of the organization and slowly spreading it to other parts. This may be necessary in a large or widely located organization.

(ii) Vertical phasing: It means, introducing the system at one or a few levels in the organization and expanding up or down gradually.

(iii) Functional phasing: It means, introducing one function or subsystem followed by other functions. For example, introducing job specifications (identification of critical attributes of jobs) before introducing a complete potential-appraisal system.

(iv) Sophistication phasing: It means, introducing simple forms of subsystems, followed after some time, by more sophisticated forms.

4.8 GRIEVANCE

A grievance may be defined as any genuine or ingenuine feeling of discontent or dissatisfaction, whether expressed or unexpressed arising out of anything connected with the company that an employee thinks, believes or even feels is unfair, unjust or inequitable.

4.8.1 Grievance Handling Procedure

A good grievance handling procedure should be simple, and easy to understand and operate. The grievances should be settled as far as possible, at lower levels. Depending upon the nature of grievance, it should be referred to the appropriate authorities. The grievance procedure should permit the worker to appeal against the decision taken at lower levels. The importance of industrial harmony and good labour relations should always be borne in mind.

4.9 ORGANIZATIONAL CONFLICTS

The term conflict is used in four ways to describe:

- antecedent conditions of conflictful behaviour, such as scarcity of resources or policy differences;
- affective stages of individuals involved, such as stress, tension, hostility, anxiety, etc;
- cognitive states of individuals i.e. their perception or awareness of conflictual situation; and
- conflictual behaviour, ranging from passive resistance to overaggression.

4.9.1 Positive Aspects of Conflicts

Conflicts, though, are harmful for both the individual and the organization, it also holds some benefits. These are:

1. Conflicts provide opportunities to individuals and groups to think again and take a more concrete view of the situation.
2. These lead to innovation as conflicting situations always present threats to the working. In order to overcome this threat, the individuals and groups have to find out new ways of working.
3. Conflicts bring cohesiveness in groups. This happens more in the case of intergroup conflicts.
4. Conflicts provide challenging work environment as these develop high degree of competition.
5. As conflicts develop among various individuals and groups, these indicate the shortcomings in the existing system of organizational functioning, and hence, management attention can be drawn for overcoming such as shortcomings.
6. Conflicts may be used as a device to overcome many frustrations and tensions because people often express their frustration and tension by means of conflicts and thus, feel relieved.

4.9.2 Individual Level Conflict

Individual level conflict or goal conflict occurs when two or more motives block each other. There can be three forms of goal conflict; approach–approach conflict, approach–avoidance conflict, and avoidance–avoidance conflict.

4.9.2.1 Approach—Approach Conflict

In this situation, the individual is caught between trying to decide upon one of the two attractive goals, which are mutually exclusive. The problem comes in when the desirabilities are roughly equal. This type of conflict has probably least impact on organizational behaviour.

4.9.2.2 Approach–Avoidance Conflict

In this situation, the individual has both positive and negative feelings about trying a goal because the goal possesses both attractive and repulsive characteristics. The result is a stable or self-maintaining conflict that tends to keep the organism at the point where the two tendencies cross. This type of conflict is quite relevant for organization's behaviour.

4.9.2.3 Avoidance–Avoidance Conflict

This is the situation where the individual must choose between mutually exclusive goals, each of which possesses unattractive qualities. Unless other alternatives are available, such a conflict has a tendency to stay unresolved.

4.9.3 Role Conflict

An individual performs a number of roles. Although all the roles which he brings into the organization are relevant to his behaviour, his organizational role is most important. In the organization, every person is expected to behave in a particular manner while performing a specific role. When expectations of a role are materially different or opposite from the behaviour anticipated by the individual in that role, he tends to be in a role conflict because there is no way to meet one expectation without rejecting the other. Role conflict occurs in three situations: (i) when the individual occupies a role which is not consistent with the images, need, and expectations of the self, (ii) when the individual is physiologically unfit to fulfill the role expectations, and (iii) when due to gaps or deficiencies in the process of development of self, the person fails to perceive accurately the expected behaviours associated with the role.

4.9.3.1 Factors in Role Conflict

Mainly, there are three factors that lead to role conflict:

(i) Role ambiguity: When role expectations are inadequately defined or substantially unknown, role ambiguity exists causing role conflict.

(ii) Organizational position: A set of expectations is that an employee is a separate link between management and workers and should have his own unique set of values and attitudes. Conflict arises in the mind of the supervisor as to which expectations he should fulfill.

(iii) Personal characteristics: Role conflict also arises because of personal characteristics. These personality dimensions include emotional sensitivity, introversion-extroversion, flexibility-rigidity and need for career achievement.

4.9.3.2 Variables Affecting Role Conflict

The extent of the undesirable effects from role conflict depends upon the following four major variables:

1. Awareness of role conflict
2. Acceptance of conflicting job pressures
3. Ability to tolerate stress
4. General personality make-up

The management's attempt towards managing role conflict should be to avoid the situations where role conflict arises.

4.9.4 Interpersonal Conflict

In an organization, two types of interpersonal conflict arises:

(i) Vertical conflict: Vertical relationship, that is mostly in the form of superior-subordinate relationship, results into vertical conflicts which usually arise because superior attempts to control the behaviour of his subordinates, and subordinates resist such control.

(ii) Horizontal conflict: Horizontal conflict at interpersonal level is among the persons at the same hierarchical level in the same function or in different functions. Resource sharing may be one of the reasons for horizontal conflict.

4.9.4.1 Factors Affecting Interpersonal Conflict

The types of persons involved in the interaction process determine to a great extent the degree to which the interaction may be cooperative or conflicting. Following factors are important in this context.

(i) Ego states: People interact with particular ego states. Ego states are the person's way of thinking, feeling, and behaving at any particular time. If ego states are not complementary, the conflicting situations take place. Since people are not aware about others adequately, often such situation arise. Lack of complementary ego states may ultimately lead to interpersonal conflict.

(ii) Value systems: People having different dominant value systems may develop conflict in their interaction. A value system is a framework of personal philosophy which governs and influences individual reactions to any situation. Thus, people having different value systems may interpret the things and situations differently which may reflect the choice of different methods of working and behaving. Such differences become the basis of interpersonal conflict.

(iii) Situational variable: There may be several situational factors which also generate interpersonal conflict. These factors generate the conditions which either hightens the personal differences or may sink these. If the differences are heightened, these may lead to conflicts. Following are the major situational variables which generate conflicting relationships.

(a) Interest conflict: The most important situational variable is when people in a group or in intergroup see their interest differently.

(b) Role ambiguity: This may also develop into interrole conflict specially if various interacting roles have not been clearly specified. Thus, organization structure itself may be responsible for such type of conflicts.

4.9.5 Intragroup Conflict

Intragroup may be thought of in terms of group characteristics and to some extent interpersonal conflict, specially if two persons are from the same group. Intragroup conflict may arise in three situations:

(i) when groups face a novel problem or task;
(ii) where new values are imported from the social environment into the group; and
(iii) where a person's extragroup role comes into conflict with his intragroup role.

Intragroup conflict is visualized more when people come from different socio-economic backgrounds and have different political and religious views. The disagreement may be over ethics, the way power should be exercised, or moral considerations of assumptions, justice, fairness etc. Such differences may affect either the choice of goals or methods of achieving it.

4.9.6 Intergroup Conflict

Intergroup conflict arises out of the interaction among various groups. There are many factors in the organization which determine the intergroup relationships. These factors can influence relations between two or more groups. If these factors are not positive, they tend to create conflict among groups. These factors are goal incompatibility, resource sharing, task relationship, uncertainty absorption, and attitudinal set. These factors are described below to show how these can lead to cooperative or conflicting relations among groups.

Goal incompatibility: The goals of two groups can have a powerful impact on their relationship. Decision-makers often use goals to indicate their relative preference. The accomplishment of the stated goals of each group may require interaction with one or more groups.

Resource sharing: The relations between two groups can be affected by the degree to which the two groups draw from a common pool of resources, and the degree to which this common pool of resources is adequate to meet the demands of both the groups. Thus, conflict of this nature arises because of the discrepancy between aggregated demand and available resources.

Task relationship: Organization structure is the result of organizing process through which departments are created for achieving organizational goals. Thus, each group, in some way or the other, is interrelated. Depending upon the nature of such functional relationship, various groups may be related due to: interdependence or dependence. Two groups are independent if both of them have the discretion to withdraw from the relationship at will. Depending upon the type of task relationship, groups may perceive conflict.

Absorption of uncertainty: Uncertainty is the gap between what is known and what needs to be known to make correct decisions. In order to manage uncertainty, organizations assign certain groups or individuals to deal with it. Thus, a group may absorb uncertainty of other groups. The group may make decisions or set premises for decision-making for other groups, thereby avoiding the uncertainty.

Attitudinal sets: The set of attitude that members of various groups hold towards each other can be a cause and a consequence of the nature of their relationship. If the group relations begin with the attitudes of distrust, competitiveness, secrecy, and closed communications, there is a possibility of various factors of group relationship being emphasized in a negative way, consequently leading to conflicts. Alternatively, the group relationship may be cooperative characterized by mutual trust and respect, greater acceptance of responsibility for mutual problems, greater consideration for others' point of view, greater willingness to avoid blaming each other, more open communication etc. In such cases, cooperation, instead of conflict, is visible.

4.10 CONFLICT MANAGEMENT

Among several available strategies, two main strategies of conflict management are: (i) changing structural arrangement, and (ii) taking conflict resolution actions, are briefly being discussed here.

4.10.1 CHANGING STRUCTURAL ARRANGEMENT

This type of conflict management strategy requires the following actions to be taken:

1. Reduction in interdependence: Physically separating the conflicting groups has the distinct advantage of preventing furhter damage and the creation of rationale for fighting. However, this tactic may require continuous surveillance to keep the parties separate, especially, if tempers are hot and energy levels high. Physical separation, however, is not a permanent measure for managing conflict.

2. Reduction in shared resources: When two or more units are required to share resources, particularly scarce ones, the potential for conflict increases. One technique for reducing such conflict is to increase such resources so that each unit is independent in using them. However, since resources are scarce, it is not always possible to do so. As such, measures may be adopted for their optimum allocation.

3. Exchange of personnel: Personnel of the conflicting groups may be exchanged for a specified period as a way to reducing and managing conflict. An exchange of people is very similar to role reversal, which is aimed at developing greater understanding between people by forcing each to present and defend the other's position.

4. Creation of special integrators: To resolve conflict, organization may create positions for the appointment of special integrators who may manage the interdependence of various groups so that unresolved matters can be solved through them.

5. Reference to superior's authority: Conflicts may be resolved through the hierarchy. If resolution cannot be attained by two organizational members, they may take the issue to a common supervisor who resolves the conflicts by making a decision.

4.10.2 TAKING CONFLICT—RESOLUTION ACTIONS

Taking conflict-resolution actions is also a frequently adopted strategy for managing conflicts. It includes:

1. Problem–solving: The problem-solving technique is considered to be the most positive technique available for conflict resolution because it emphasises on finding a common interest for both conflicting parties.

2. Avoidance: Another method of overcoming conflict is its avoidance, i.e. parties to the conflict may either withdraw from the conflict or conceal the incompatibility.

3. Smoothing: Smoothing can be defined as the process of playing down differences that exist between individual groups while emphasizing common interest. Differences are suppressed and similarities are accentuated in smoothing process. However, this is not a long-term solution for the conflicts.

4. Compromise: Compromise is a widely accepted technique for resolving conflict, yielding neither a definite loser nor a distinct winner. Included here are external or third party interventions, plus internal compromise between conflicting parties through both total group and representative negotiations and voting.

5. Confrontation: The parties concerned may settle their score by applying their strength against each other. Confrontation may be used for organization development and increasing organizational effectiveness.

4.11 AREAS OF CONFLICTS

Conflicts in an organization may be:

- Regarding wage structure, wage calculation etc.
- Regarding factory working conditions
- Regarding supervision such as rigid rules etc.
- Regarding partial attitude of management
- Regarding collective bargaining

4.12 WORKERS' PARTICIPATION IN MANAGEMENT

Workers' participation in management can be in any shape from establishing work-committee to auto-management by the employees. Workers, if permitted to participate and involve themselves in some of the decisions relating to work situation, can help the company to achieve its objectives very effectively.

4.12.1 Objectives

The objectives or the necessity of permitting workers to participate in management can be:

1. To achieve industrial peace and harmony.
2. To develop internal motivation in the workers.
3. To boost the morale of employees.
4. To raise the levels of the employee production, productivity, and product quality.
5. To satisfy workers by making them feel that they also have their voice in the management.
6. To give workers a better understanding of their role in the working of the industry.
7. To develop better mutual understanding so that workers do not resist a change (new technology) for their betterment.
8. To reduce labour turn-over, absenteeism and tardiness.
9. To minimize the number of grievances and therefore industrial disputes.
10. To make managing subordinates, easy.

4.12.2 Types of Worker Participation

The formal and informal participation are discussed briefly:

4.12.2.1 Formal Participation

It consists of some plan for labour management cooperation. To some degree, it is recognized as a modus operandi between management and workers, frequently through a union. Workers and management may work together on such plans as accident prevention, elimination of waste and defective work, attendance and absenteeism, employee insurance plans, and so on. Individually, workers can participate in management through suggestion systems, delegation and job enlargement in which workers plan and decide their own work.

Types of formal participation: Formal participation can either be ascending type or descending type. In ascending type of participation, the elected representatives of workers participate in managerial decisions at higher levels such as in the board of directors meeting. In descending type of participation, workers participate in planning and deciding their own work on the shop floor.

Collectively, workers can participate in the following:

(i) Works committees: These are meant for promoting measures for securing and preserving amity and good relations between workers and management. A works committee comments upon matters of common interest, and attempts to settle any material difference of opinion between the two parties.

(ii) Joint-councils: Joint-council of workers and management may decide the issues on which interests of management and workers are identical. For example, accident prevention and safety measures, determination of production standards, worker's training, welfare measures, etc.

(iii) Information sharing: It refers to those informations in which workers are told about certain aspects of the company. For example, information regarding expansion plans, financial position of the company etc.

(iv) Employee's director: Employee's Director is an elected representative of the employees who is also one of the member of Board of Directors.

4.12.2.2 Informal Participation

It is more typically at the work-group level where the foreman develops the opportunity for the group of workers to take part in a problem-solving or decision-making process. Typically, the matters on which decisions are taken are those within the prerogatives of the foreman or supervisor.

4.12.3 Success of Workers' Participation In Management

The success of the scheme depends on the following points.

1. There should be an atmosphere of cooperation and trust between the management and the workers.

2. Workers who are participating must be capable of understanding the problems, their complexities and interactions.
3. The participating workers should be able to express themselves to their own satisfaction.
4. Workers should be permitted to participate in decision-making on company matters as in introducing new machinery or newer methods of operation.
5. The participation of a worker must not adversely affect his status or role.
6. Discussions should be frank and free and without any reservation.
7. Both the parties should respect each other's interests.

It is generally commented that most of the relatively rare successes of such consultations seems to occur where an unusually progressive manager is blessed with unusually competent union officials.

Review Questions

1. Define staffing. What are the key staffing activities?
2. What are the procedural steps involved in the process of selection?
3. Why is human resource planning necessary? What factors must managers of a human resource planning programme consider?
4. What methods of recruitment can managers use? What are the advantages and disadvantages of recruitment from within?
5. What are the defects of in-depth interviews? How can they be minimized?
6. Explain in detail the various HRD subsystems and their contributions.
7. What is the difference between training and development?
8. How good are the internal sources of recruitment of key personnel, especially in middle level positions? Explain.
9. Explain organizational conflict. Is conflict desirable in certain situations? If so, then describe some of these situations.
10. Define inter-group dependence and give examples where work of one group depends upon the work of another group. How can each interdependence cause conflicts among groups?
11. Explain in detail the various types of conflict that are inherent in the very nature of human beings. Give examples that are relevant to each type of conflict.

Caselets

GROUP BEHAVIOUR

JJ Industries is a manufacturing company with line and staff organization. Pandian, a young staff officer developed a plan of increasing the life of certain equipments in the plant. He took the plan directly to the foreman of the department but was rebuffed by the supervisior who privately acknowledged the merit of the plan but resented the staff officer trying to show off his talents. The staff officer's association condemned the behaviour of Pandian that he should have allowed the plan to appear as a contribution of the staff group rather than his own.

Question 1: Analyze the situation in terms of the possible causes of the reaction of the supervisor and staff officer's group.

Question 2: Suggest measures to diffuse the situation.

HUMAN RESOURCE PLANNING

Chamber Chemicals Limited has planned for computerization of nearly 50% of its production, operation and control activities They have taken into account all resources including human. The human resource planners suggested the redeployment of chemical engineers in their newly started sister concern and retrenchment of surplus employees in all other categories. They also recommended to the management that there was no need for further recruitment or for any other action plan. The computerization was over by 1998. When the management wanted to start the production on the newly computerized process, it was shocked to note that not many employees in the production department were suitable to the new jobs and the information supplied by the human resource planners in this regard did not match with the reality.

Question 1: Identify the problem in this case.

Question 2: What should the management do now to deal with the problem taking into account both the short- and long-term perspectives?

CHAPTER 5

Directing

Leadership is the activity of influencing people to strive willingly for group objectives. Leadership is "interpersonal influence exercised in a situation and directed through the communication process, toward the attainment of a specialized goal or goals". A supervisor is the leader of a group or has a set target to be achieved in a given time. His leadership comes into play when the group goes adrift when there is a problem and a quick decision is to be made.

5.1 SUPERVISION AND LEADERSHIP

The essence of supervision and leadership are discussed below:

5.1.1 SUPERVISION

Supervision can broadly be classified as:

(i) close supervision
(ii) general supervision

5.1.1.1 Close Supervision

Close supervision reduces the worker's effectiveness. Most workers want enough supervision to be sure that they are doing their work correctly. Close supervision implies that the workers are incompetent and might lack in morale. Jobs requiring high quality and low time limit need close supervision. New workers need close supervision than old workers. This helps to develop good working habits.

5.1.1.2 General Supervision

General supervision gives the employees a chance to develop their talents; they learn to make decisions by being in a position to make them. Since the work is a result of their own efforts, they take pride in their work, improve productivity and show less absenteeism. It is likely that an employee takes a better decision since he is closest to the problems. The supervisor also gets more time to spend on his other functions.

5.1.2 LEADERSHIP

Leadership, as defined earlier, is interpersonal influence exercised in order to guide people toward goal achievement. The person exercising this influence is called a leader. He can be relied upon for the performance of leadership functions continuously.

Leaders derive their authority from the group rather than imposing it upon them. He earns leadership by being popular and dependable or mostly the latter. It is this leadership that gives him the power to act. To clarify the difference between power and authority, it is being discussed below.

Authority is the right or privilege of directing or requesting workers to do or to refrain from doing something. It includes the right to take disiciplinary action. *Power* is the ability to achieve the expected outcomes that emerge from supervisory directives. Authority is the right to tell a subordinate what to do; power is the ability to get the subordinate to do it.

5.1.3 LEADERSHIP TRAITS

Following are the traits of a leader found in general:

1. Leaders are self confident, well-integrated, and emotionally stable.
2. Leaders want to take leadership responsibility and are competent in handling new situations.
3. Leaders identify with the goals and values of the groups they lead.
4. They are warm, sensitive, and sympathetic toward other people, and give practical suggestions.
5. They are intelligent in relation to other group members.

5.1.4 LEADERSHIP STYLES

Studies reveal that leaders use leadership styles that are consistent with their personalities. The *style* reflects the leader's desire to be efficient, not the need to be autocratic. Leaders are not *born* but developed. Autocratic, participative, and free-reign are the three general classification of leadership styles.

5.1.4.1 Autocratic Leaders

As the name suggests, these leaders give orders for everything and provide no freedom of work for subordinates. Their instructions are straightforward and the doubts can be cleared easily. Some workers may feel that they are not given freedom to make decisions. This one-way communication might lead to misunderstanding and subsequent errors. It can also result in poor decisions. Such styles are needed during crises.

5.1.4.2 Participative Leaders

These leaders invite participation from subordinates to exercise their responsibility and freedom. They are concerned about their relations with the employees. Democratic leaders confer final authority on the group. Consultative leaders require a great deal of involvement, but they alone have the authority to make final decisions. Participative leaders expect constant feedback. This style of functioning consumes time.

5.1.4.3 Free-reign Leaders

They are completely non-directional. They give the group complete freedom to decide, having made clear the goals and guidelines to achieve it. This offers the greatest use of time and resources. This approach can motivate people to initiate and carry out complex work plans efficiently and responsibly. This style of functioning is seen, to some degree, among professionals like engineers, teachers and scientists.

5.2 MORALE

Success and high morale begin with a self-confident supervisor, and that feeling of confidence can be contagious. An effective supervisor is a listening supervisor. Listening is an active, not a passive action. Some people are thinkers, who are well organized and slow in decision-making. Some are feelers who like to be adventurous and are involved with people and their problems. Such people may be impulsive and creative but impatient and uncompromising. Morale is the attitude of each individual in a group toward the group's purpose and goals. People need encouragement both inwardly and outwardly i.e. employees need to be encouraged through raise in salary, promotions and also other benefits like vacation etc. A survey of such records, like labour turnover, production records, waste and spillage, absenteeism, tardiness, pilferage and safety records, suggestion boxes etc. will indicate the employee morale. Morale is subjective and a supervisor to be effective, should know that motives are very important in understanding the employees. Various motives are power, affiliation, achievement, status, and security. Young workers look for praise and recognition. Older workers need the sense of belonging. Need for security dominates the preretirement age.

5.2.1 Improving Morale

Following actions can help improve the employee morale:

1. Delegating power to an employee to carry out a task without interference from top-level management.
2. Group decisions can be taken and flexibility in working hours can be allowed.
3. Job rotation and job enrichment relieve monotony and make the person to work hard. Over specializing leads to boredom.

5.3 MANAGERIAL GRID

The managerial grid (Figure 5.1) is a tool to help supervisors assess their leadership style. The grid was developed by Blake and Mouton to point out two major aspects of the supervisor's job. These variables are plotted on the chart based on supervisory self-assessment to determine which of the 5 styles of leadership best characterizes the supervisor.

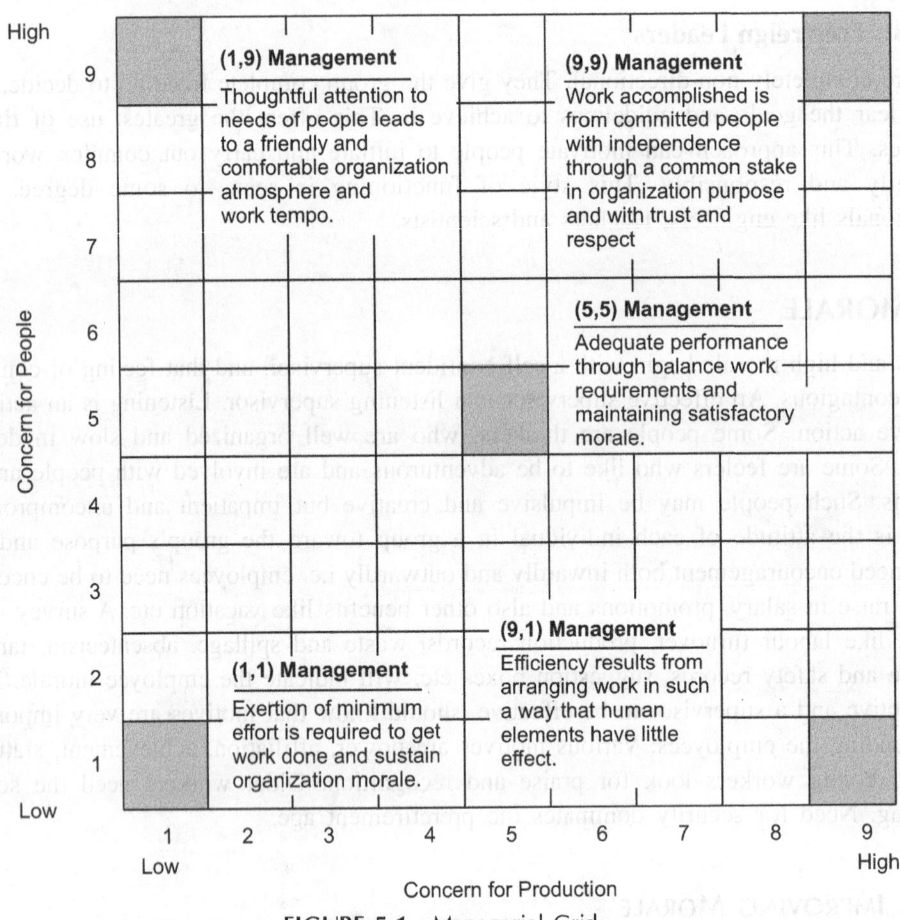

FIGURE 5.1 Managerial Grid.

5.3.1 Blake–Mouton Leadership Styles

Brief summaries of the five possible leadership styles on the basis of Blake–Mouton managerial grid are as follows:

Style (1,1): A leadership style that places low concern for employees and the job. This style suggests that maximum production is not possible because employees are lazy and indifferent.

Style (1,9): A leadership style that places high concern for employees and low concern for job. Here, the supervisor works at creating good fellowship and pleasant relationships instead of getting the job done.

Style (9,1): A leadership style that places high concern for the job and low concern for the employees. The employees are expected to produce or suffer consequences. The workers are thought of as machines.

Style (9,9): A leadership style that places high concern for employees as well as high concern for the job. This is the best style. It views the supervisor's job as one that requires a blend of job interests and people interests.

Style (5,5): A middle-of-the-road leadership style that places some concern for employees and some concern for the job. The supervisor does not go all out for either the job or the people but does not ignore each category, either.

5.4 TRI-DIMENSIONAL GRID

Reddin conceptualized a 3-dimensional grid, also known as 3-D management, borrowing some of the ideas from managerial grid. Reddin has integrated the concepts of leadership styles with the situational demand of a specific environment. 3-dimensional axes represent task orientation, relationship orientation, and effectiveness.

Task Orientation (TO) is defined as the extent to which a manager directs his subordinate's efforts towards goal attainment; *Relationship Orientation (RO)* is defined as the extent to which a manager has personal relationship; and *Effectiveness* is defined as the extent to which a manager is successful in his positions.

5.5 COMMUNICATION

Communication is one of the most important facilitators of managerial activities. Without it, facts, ideas, and experiences cannot be exchanged. Understanding is the target in communicating. This emphasizes the need for knowing the subject, finding out what the recipient knows about it, and anticipating questions and answers. Communication is essentially a human transaction, and the influence and importance of human behaviour confront any person who wants to communicate with another. Being sensitive to the other person's needs and feelings is an important part of the communication effort. Communication helps managerial planning to be performed organizing to be carried out actuating to be followed and controlling to be applied, effectively. Successful communication is the result of competent management. Conceivably, one might be an excellent communicator, but a poor manager. However, a competent manager is nearly always a good communicator. Excellent communicative efforts may result in total failure if the management is ineffective.

5.5.1 Types of Communication

Communication may be classified as follows:

- On the basis of relationships between concerned parties i.e. formal or informal.
- On the basis of its flow or direction i.e. downward, upward or horizontal.
- On the basis of methods used for the purpose i.e. oral, written or by gestures.

Formal communication follows the chain of command of the formal organization. For any such communication, the path of transmission is prescribed, the form designated, and official sanction provided. This may include executive orders regarding new bonus systems or stock option plans, technical information for decision-making purposes, and procedural policies and rules as set forth in company manuals. *Informal communication,* also called grapevine are not provided in the organization structure. It may be used to spread false or distorted messages.

Downward communication refers to the flow of messages from the top-level to the lower level of the organization. *Upward communication* refers to the movement of messages from the lower level to the higher level management. *Horizontal communication* refers to the passing of messages within a department as in case of staff relationship.

Communication taking place verbally without any kind of written instructions comes under *Oral communication. Written communication* on the other hand implies messsages circulated in written form e.g. circulars issued in an organization. *Communication by gtestures* takes place when bodily expressions come into play for passing messages.

5.5.2 Efficient and Effective Communication

Efficient communication attempts to minimize time and cost in the total information exchange effort. Cost may include monetary expenses, foregone comfort, and the amount of energy and effort expended in communicating. A manager must always consider the costs and consequences of efficient versus effective communication in choosing the formal or informal channels of communication to maximize company performance and employee growth.

5.5.3 Purpose of Communication

1. To increase acceptance of organizational rules by subordinates in allowing them to exchange views, resolve ambiguities about their jobs, and settle conflicts among groups and individuals.
2. To gain greater commitment to organizational objectives by motivating, controlling, and evaluating the performance of organizational personnel. Assigning tasks, issuing orders, praising performance, and criticizing mistakes involve some degree of effective communication.
3. To provide data necessary for decision-making. Communication is a vital information function for solving simple or complex problems and making accurate decisions to positively influence organizational performance.

4. To clarify task responsibilities, identify authority positions, and provide accountability for performance. Organizational charts, information programs, and standard operating procedures attempt to routinize decision-making and provide a formal communication channel for management control in organizations.

5.5.4 Communication Process

Communication researchers have raised the following five questions, the answers to which make up the communication process.

1. Who? (Source/originator of message)
2. Says what? (Verbal and nonverbal symbols that constitute the message)
3. In which channel? (Selection of information transmission i.e. speaking, writing, etc.)
4. To whom? (Intentional or unintentional receiver of message)
5. With what effect? (Is message interpreted accurately and responded to appropriately)

5.5.4.1 General Model

The general model of communication (Figure 5.2) includes the basic elements of communication i.e. communicator, encoder, a message, a transmission medium, a decoder, a receiver, feedback, and noise.

Step 1: Sender-planner: The communicator or message sender must conceptualize the message mentally before it is encoded. This is the planning of the communication process.

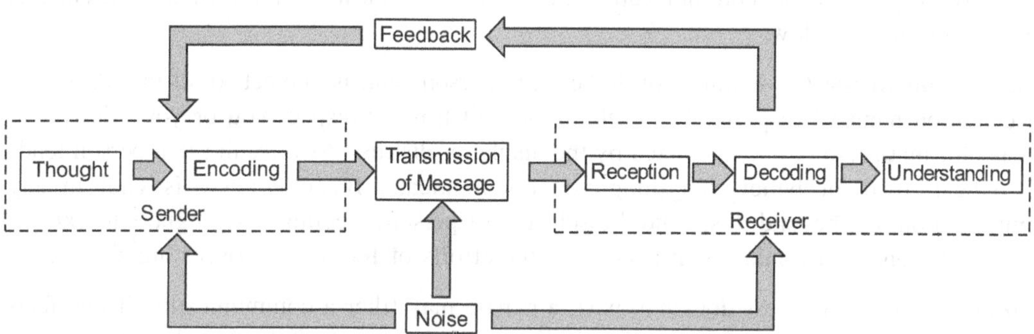

FIGURE 5.2 General Model of Communication Process.

Step 2: Encoding: It involves selecting the medium through which to communicate the planned message. Media include speaking, writing, signalling (e.g. with flags), gesturing, physical contacts (e.g. kissing, hitting.) or even attempting mental extrasensory perception. The goal is mutually of understanding between sender and receiver.

Step 3: Message and Medium: This step involves the actual physical transmission of the conceptualized message. The physical act of speaking or writing or gesturing to someone transmits a message with varying degrees of understanding by the receivers. Nonverbal transmission such as facial expression, eye contact (or lack of it), strength of grip in a handshake, or sway of certain parts of the anatomy provides powerful meanings to the intended message and can enhance or distort effective communication efforts.

Step 4: Receiving: This simply involves the physical reception of the message; hearing, seeing, feeling, sensing and so on.

Steps 5 and 6: Decoding and response: Decoding is the receiver's interpretation of the message. It involves the mental process of asking: What does this mean to me and what should I do about it? This is affected by many factors—perception of the sender, past experience with similar communication, interpretation of body language, personal desire, etc.

Step 7: Feedback: The receiver's reaction to the message is a form of communication back to the sender and actually follows the same step-by-step process as the initial sender sequence. Feedback can be written, spoken, signalled, or given through other means. All these reactions condition the initial message sender (who now becomes a receiver for a subsequent communication response).

5.5.5 BARRIERS TO EFFECTIVE COMMUNICATION

A lack of understanding about what really transpires in a communication exchange is a major barrier to good communication in organizations, but there are several other common barriers to effective organizational communication that cause breakdowns in information exchange. These are discussed below.

1. Lack of openness: Communication is between persons and is subject to all the influences that condition human behaviour. If somebody doesn't trust or respect you or your viewpoint, it's easy for that person to be distracted by the dislike or distrust. As a result , that person tends not to hear, read, or believe anything you communicate. Basic honesty is vital in any communication, but beyond this, candid disclosure of personal feelings, willingness to express contrary opinions, and frankness in evaluating the efforts of fellow employees are significant.

2. Filtering: When openness does not exist, a person may filter a communication if one feels it will harm one's chances of promotion. Employees tend to shape their behaviour to reap satisfying rewards. It is not uncommon for subordinates to refrain from communicating information that is potentially threatening to them or their superiors. Likewise, a communication issued at the top management level may be considerably altered by the time it reaches the bottom level.

3. Degree of motivation: When communicating, people have various motives – to persuade, to tell, to entertain, and to reinforce ideas. The enthusiasm displayed and the interests shown definitely condition the communication. When it is planned to appeal to the assumed motives of the participant, it usually is more effective.

4. Either–or thinking: There is also the consideration of a person behaving under the influence of "either-or" thinking. Early in life we learn to use such terms as near/far, objective/subjective, black/white, and we think and speak in this way. Actually most things don't conform to these convenient extremes. By taking the position of either-or, a person is committed to a position where compromising or viewing a situation correctly is not feasible. This places rigidities in communication.

5. Assumptions: Everyone makes assumptions about a working environment and the people in it. But when a high or low-level assumption is made without checking the facts, trouble and communication breakdown can occur. Mutual understanding must not be taken for granted. This assumption is one of the biggest causes of communication failure.

6. Snap reactions: When the receiver feels that little will be gained by listening or reading carefully, the communication is almost certain to be ineffective. The possibility that the given message has a new idea, fact, or point of view doesn't occur to the receiver. Frequently, this condition exists in communication between two persons in conflict or when one person is short-tempered.

7. Fear: Fear plays an important part in communication when emotionally loaded words like failure, death, strike, liar, and defeat are used. Fear can affect the translation of information. When communication is expressed under tension or nervousness, its effectiveness can be changed considerably by increasing mental and physical energy and alertness.

8. Language: The meaning of words is influenced by association. For example, the word 'pay' brings to mind different words to different persons. To the executive it might suggest bonus, checking account, cheque or bills. To clerks of the personnel department, promotion, job evaluation, or increase in salary may be thought of, while to another employee it may be associated with food, clothes, car, family, date, or blonde. There is also body language, which includes facial expressions, the twinkle in the eye, gestures made, and tone of voice. For example, a word spoken in anger can have an entirely different meaning from the same word spoken in friendliness.

9. Time constraints: When a manager or employee is placed under a severe time constraint, he or she is likely to hurry the conceptualization and encoding process or emotionally decode a received message that can result in extremely poor communication and performance.

10. Perception: Perception is the way in which we individually interpret messages from other people or sources. We are products of our past experiences and these cumulatively affect our perception and cause us to view people, events and other messages differently. Several perceptual factors restrict our accuracy, effectiveness, and efficiency in communicating.

11. Stereotyping: Stereotyping is generalizing "about a class of people, objects, or events that are widely held by a given culture." This orientation expresses itself in such statements and mindsets as All roadside automobile mechanics cheat their stranded customers.

12. Halo effect: A halo effect is "a process in which a general impression which is favourable or unfavourable is used by judges to evaluate several specific traits". The halo serves as a screen keeping the receiver from actually seeing the trait he is judging. For example, a manager might single out one trait, such as an excellent attendance record, and perceive that the employee's productivity and quality of work must also be outstanding.

13. Projection: Projection is tending to attribute one's own undesirable personal trait(s) to another. For instance, if you are personally disorganized and tend always to be a few minutes late to meetings, you will probably be extremely aware of this trait in another individual who has a similar habit and dislike it very much. This is a sort of defense mechanism that allows a person to relieve feelings of guilt by projecting blame and incompetence onto some other person.

5.5.6 Means to Effective Communication

Since communication is an inseparable part of management that facilitates other basic managerial functions, it is important that it be effective. To make it effective and improve comminication results, some actions need to be taken. These are discussed below.

5.5.6.1 Improving Perception

1. Recognize the role of the receiver as active. The active receiver should seek as much information as possible about the subject to improve the accuracy of the perception.
2. Develop a close relationship with the subject being assessed. People's perception of each other significantly changes after they work together.
3. Create a climate that is favourable to the free flow of information in all directions. Considerate attitude and trust nourish accurate perception.
4. Be aware of the uniqueness of your own frame of reference. Realize that each of us view the world in our own way and that everyone else will not have our level of concern excitement, or disturbance.

5.5.6.2 Recognizing Essentiality

A major step in improving communication is to believe in its essentiality in management. By means of communication, a manager finds out about problems, draws up plans, assists employees to satisfy their basic wants, gives instruction, and checks results. Each manager is obligated to communicate clearly, to listen sympathetically, to respond considerately and to act promptly.

5.5.6.3 Using Human Relation Tool

The most effective communication takes place among people with common points of view. The manager who fosters good relationship with group members will have less difficulty in communicating with them. Human behaviour must be taken into account and human relation tool utilisted. It includes the following.

1. Plan, Plan: Take time to plan effective communication. This boils down to expressing the message clearly and being a good listener and reader. What to communicate is vital but consideration for how and when to communicate is also essential.

2. Create positive climate: Seek to establish a work environment that encourages upward communication. Upward communication is also encouraged by the manager expressing an interest in the problems and views of the subordinates, and not discriminating against any one because of the information given.

3. Use the grapevine: The grapevine is an informal means of circulating information or gossip or even a baseless rumour. In the context of an enterprise the grapevine takes on the role of spreading official information and messages among its members. The grapevine provides a better channel for propagating official policies and procedures among the members than the formal channels of communication. A good system of communication should treat grapevine as a supplementary to the formal communication.

4. Empathize: When the information being communicated is vital to the participants' needs, the communication will tend to be more effective. Among the list of items that usually rank high in employees' interest are company and industry outlook, expansion plans, labour policies, personnel changes, organization changes, company finances, research activities, company ethics, and taxations.

5. Use pictures: "One picture is worth a thousand words". Hence, use appropriate illustrations and charts to get your ideas across. Be sure the visual is relevant to the idea being communicated. If possible, add glamour to the communication.

6. Be open to feedback: Utilize communication feedback. The feedback can reveal whether the communication is effective or not, and why. It enables a manager to improve personal communication.

7. Kiss (Keep it short, stupid): Finally, avoid overcommunicating. Too much communication is as bad as too little communication. If people are deluged with company communication, many of its aims are probably lost or defeated.

5.6 MOTIVATION

Motivation is a predisposition to act in a specific goal-directed manner. Motivation may be defined as the state of an individual's perspective, which represents the strength of his or her propensity to exert effort towards some particular behaviour. An internal need energizes and activates human behaviour. Drive is the inner force that propels behaviour in a specific direction and goals are the incentives or payoffs that reinforce personal satisfaction, that in turn reinforces the perpetuation of needs. The extent of drive depends on the perceived level of satisfaction that can be achieved by the goal. Generally speaking, when employees enjoy their jobs, find the work challenging, and like the work environment, they will usually put forth their best efforts and perform their tasks enthusiastically. In other words, they are motivated to produce at optimal output.

5.6.1 TRADITIONAL APPROACH TO MOTIVATION

Many people argue that the traditional "carrot and stick" method of motivation still works today, the carrot being money and the stick being physical, financial, or social punishment. The assumption has been that people will work harder and produce more if substantial financial rewards are placed before them or if they are threatened with dismissal or peer embarrassment or physical punishment.

5.7 NEED THEORIES

Need theories focus on the importance of analyzing and understanding the psychological factors with individuals that cause them to behave in certain ways. Various need theories have been put forward by scholars during the years from which four are being disucssed here.

5.7.1 MASLOW'S NEED HIERARCHY

Maslow recognized five basic human needs which constitute a "hierarchy" (Figure 5.3).

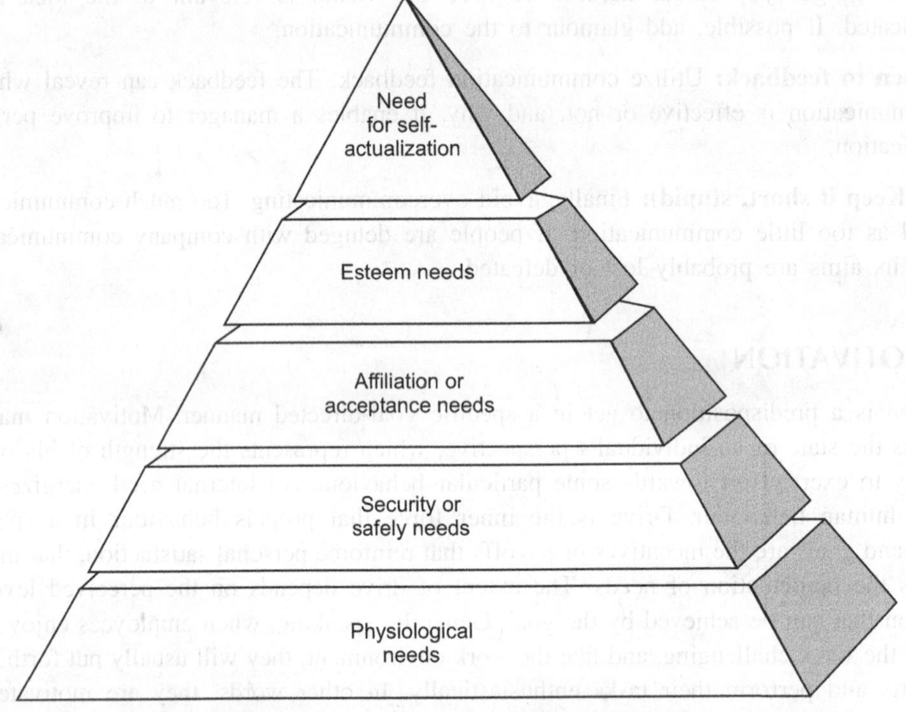

FIGURE 5.3 Maslow's Need Hierarchy Model.

Level 1: The first level of physiological needs includes food, air, water, sleep, shelter, sex, and any other necessities to sustain and preserve life. These are the most basic needs, and people will be motivated to fulfill them first through whatever behaviour. Once satisfied, the needs cease to operate as a prime motivator of behaviour.

Level 2: The safety needs consists of the need for clothing, shelter, and an environment with a predictable pattern such as job security, pension, and insurance. People are motivated to fulfill these needs only when the physiological needs are mostly satisfied.

Level 3: Love or social needs include the need to be liked by others, to be a wanted member, and to belong to a group other than just a family. Developing meaningful relationships on the job, becoming a member in good standing of the informal organization, and receiving the grapevine communication are means of fulfilling this need in a person's worklife.

Level 4: Esteem needs include the need for self respect, sense of achievement, and recognition from others. The desire for status and prestige is an important aspect of the need for esteem. "Satisfaction of the self-esteem need leads to feelings of self-confidence, worth, strength, capability, adequacy, and being useful and necessary in the world.

Level 5: Self-actualization is the concept of fulfilling one's potential and becoming everything one is capable of becoming. To some, it may mean becoming the ideal mother or father, to another becoming the best jogger in the office, or to another developing the reputation of becoming the most daring investor in the firm.

5.7.1.1 Practical Implications

If an employee is concerned with the basic physiological needs of making the house, payment, and purchasing food for the family, attention must be devoted to wages and salary for that employee. Compliments and offer of future advancement (esteem) will not do much to motivate that individual until the physiological needs are first satisfied. Even when compensation needs are fulfilled, employees want to have a sense of job security. Managers can do much to satisfy such security needs by proper and adequate communication and personal relationships. New employees have social needs of being quickly accepted into the work group, and a well-implemented orientation program can expeditiously satisfy this need. In contemporary society, the needs lower in the hierarchy are more completely satisfied than the higher needs. Many people have their physiological and safety needs fulfilled. It is the affection and esteem needs that require satisfaction while for the people at the highest level, self-actualization needs are of prime importance. The hierarchy of needs is not always followed in a rigid pattern, there are reversals and substitutions. Some persons centre on esteem needs, the acquisition of wealth, for example, almost to the exclusion of affection needs i.e. the need to belong to a group. Such a situation may have developed due to a suppression of affection needs early in life with a resultant emphasis on esteem needs as a substitute. Needs are relative in their strength and are individualistic. A lower need does not necessarily have to be fulfilled completely before higher need emerges.

5.7.2 Herzberg's Motivation—Hygiene Theory

Herzberg developed his theory after surveying hundreds of accountants, engineers, and other managerial personnel. Herzberg's research caused him to categorize various needs of individuals into two groups (Table 5.1):

1. Hygiene factors or "dissatisfiers", and
2. Motivation factors or "satisfiers".

Table 5.1 Herzberg's hygiene and motivating factors.

Group I: Hygiene factors	*Group II: Motivation factors*
Money and compensation	Challenging work
Personal life	Added responsibility
Working conditions	Advancement
Working relationships	Recognition of good work
Status	Personal growth
Job security	
Company policy and administration	
Quality of supervision	

Herzberg's model is shown in Figure 5.4.

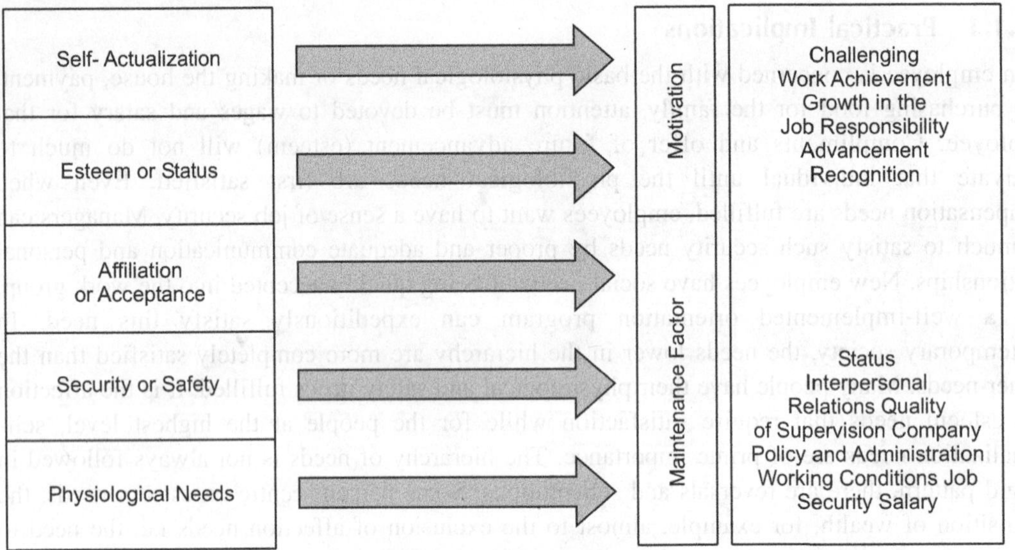

FIGURE 5.4 Herzberg's Modeling.

5.7.2.1 Hygiene Factors

The hygiene factors are dissatisfiers because if all of them are adequately met with in a work situation, people will not be dissatisfied. Their adequacy, hence, does not really motivate people. However, if any of the hygiene factors is not attended to properly in a job, dissatisfaction can occur. For example, lower pay, bad supervision, or a hazardous or uncomfortable workplace can create substantial dissatisfaction among employees.

5.7.2.2 Motivating Factors

These factors are aspects of the task or work itself. They include challenge, chance for personal growth and performance feedback. In other words, as viewed by the employee, a job with these characteristics means it bears the motivational factors. These factors contribute heavily to the satisfaction of the employee and have a positive effect on his or her performance.

5.7.3 McClellands's Three Needs Model

The model is concerned with three motives, namely, the need for achievement, the need for power, and the need for affiliation. Everyone possesses these needs in varying degrees. Individuals with a high need for achievement thrive on jobs and projects that tax their skills and abilities. Such individuals are goal-oriented in their activities. Individuals with high affiliation needs value interpersonal relationships and exhibit sensitivity towards other peoples' feelings. Individuals with high power needs seek to dominate, influence or have control over people. McClelland's concept of achievement motivation is related to Herzberg's motivation–hygiene theory. His research revealed that managers generally score high in the need for achievement.

5.7.4 Vroom's Valence–Expectancy Theory

According to this theory, a person's motivation towards an action at any time would be determined by his perception that a certain type of action would lead to a specific outcome. There are three variables and they have high positive values to imply motivated performance choices. If any one of the variables approaches zero, the probability of motivated performance approaches zero. Valence is the strength of an individual's preference for a reward expectancy is the probability that a particular action will lead to a desired reward and instrumentality denotes an individual's estimate that performance will result in achieving the reward. This can be expressed as follows:

$$\text{Motivation} = \text{Valence} \times \text{Expectancy} \times \text{Instrumentality}$$

The combination that produces the strongest motivation comprises high positive valence, high expectancy and high instrumentality. If all the three are low, the resulting motivation will be weak. In brief, Vroom's model attempts to explain how individual's goals influence his efforts.

Review Questions

1. Define leadership. What are the leadership traits?
2. Explain the various forms of leadership styles.

3. What is morale? How can it be improved?
4. Explain managerial grid.
5. What is the purpose of communication?
6. Distinguish between formal and informal communication.
7. How important is the informal communication networks in the efficient and effective operations of the organization.
8. What are the barriers to effective communication?
9. What steps can you take to overcome noise?
10. How is Maslows's theory of hierarchy of needs related to motivation in organizations?
11. What is Herzberg's two factor approach to job satisfaction and dissatisfaction? Why has this approach been criticized?
12. According to McClelland's theory of needs, the primary motive is the need to succeed in competitive situations. Do you agree with this concept? Explain.

Caselets

IMPORTANCE OF COMMUNICATION

On January 28, 1986, the Challenger Space Shuttle crashed killing seven people. The Challenger mission consisted of two complex systems—the technical, and the management systems. The technical problem was the troublesome O-rings, which under pressure and low temperatures became ineffective and did not provide the required seal. Engineers and managers were aware of the problem. The engineers of the contracting firm for the booster rocket argued against the launch. Management may have been pressurised by NASA to go ahead with the launch. Finally, the go-ahead signal was given by managers. Engineers were excluded from the final decision. The result was the death of seven Americans. Was it a lack of communication between engineers and managers, or was it due to safety versus on-time launching? Perhaps there was also false confidence in the mission because of past luck.

Question 1: Could this accident been prevented? Explain.

LEADERSHIP

In 1994, Sanjay, a professional manager was elected Chairman of General Insurance Company, which was at that time the largest general insurance company in the country. During the next five years, while the business increased, it did not grow as fast as its major competitors had, and the company dropped from 1st to 5th place. After deliberations, the board of directors concluded that lack of leadership in the sales of both fire and marine policies was the major cause for the company's slow progress. It also concluded that the two directors in charge of sales in these two major areas of business were competent executives and leaders, but the regional and district managers working under them were not so competent. Sanjay called the two directors responsible for fire and marine policies and asked them to ensure strong leadership at the regional and district levels or else quit their jobs. After the meeting, one director told the other, "How do we make people leaders. How can we be sure whether or not a person is a leader".

Question 1: If you were one of the directors, how would you have answered the other director?

Question 2: How would you go about developing competent and strong leaders.

CHAPTER 6

Controlling

Controlling is determining what is being accomplished i.e. evaluating the performance and, if necessary, applying corrective measures so that the performance takes place according to plans. Controlling can be viewed as detecting and correcting significant variations in the results obtained from planned activities. Controlling is a managerial necessity and not an impediment or a hindrance.

6.1 CONTROLLING AND PLANNING

Planning bears a close relationship to controlling. Planning identifies commitments to action intended for future accomplishments. Controlling function is performed to ensure that the commitments are carried out. When controlling clearly demonstrates that the planning cannot be implemented, a modified or new plan must be developed. When unacceptable performance under a plan becomes common, controlling facilitates the decision regarding altering the plan or abandoning it. A plan should identify and specify the controls needed, otherwise it is not a viable plan. Effective controlling assists in the effort to regulate actual performance to assure that it takes place as planned.

6.2 CONTROL PROCESS

Controlling (Figure 6.1) consists of a process made up of the following three definite steps which are universal:

1. Measuring performance.
2. Comparing performance with the standard, and ascertaining the difference, if any.
3. Correcting unfavourable deviation by means of remedial action.

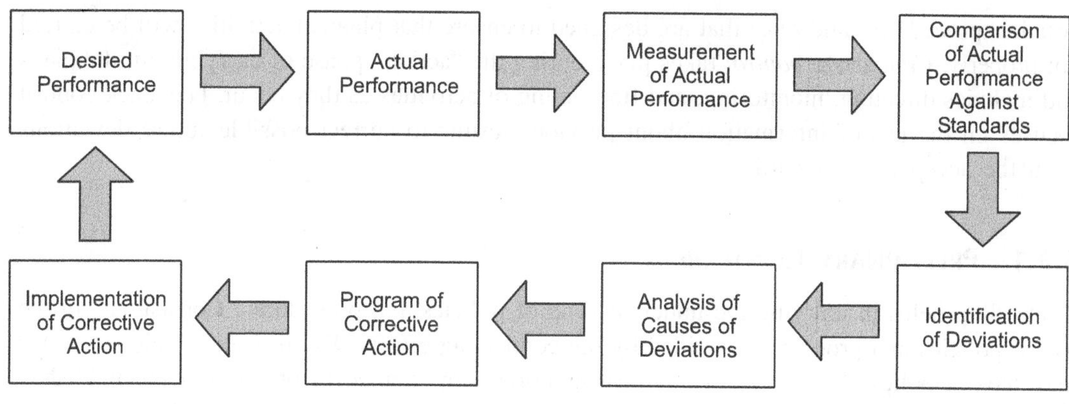

FIGURE 6.1 Control Process.

6.2.1 Measuring Performance

Measurement is the determination of the quantity or capacity of a well-defined entity. Without measurement, a manager is forced to guess or use rule-of-thumb methods, which may or may not be reliable. Measurement requires a measuring unit and a count of how many times the entity is under consideration.

6.2.2 Comparing Performance with Standards

When there is a difference between the performance and the standard, judgment is frequently required to assess its significance. To establish a rigid absolute variation, or even a range for what is satisfactory, is inadequate. Relatively small deviations from the standard are approved for the performance of some activities, while in other cases a slight deviation may be serious.

6.2.3 Correcting Deviations

This step ensures that operations are adjusted and efforts are made to achieve the results initially planned. Wherever significant variances are uncovered, vigorous and immediate action is imperative. Effective control cannot tolerate needless delays, excuses, or excessive exceptions. For maximum effectiveness, correcting the deviation should be accompanied by fixed and individual responsibility. Fixed individual responsibility tends to personalize the work. It becomes one's job, one's responsibility to take the necessary action to reach satisfactory performance, and one's responsibility to make any correction that might be necessary.

6.3 TYPES OF CONTROL

Controls have been designated as preliminary control, concurrent control, and feedback control. *Preliminary control* takes place before operations begin and includes the development of policies, procedures, and rules that are designed to ensure that planned activities will be carried out properly. *Concurrent control* takes place during the "action" phase of carrying out the plans and includes directing, monitoring, and fine-tuning of activities as they occur. Feedback control focuses on the use of information about previous results to correct possible future deviations from the acceptable standard.

6.3.1 PRELIMINARY CONTROL

Controlling helps in unifying the understanding of policies and procedures. Consistency in the use of policies and procedures is aided by the controlling efforts. To illustrate, a sales manager may have a policy that the manager must authorize any change in price from the published prices in writing; no salesperson is permitted to change any price. In effect, this clarifies the existent policy and provides control to the sales manager, who can know what is going on and exercise regulation and restraint over it.

6.3.2 CONCURRENT CONTROL

Concurrent control is the heart of any operating control system. On the production floor, all efforts are directed toward getting out the right quantity of the right product at the right time. In an airline terminal, the baggage crew must get the right bags to the right airplanes at the right time. Concurrent control can assist in guaranteeing that the plan will be carried out at the specified time and under required conditions.

6.3.3 FEEDBACK CONTROL

Feedback control implies that some data have been gathered and analyzed and the results returned to someone or something in the process being controlled so that corrections may be made. Timing is critical, if feedback control is to have any benefit. A process may be under real time control, such as a computer controlled robot or an assembly line. These units have sensing units, which determine whether they are in the correct position to perform their function. If not, there is a built-in control device that will make corrections. As a contrast, banks, which are trying to move toward real time transactions with electronic funds transfer (EFT) systems, must cope with slow manual systems that take days to clear a cheque.

6.4 CONTROL AT ORGANIZATIONAL LEVELS

Top management is most concerned with preliminary control and with obtaining feedback to indicate the degree to which long-range plans are being successfully carried out. Due to the intangible nature of their work, it is difficult for top management to apply concurrent control. Assessing top management by such short-term results as return on investment, or market share increases have often created long-term problems for the firm. Middle level management is concerned with preliminary control in the form of operating policies and procedures. They are also charged with the responsibility of developing and justifying requests for new products, capital investment programs, and productivity improvement projects and of reporting on progress and controlling it. In these areas, feedback control is important. First-line (operating) management is concerned with immediate events and typically deals with a short time horizon. Anything that happened a month ago is ancient history, and anything that anticipates requirements for a month in the future is long-range planning to the first-line manager. This manager is interested in information that will help control quality, inventory, personnel, and costs on a day-to-day and even an hour-by-hour basis. Interchange of ideas among different levels is healthy and does not violate the control concepts discussed here.

6.5 INFORMATION AND CONTROL

The role of information in the control process is critical. Without accurate and timely information that can be used easily for decision-making, a control system will fall apart. With the increasing capabilities and decreasing costs of computers, it is relatively easy for large or small companies to gather huge amounts of data in a short time. It is much more difficult to summarize, analyze, and interpret the data in such a way as to change them into information that is useful for managerial decision-making.

6.5.1 DATA SOURCES FOR PERFORMANCE MEASUREMENT

Let us review the means commonly used to obtain data for measuring performance.

6.5.1.1 Personal Observations

The personal observations approach means going to the area of activities and taking notice of what is being done. The methods followed, the quality and quantity of work, the attitudes of employees, and the general operation are the types of things that might be observed.

Use of the personal observation approach has the following disadvantages.

1. It does not provide accurate quantitative values, and the information acquired is in broad and general terms.
2. It is time consuming and take the executive away from other tasks. Also, there is the possibility that the good intentions of the executive might be misunderstood by the employees.
3. Direct contact is limited to a few employees and happenings.

6.5.1.2 Oral Reports

One common example of oral reports is the practice of sales people reporting personally to their immediate manager at the close of each business day on the accomplishments, problems, or customers' reactions encountered. Frequently, oral reports are supplemented with direct observations and personal calls on customers. Oral reports maintain certain elements of the personal observation method, in that, information is transmitted orally and personal contact is included. The facial expressions, tone of voice, and general evaluation of the performance by the reporter can be observed, and questions can be asked at the most opportune time to clear any misunderstandings or to gain additional information. Tentative answers to conditions that need remedial action can also be worked out at the time of discussion. Oral reports can provide wide and complete coverage which is not always possible with the personal observation method.

6.5.1.3 Written Reports

These reports lend themselves to comprehensive data and are adaptable for statistics that are somewhat involved and detailed. Written reports also supply a permanent record for comparison or study at a future date. Frequently, written reports are supplemented by oral reports and direct observation. Care must be taken to ensure that meaningful information is conveyed by the report. Incorrect data or inadequate summarization makes a report useless for managerial decision-making (garbage in, garbage out). There are numerous types of written reports; some are primarily descriptive, others are statistical; some cover limited areas of operation, others deal with the entire enterprise. Reports should be reviewed periodically to be sure they are useful.

6.6 ANTICIPATORY CONTROLLING

Any activity can be controlled with respect to any or all of the following factors: (1) quality, (2) quantity, (3) time use, and (4) cost. For example, sales control is accomplished by controlling the quantity of sales and the cost of sales. The critical areas or happenings result from numerous conditions, but the most common are: human error, strikes, material shortages, failure of new processes, machines and shipments, and uncertainties.

6.7 MAJOR GUIDELINES TO EFFECTIVE CONTROLLING

Controlling results from action and must be continued to provide current valid data. The orientation is toward the future, control reports, for example, are not merely reports of the past. Furthermore, controlling is concentrated at points or interfaces where change occurs. The control process does not cover an operation in totality. This suggests that the location of control points should be selected carefully, with special attention given to avoid strains among organizational relationships. The inception and adoption of the controlling must contain reasonable certainty that it will work. It must be practical and it must fulfill a known and stated objective. Also, controls must be enforceable. The standard is the key in controlling. This is the basis for the evaluation, and the standard should use some form of measurement. Controlling diminishes in effectiveness as standards become inexact. When the plan is achieved or discarded, controlling can be stopped. The consensus of most managers is that multiple controls should be used. Among the more common controls are inventory control, production control, maintenance control, quality control, salary control, sales control, advertising control, and cost control. It is entirely possible to have good controlling at low cost and also poor controlling at high cost. A person controlling must be free to control, and this means freedom from being buried in details yet keeping in close touch with what is going on. Usually, the person with line authority should handle any corrective measures taken, while the staff authority is involved only in the control steps of measurement and comparison of performance.

6.8 MANAGEMENT AUDIT

Management audits have developed over the years as a way to evaluate the effectiveness and efficiency of various systems within an organization, from social responsibility to accounting control. Management audits may be performed for either internal or external purposes.

6.8.1 External Audit

An external audit is directed towards the evaluation of firms outside the boundaries of the corporation. The results of an external audit are generally used primarily for planning purposes. Some typical situations in which such an analysis might be beneficial are to:

(1) investigate other firms for possible merger or acquisition
(2) determine the soundness of the firm to be used as a major supplier, or
(3) find out the strengths and weaknesses of a competing firm to better exploit its own competitive advantages. Typically, publicly available data are used for such evaluations.

6.8.2 Internal Audit

Internal management audits may be used to improve the planning process as well as internal control systems. The periodic assessment of a company's managerial planning, organizing, actuating, and controlling by comparing it to what might be called the norm of successful operation is the essential meaning of an internal management audit. It reviews the company's past, present, and future performances. The areas covered by the company are examined with a view to determine whether the company is achieving maximum results from its endeavours, identifying areas where improvements are needed, and keeping expenditures to a minimum while carrying out required operations.

6.8.3 Merits of Auditing

A management audit cannot be conducted until the company has been operating for a sufficient time to establish its behaviour pattern. However, a company goes in favour of a management audit for the following reasons.

- To check on new policies and practices for both suitability and compliance.
- To identify areas that needs shoring up.

- To ensure better use of organizational units.
- To have an improved communication on state of the company.
- To measure the effectiveness of current managerial controls.
- To determine the reliability of data developed within the organization.

6.8.4 Identifying Areas for Audit

A management audit should uncover the performance of unnecessary work; duplication of work; poor inventory control; use of an improper number of employees for a specific quantity, quality, or type of work; uneconomical use of equipment and machines; wasteful use of resources; and procedures that are more costly than necessary. If social goals are included in a company's objectives, the audit should determine whether the efforts and expenditures made are achieving reasonable accomplishments in the social objectives sought.

6.8.4.1 Techniques for Identifying Audit Areas

First is to review the internal reports of managers to obtain data on progress, accomplishment, and present status of work. Of special interest are disclosures of projects on which management has not acted. Inquiries about such inaction and its justification may point out weaknesses that need correction. *Second* is to select key systems or procedures used by the company and follow them from start to finish. This approach provides an insight into present efficiency and the way the work is being done. For example, by noting the capabilities of the personnel involved, the usefulness of the prescribed systems and procedures, and the degree of participation by employees, the audit can uncover possible inadequacies and suggest possible areas for improvement. Also, interviews with managers and nonmanagers are important sources of valuable information. Discussion with responsible personnel must be handled carefully. Prior to any formal interview, the interviewer should have some background and knowledge of the company so that constructive and pertinent questions can be asked. Also, the atmosphere should be conducive to response. Whom to talk to is significant and the selection should be made only after appropriate thought.

6.8.5 Attributes Used in Auditing

To perform a management audit, it is helpful to draw up a list of qualifications desired and attach a credit valuation to each. The selection and respective weights given to these qualifying factors are highly favoured with judgment and in many cases quite controversial. The audit assesses what the company has done for itself and also what it has done for its customers or recipients of the products or services provided. To reach these assessments, evaluations on a number of factors may be deemed necessary. These include attributes dealing with financial stability, production efficiency, sales effectiveness, economic and social affluence, personnel development, earnings growth, public relations, and civic responsibility.

6.9 AREAS FOR OVERALL CONTROLLING

While the term overall controlling usually connotes control efforts over the entire enterprise, popular use of the term has made it apply to control efforts over major areas. Usually such controlling is relatively intensive and includes the following areas.

1. Market standing of the enterprise,
2. Innovation
3. Profitability
4. Materials acquisition and use
5. Employee performance (both managerial and nonmanagerial) development
6. Capital or financial resources
7. Productivity
8. Physical resources
9. Public responsibility.

Applying controlling to these broad areas helps to minimize losses in sales, material, time, profit, manpower, capital, and facilities.

6.9.1 OVERALL CONTROL REPORTS

Financial statements that are most helpful for controlling overall performance are: (i) the balance sheet, (ii) the profit and loss statement, and (iii) special reports designed to show selected pertinent data. In each type of report, information for several consecutive years reveals important trends. Such reports are called comparative i.e. a comparative balance sheet shows data in balance sheet format for several consecutive years.

6.9.1.1 Comparative Balance Sheet

This is an important accounting document showing the financial picture of a company at a given moment. An accounting statement contains three elements: (i) assets, (ii) liabilities, (iii) shareholders' equity. Assets are the value of the various items owned by the corporation; liabilities are the amounts owed to various creditors by the corporation; and stockholders' equity is the amount accruing to the corporation's owners. The relationship among these three elements is: Assets equal liabilities plus stockholders' equity. This is called the balance sheet equation.

6.9.1.2 Profit and Loss Statement

This is an itemized financial statement of the income and expenses resulting from the company's operations during a stated or accounting period of time. Controlling by profit and loss is applied most commonly to an entire enterprise. However, if controlling by departments is followed, a profit and loss statement is drawn for each department. Thus, the contribution of each department to the net income of the entire enterprise is ascertained. The department's achievement of net income against an expected amount is considered a standard for measuring its performance. To illustrate, suppose a manufacturer has three departments: punching, welding, and assembling. The punching department produces and sells its products and services to the welding department, which in turn sells its products and services to the assembling department. Each department is thought of as a separate enterprise with its own profit and loss statement. This approach works satisfactorily for departments that produce tangible or physical results. However, where a department's output is predominantly intangible, as with certain staff and service units, control by profit and loss statements is unsatisfactory and other approaches should be used.

6.10 PRINCIPLE OF PREVENTIVE CONTROL

The principle of preventive control reflects the idea that most of the responsibility for negative deviation from standards can be fixed by applying fundamentals of management. The principle can be stated as–"the higher the quality of managers and their subordinates, the less will be the need for direct controls".

The principle of preventive control rests on three assumptions:

1. Qualified managers make a minimum of errors.
2. Managerial performance can be measured, and management concept, principles, and techniques are useful diagnostic standards in measuring managerial performance.
3. The application of management fundamentals can be evaluated.

6.10.1 ADVANTAGES OF PREVENTIVE CONTROL

Preventive control has the following advantages:

1. Greater accuracy is achieved in assigning personal responsibility. The ongoing evaluation of managers is certain to uncover deficiency and should provide a basis for specific training to eliminate them.
2. Preventive control hastens corrective action and make it more effective.
3. Preventive control may lighten the managerial burden caused by direct controls.
4. The psychological advantage of preventive control is impressive. Many subordinates feel that superiors do not rate fairly, that they rely on hunch and personality, and that they use improper measuring standards. This can be avoided to a great extent by preventive control.

Review Questions

1. What part should the employees play in setting up the requirements for an effective control system?
2. Describe some of the benefits of budgetary control?

3. Describe some of the characteristics of effective budgetary control systems.
4. Discuss the steps in the control process.
5. Explain why key performance areas and strategic control points are important in designing control systems.
6. What are the major types of financial statements? What information does each type provide?
7. Why are budgets so widely used by organizations?

Caselets

HIERARCHY OF NEEDS

Rahul, an accountant, is a reliable employee of Precision Plastic Limited. He can always be counted on to get his work done accurately and on time. He is punctual, works steadily and gets along with other people. He has been an accounting specialist for 7 years. The fact that he has not been promoted recently is not of great concern to him. The pay is good, the supervision is fair, his work area is well equipped, he likes the people he works with, and company treats him well. Nevertheless, he looks forward to 5 pm. He is active outside, especially with hobbies and recreational pursuits. He is a member of the company's hockey and basketball teams. He is also a good painter. He is a boy scout leader and enjoys helping friends in all matters.

Question 1: Which of the needs in Maslow's hierarchy seem to be most important to Rahul?

Question 2: What types of job factors – motivators or hygiene – are determining the course of Rahul's behaviour?

RESISTANCE TO CHANGE

Rex is a well-established ready-made garment manufacturing company. The company has 100 employees including the supervisory staff. The entire output is exported to European countries. The company is planning to introduce new machines, and new methods of production to reduce the cost and have new designs. The management is apprehensive of the change because it will be resisted in many ways.

Question 1: You have a senior position in the company. You are required to advise the management about: (a) reasons for human resistance to change. (b) strategies to overcome the resistance to change.

CHAPTER 7

Decision Making

Decision-making is the process of selecting a course of action from among alternatives. It is a core of planning. Matters relating to all managerial functions are settled through decisions and the decisions are executed by the company personnel. A decision involves a choice; it is rational and means a commitment to action i.e. it is goal-oriented.

7.1 DEFINITION

Managerial decision-making involves an entire process of establishing the goals, designing tasks, searching for alternatives and developing plans in order to find the best solution to the decision problem. The elements of a decision-making process are:

- The decision-maker
- The decision problem
- The environment in which the decision is to be taken
- Objectives of the decision-maker
- The available alternative course of action
- The outcome expected from various alternatives
- The final choice of the alternative taken

7.2 CHARACTERISTICS OF DECISION MAKING

1. It is a process of selecting the best possible alternative
2. It is a rational process involving the application of intellectual ability
3. It is a goal oriented process
4. It is always related to the environment
5. It involves all actions like defining the problem, probing etc.
6. Decision is the end product

7.3 NATURE OF DECISION MAKING

Managerial decisions help in maintaining group effectiveness. Decision problems necessitate a choice from different available alternatives. A decision requires some sort of forecasting on the basis of past and present available informations. The effect of the decision is to be felt in the future. If the decision outcome is not as expected, then the decision itself may be wrong.

7.4 DECISION MAKING PROCESS

Decision-making involves a sequence of procedures as listed below.

1. Defining the problem: Precise definition and identification of main and sub-problems needed

2. Classifying objectives: Classification with reference to criticality and order of importance is required.

3. Identifying evaluation criteria: Cost, performance and risk involved are to be assessed quantitatively.

4. Model building: It may be mathematical or analytic through computer simulation; to assess the likely consequences of various alternatives.

5. Evaluating results: The analysis should lead to a recommendation for some type of action.

6. Taking final decision: The best possible solution is selected after taking into account the risks involved and the uncertain future.

7. Feedback or following up the decision: It is ensured that the decision is properly implemented and that no deviations occur.

7.5 TECHNIQUES OF DECISION MAKING

In order to assist management in the field of decision-making various theories have been developed and new techniques have been introduced. Some of the approaches are as follows:

Scientific management techniques: Cost control and managerial control could be effectively exercised with the help of work measurement and time study.

Human relation techniques: The concept given by Elton Mayo is concerned with the problem of motivation and leadership.

Empirical techniques: Experiences of successful managers could provide the key to effectiveness and success and the formulas could be deduced for other managers to follow.

Financial techniques: Development of accounting methods and procedures, cost accounting and budgetary planning have resulted in the identification of managerial control of the company connected with financial implications.

Mathematical model techniques: Operations Research techniques are based upon expressing the problems in a mathematical way to build up a conceptual method for the given situation. Manipulation of such models helps the managers in decision-making problems.

Decision theory techniques: Both quantitative and qualitative aspects are investigated in the analysis of decision problems.

Decision support system: In this approach the main focus is on understanding and improving the manager's decision-making ability by adopting available and suitable technology.

7.6 CLASSIFICATION OF DECISIONS

Managerial decisions may be classified as:

1. Organizational and Personal
2. Routine and Strategic
3. Programmed and Non-Programmed
4. Policy and Operative
5. Individual and Group
6. Major and Minor
7. Long-term departmental and Non-economic

7.6.1 ORGANIZATIONAL AND PERSONAL DECISIONS

When a person takes a decision in the organization as an executive, it will be an organizational decision. The power to take organizational decision can be delegated from the superior to the subordinate. Personal decisions are those taken by an executive about himself.

7.6.2 ROUTINE AND STRATEGIC DECISIONS

Routine decisions are made by following certain established rules or procedures and policies. These decisions do not require fresh information or knowledge. Routine decisions are taken at middle or lower level of management. Strategic decisions are taken at top-level management and these are related to policy matters. Such decisions influence organizational structure, working condition, objectives etc.

7.6.3 PROGRAMMED AND NON-PROGRAMMED DECISIONS

These are structured decisions and are applied to routine problems. They rely primarily on previously established criteria. They are intended to free the managers from routine matters so that the mangers can engage themselves in challenging and difficult tasks. Non-programmed decisions are open decisions and deal with unique problems. All strategic decisions are non-programmed decisions. Allocation of resources, improving customer satisfaction, taking over sick units etc. demand non-programmed decisions.

7.6.4 Policy and Operative Decisions

Policy decisions determine the basic policy of the organization and are taken up at top-level management. Operative decisions are less important and are related to day-to-day operations of the business.

7.6.5 Individual and Group Decisions

In small concerns only the owner takes all-important decisions. Even in big organizations, a person may be allowed to take a decision about a particular matter. These individual decisions are programmed and are less important. Group decisions are taken by group of persons. These decisions are taken after thorough deliberation among people who are assigned this job.

7.6.6 Major and Minor Decisions

These can be categorized on the basis of intensity of the decisions. A decision related to a purchase of a CNC machine costing Rs.10 lakhs is a major decision while purchase of stationery items involves a minor decision.

7.6.7 Long-Term Departmental and Non-economic Decisions

In long-term decisions the period involved is long and risk involved is more. Decisions relating to non-economic factors such as technical values, moral behavior etc. may be called non-economic decision.

7.7 EVALUATING THE ALTERNATIVE

In most planning, there are certain tangible factors to be assessed in terms of rupees, man-hours, machine-hours, unit of output, rates of return on investment, or some other quantitative unit, although they may carry a wide margin of error. Along with these, there are other factors also that can hardly be quantified. Nevertheless, both the tangible and the intangible factors must be weighed while deciding upon a course of action.

7.7.1 Principle of Limiting Factor

In choosing from among alternatives, primary attention must be given to those factors that are limiting or strategic to the decision involved. For instance, if a machine fails to operate for lack of a screw, the screw is the limiting factor. The search for and recognition of limiting factors in planning never ends. Discovery of the limiting factor is a fundamental criteria for selection from alternatives and hence, of planning.

7.7.2 Bases for Selection from Alternatives

In selecting from among alternatives, three bases for decision are open to the manager – experience, experimentation and research.

The manager may sometimes analyse the pros and cons of an alternative solely on the basis of his experience. In this case the manager decides upon the effectiveness of an alternative by recalling the use of similar solution in similar problem situation in the past and its result thereof. Experience comes into play when prompt decisions are to be made.

Decisions made on the basis of experimentation are also very effective. In this case, alternatives are put to test by applying it in a non-real, though real-like, situation and analysing its effect. The alternative giving the best result is selected.

Research is a widely used basis for making decisions specially when the decisions concern major issues. In this case the research team gathers information regarding the pros and cons of the promising alternatives and provides it to the concerned manager who finally takes the decision as to which alternative should be selected.

7.7.3 Evaluating the Decision's Importance

The importance of a decision depends upon the extent of responsibility. There are useful criteria of importance as discussed below.

1. Size or length of commitment: If a decision commits the enterprise to heavy expenditure of funds or if the commitment can be fulfilled only over a long period, it should be subjected to suitable attention by the top-level management.

2. Flexibility of plans: Decisions involving inflexible courses of action must carry priority over those plans which could easily be changed.

3. Certainty of goals and premises: If goals and premises are fairly certain, a decision resting on them tends to be less important than where they are highly uncertain

4. Human impact: Where the human impact of a decision is great, its importance is high e.g. a decision to put payroll or purchasing procedures on computers.

7.8 DIFFICULTIES IN DECISION MAKING

Some difficulties normally experienced in decision-making are given below:

- Incomplete information
- Unsupporting environment
- Ineffective communication
- Incorrect timing
- Non-acceptance by subordinates

Review Questions

1. How do you define a problem? How do you know that a problem exists? How would you test the severity of the problem?
2. Classify problems into relevant categories and give examples of problems that fit into each category.
3. Explain some of the factors and personal characteristics that have an impact on the decision-maker.
4. Explain briefly the ten steps in the process of rational decision-making.
5. Differentiate between: facts, inferences, speculations, and assumptions.
6. What is the synectic approach of generating alternative solutions? How does it contribute to the decision-making process?
7. What are the different criteria that can be used to evaluate alternatives? Under what circumstances would each criterion be used?
8. What are the advantages and disadvantages of group decision-making? What guidelines can be prescribed so as to dilute the impact of disadvantages?

Caselets

WORKING CONDITION

Twenty female employees of a large company were grouped together daily in an area measuring 40 × 40 feet to perform semi-skilled assembly work. Though the layout was far from ideal, it was accepted as livable, at least as temporary quarters, until construction of the new manufacturing facility was completed. These women enjoyed their work; they could talk freely about any subject that came to mind and still be able to do their jobs. They worked elbow to elbow and rarely failed to assemble their daily quota. When the new manufacturing facility finally opened, they were assigned to an area several times as large as their former quarters. The new plant was equipped with superior lighting, water fountains, windows, and piped music. On the surface, these work conditions appeared ideal. However, management became perplexed when after a few weeks in the new facility, absenteeism increased and production went down. Complaints and grievances became numerous and two of the women quit their jobs. In a closed door meeting with the production supervisor, the plant engineer, and the manufacturing manager, the personnel director voiced his opinion about the unforeseen problems in the assembly department. In his opinion, the women missed personal contact with each other, the continuous conversation and other accustomed form of social interaction and basically were resisting the change to the new location. The personnel director recommended that the plant engineer should do something about the redesigning of the layout to bring the women closer together even if it meant spending several thousand rupees.

Question 1. Make a comprehensive analysis of the case.

Question 2. If the employees were men, would the same situation prevail?

CHAPTER 8 Productivity and Operations Management

Operations management is important to managers for at least two reasons. First, it can improve productivity which in turn improves the financial health of the organization. Second, it can help organizations meet customers' competitive priorities.

8.1 PRODUCTIVITY

Productivity is of great importance, specially, for underdeveloped and developing countries, since it is a measure of how well the resources are utilized to get the maximum output. So there should be a tendency to perform a job by cheaper and quicker means. Other way round the goal should be optimum utilization of input resources so as to achieve maximum satisfaction with minimum efforts and expenditure.

8.1.1 DIFFERENCE BETWEEN PRODUCTION AND PRODUCTIVITY

The concept of production and productivity are totally different. Production of any commodity or service is the volume of output irrespective of the quantity and quality of resources employed to achieve it. Thus, production may improve without corresponding improvement in productivity and vice-versa. If the input remains the same and the production output increases, there is an improvement in productivity. Production, therefore, value the output in terms of value whereas productivity is the efficiency of the system used for production.

8.1.2 FACTORS OF PRODUCTIVITY

The important factors affecting productivity can be classified into external factors and internal factors.

8.1.2.1 External Factors

The various external factors are:

1. Capital availability
2. Natural resources
3. Taxation
4. Laws and restrictions imposed by Government
5. Competition in the market
6. Technical and other training facilities
7. Political, social and economic conditions
8. Availability of water, power and other input supplies

8.1.2.2 Internal Factors

The various internal factors are:

1. Product design
2. Input materials
3. Technological developments and innovations
4. Plant layout
5. Material handling techniques utilized
6. Work study
7. Method study
8. Inspection and quality control
9. Production planning and control
10. Management techniques used

8.1.3 Reasons for Low Productivity

The factors responsible for low productivity are:

1. Poor product design
2. Lack of standardization (of products, input materials etc.)
3. Improper equipment/machines/cutting tools and non-optimal machining parameters (like speed feed and depth of cut etc.)
4. Poor process planning
5. Poor plant layout leading to unnecessary and avoidable movement of manpower and materials
6. Non-standardization of methods of production
7. Unnecessary variety of products
8. Shortage of input materials, tools, jigs and fixtures
9. Frequent changes in product design
10. Frequent breakdown of machines due to poor preventive maintenance
11. Poor working conditions and environment
12. More absenteeism of workers without prior permission

13. Idleness of workers, careless and poor workmanship
14. Lack of motivation among workers.

8.1.4 Factors Increasing Productivity

In order to improve productivity the following factors are to be taken into consideration and need to be controlled.

1. Wastage of materials
2. Breakdown of machines
3. Waiting time concerning manpower and machines time concerning
4. Poor working conditions
5. Political interference
6. Poor management
7. Material handling

Hence, considering the above factors, the wastage at each stage of production can be reduced, which ultimately will help to provide the consumers with cheaper and better quality products/items. Thus, management can play an important role in improving productivity, as—

(i) It brings the resources together.
(ii) It directs and controls the workers.
(iii) It helps in bringing latest techniques and puts in efforts to see that the techniques are being used.

The supervisory staff—foremen and supervisors are in the frontline of management—is the main line of communication between top management, middle management and the general body of operators/workers. Hence, to improve productivity, it is essential for the management to see the level of education and technical ability of workers. Therefore, it is important that the management should make investment in education, human relations and necessary training of workers.

8.1.5 Productivity Ratios

Ratios that usually relate units of one single input to one single output are termed as productivity ratios. There are two basic types of productivity ratios. The first, total productivity relates the value of all output to the value of all inputs (total output / total input). The second, partial productivity, relates value of all output to the value of major category of input (total output/ partial input). Productivity ratios can be calculated for a specific time period, which measures the efficiency of operation at that time, or they can be compared with other ratios over time.

8.1.6 Productivity Index

Since productivity is a ratio of comparison within a period of time, the productivity Index can be taken as a basis of measurement.

Productivity indicates a combined effect of resource utilization (i.e. efficiency and performance i.e. effectiveness). The combined effect of efficiency and effectiveness is utilized in defining a term called productivity index, which is used as basis of measurement.

$$\text{Productivity Index} = \frac{\text{Current year productivity}}{\text{Base year productivity}}$$

$$= \frac{\text{Current year results/current year resources}}{\text{Base year results/Base year resources}}$$

Now, how well resources are utilized to accomplish a target or result indicates efficiency and how well a set of targets or results are accomplished indicate effectiveness. So,

$$\text{Productivity Index} = \frac{\text{Effectiveness}}{\text{Efficiency}}$$

8.1.7 Productivity Measurements

Productivity is an effective tool for judging how a system is performing over a period of time. It is important to measure it quantitatively and the following techniques are commonly used to measure productivity.

8.1.7.1 Material Productivity

There are many industries in which the cost of raw material is in appreciable proportion to cost to finished product. Under such conditions, the productivity of materials becomes a key factor in economic production.

$$\text{Material productivity} = \frac{\text{Output}}{\text{Material input}}$$

Raw material productivity can be improved by ensuring:

1. Changes in product design
2. Proper training and motivation of workers
3. Better material planning and control
4. Waste reduction and scrap control
5. Ability of alternative cheaper materials

8.1.7.2 Labour Productivity

$$\text{Labour or Human productivity} = \frac{\text{Output}}{\text{Human input}}$$

Output and labour can also be measured in terms of their money value. Thus,

$$\text{Labour productivity} = \frac{\text{Total revenue from production}}{\text{Expenditure on labour}}$$

The labour productivity can be improved by:

1. Providing training to workers to utilize best methods of production.
2. Selecting such product designs and process of manufacture that it ensures most economic use of labour.
3. Constant motivation of workers through financial and non-financial incentives.
4. By boosting the morale of employees.
5. Improving working conditions in the plant.

8.1.7.3 Capital Productivity

$$\text{Capital productivity} = \frac{\text{Turnover}}{\text{Capital input}}$$

It can be improved by:

1. Making rational make or buy decisions.
2. Better utilization of capital resources like land, building and machines.
3. Adopting modern manufacturing techniques, like flexible manufacturing system, improved techniques of maintenance and proper plant layout etc.

8.1.7.4 Machine Productivity

$$\text{Machine productivity} = \frac{\text{Output}}{\text{Actual machine hours used}}$$

Following measures can increase machine productivity:

(i) Preventive maintenance.
(ii) Utilization of proper machining parameters like speed, feed and depth of cost etc.
(iii) Use of requisite skilled and properly trained labour.
(iv) Method study.

8.1.7.5 Energy Productivity

$$\text{Energy productivity} = \frac{\text{Output}}{\text{Energy input}}$$

8.1.8 Productivity—A General View

Following formula can attain a general measure of productivity.

$$\text{Productivity} = \frac{\text{Output}}{\text{Labour} + \text{Capital} + \text{Energy} + \text{Other input}}$$

It is clear from the above relations that each kind of measure needs some specific kind of information; appropriate measure can be the basis of the information available and the main target of the investigation. Generally, the measure of productivity indicates the performance of inputs namely, labour, capital, energy or other investment required in an enterprise. So it can be said that merely an increase in output is not an indication of productivity improvement. Thus, production is an absolute measure and productivity a relative measure.

8.1.9 Low Productivity

Productivity is a combination of effectiveness or performance and efficiency. Effectiveness is affected by wastage of time while efficiency is affected by wastage of input resource. Therefore, for improving productivity both these wastages should be minimized. The factors responsible for decreasing productivity can be discussed under four categories as mentioned below.

8.1.9.1 Defects in Design of Product

1. Bad design of product prevents use of most economic production technique
2. Lack of product standardization prevents utilization of efficient production process
3. Incorrect quality standards cause unnecessary work
4. Due to faulty design excess material removal requirement is involved.

8.1.9.2 Inefficient Methods of Manufacture

1. Wrong machine used
2. Process not operated correctly or in bad condition
3. Improper or bad layout causing excessive movement
4. Operatives' bad working methods

8.1.9.3 Mismanagement of Time on Account of Management

1. Excessive product variety adds idle time due to short runs
2. Lack of standardization also adds idle time due to short runs
3. Bad planning of work and orders adds idle time, men and machines
4. Lack of raw materials due to poor inventory control results in idle men and machines
5. Frequent plant breakdown cause interruptions in production
6. Plant in bad condition adds to unproductive time due to scrap and rework
7. Bad working condition in the plant force the workers for more rest

8. Lack of motivation and low morale results in decrease of productivity
9. Bad planning in distribution of capital leads to expenditure on dispensable personnel and equipment

8.1.9.4 Mismanagement on Account of Workers

1. Late coming, idleness and deliberate slow working adds to unproductive time
2. Careless workmanship causes lot of scrap, rework and poor product quality
3. Accidents due to careless workers

The factors discussed under the above four heads should be eliminated or avoided or minimized to achieve effective utilization of resources and maximum output. This will result in higher productivity.

8.1.10 FACTORS AFFECTING PRODUCTIVITY

In any manufacturing setup or unit, all the factors related to input and output components of production process, affects productivity. These factors are of immense importance and are broadly classified into following categories:

1. Manpower
2. Equipment and machines
3. Input Materials
4. Time
5. Floor Area or space
6. Power or Energy
7. Finance
8. Movement of men and machines

Many decisions have to be taken for the effective utilization of these factors as it helps to improve productivity to a considerable amount. On the other hand, mismanagement or poor utilization of these factors deteriorate the productivity.

8.1.10.1 Manpower

Decisions to be taken are regarding:

- Selection of right man for a specific job
- Training requirements whether to be imparted in the plant itself or outside the unit to other plants within the country or abroad or in training institutes
- Number of personnel required in each of the departments.

8.1.10.2 Equipment and Machines

The management needs to decide upon:

- The number of machine tools and their capacity
- The accessories required
- The replacement policy of the organization
- The maintenance schedules

8.1.10.3 Input Materials

Decisions to be taken are regarding:

- Appropriate quality of materials
- Material requirement planning (M.R.P)
- Substitute of materials being used
- Inspection of input materials at various points
- Cost of materials procurement and handling up to stores

8.1.10.4 Time

Time is significant for the following reasons:

- Inspection of input materials i.e. raw material and semi-finished or finished items required for assembly
- For inspection of finished products
- Carrying out production or manufacturing activity
- For repair and maintenance of machines and equipment

8.1.10.5 Floor Area or Space

It takes into consideration, the following:

- Total area covered by the administrative block, production shop, and inspection and quality control departments etc.
- Location of different departments and shops etc.
- Other spaces covered by plant layout

8.1.10.6 Power or Energy

The management should ensure the following:

- Maintenance of equipment for saving energy
- Use of renewable energy devices
- Use of biogas, photovoltaic cells, solar energy and other non conventional techniques

8.1.10.7 Finance

Decisions regarding finance is very important as fund is needed to fulfill all the above requirements. The management should go for minimum rather than optimum finance.

8.1.10.8 Movement of Man and Materials

This factor also holds significance as it is concerned with the movement of manpower within the plant. The decisions concerning movement of raw material, semi-finished and finished products/items within the plant also affect productivity.

8.1.11 Methods to Improve Productivity

Various techniques to improve the productivity of a system or organization could be categorised as follows:

1. Task based techniques
2. Product based techniques
3. Technology based methods
4. Material based techniques
5. Employee based methods

8.1.11.1 Task-Based Techniques

These could be based on the following methods:

- Work measurement (Time study)
- Motion study/work simplification (Method study)
- Job analysis
- Job evaluation and merit rating
- Ergonomics (related with human factors)
- Production scheduling

8.1.11.2 Product-Based Techniques

This may include the following:

- Product classification and coding
- Research and development
- Reliability and improvement in product design
- Product standardization
- Product simplification
- Product diversification
- Product specialization

8.1.11.3 Technology-Based Methods

These may include the following:

- Computer aided design
- Computer aided process planning
- Computer aided manufacturing
- Computer integrated manufacturing (CIM)
- Computer aided engineering analysis
- Computer aided inspection
- Group technology
- Robotics and Just in time (JIT)
- Maintenance management
- Reconditioning and life predicting of equipment technology

8.1.11.4 Material-Based Techniques

These may include the following:

- Material requirement planning (MRP)
- Inventory control
- Just in time concept of inventory management
- Material management and quality control
- Material handling systems

8.1.11.5 Employee-Based Methods

Employees may be encouraged to improve productivity by adopting the following techniques:

- Incentive schemes for individual employees
- Incentive schemes for group of employees
- Management by objectives
- Fringe benefits for employees and job enlargement
- Recognition and punishment of employees
- Total quality management (TQM)
- Zero defect benefits for employees

8.1.12 CONTRIBUTORS TO PRODUCTIVITY IMPROVEMENT

Following are the main contributors to productivity improvement.

8.1.12.1 Human Relations

Good human relation result in cooperative attitude of workers which increases productivity of the system. Human relations can be improved by means of labour participation regarding goal setting, minimization of conflicts, simplification of communication techniques, and by providing encouragement to workers for their creative talents by awarding and honouring them with letters of appreciation.

8.1.12.2 Adoption of Latest Technology

In order to overcome market competition, industrialists must regularly adopt latest techniques in the field of marketing, material handling, inventory control and store management. Method study and work measurement may be utilized to improve the existing method of selecting a process and machine tools etc. Information may be gathered about all operations facilities, transportation facilities, distance moved, inspection time, storage facilities, time spent in storage, drawings and design specifications. This information will form a process flow chart. A questionnaire may be prepared for critical examination of all these activities and to find out the best possible course. Accordingly, changes may be incorporated to improve productivity.

8.1.12.3 Proper Design of Product

The product designs are not permanent; they can be improved if there is a possiblity. This may increase cost. However, consideration of the following elements may help in cost reduction.

1. Simplification of the product by reducing its parts
2. Utilization of better and economical materials
3. Installation of efficient system of quality control
4. Standardization of materials, processes, sequence of operations, and tools

These may reduce wastages in the form of scraps, and improve the durability and look of the product.

8.1.12.4 Cost Control

Productivity can be improved by reducing the production cost. It can be achieved by keeping a close watch over expenditure, minimization of material wastages, reduction in machines' breakdown period or idleness of machines, reduction in waiting time for men, power and materials, avoiding excessive material handling and minimization of overtime expenditure.

8.1.12.5 Product Simplification and Standardization

If the application of product simplification and standardization is possible in the product under consideration, and thus the enterprise, it would improve the productivity of the enterprise.

8.1.12.6 Proper Planning, Loading, and Scheduling

These industrial engineering techniques help in proper utilization of the 4 M's (i.e.) men, machines, materials and methods. Thus, improvement in these techniques will lead to improved productivity.

8.1.12.7 Supervision

Supervision prevents production inefficiency, maintenance problems, incorrect specifications, of materials and machines, and provides good working environment and coordination. Thus, it helps in improving productivity.

8.2 OPERATIONS MANAGEMENT

Operations management is the management of activities specifically related, either directly or indirectly, the organization's production of goods and services. It involves efficiently managing the transformation process from input of people, materials, tools, and money to output of goods and services.

8.2.1 Steps in Operations Management

The steps involved in operations management are listed below. However, an overview of the whole operations management system is given in Figure 8.1.

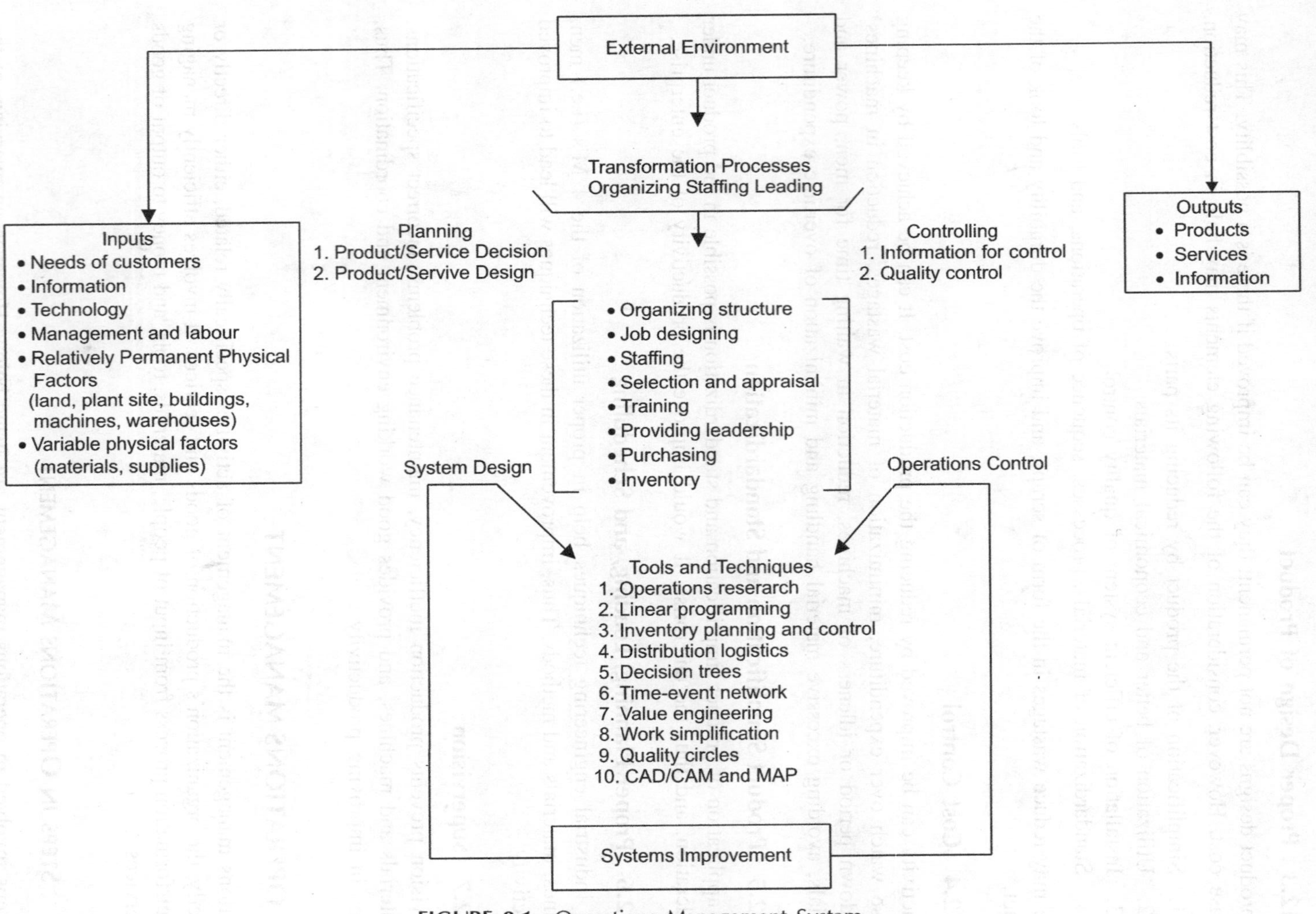

FIGURE 8.1 Operations Management System.

8.2.1.1 Selecting

This involves the selection of specific processes by which the desired goods are to be produced or services to be delivered. It includes the choice of technology to be used, smooth workflow, efficient utilization of space, sequence of activities and all the products to be routed through these facilities.

8.2.1.2 Designing

This phase includes the design of jobs as well as the design of facilities that will use the technology and the selected processes more effectively. Routine and monotonus jobs usually do not provide opportunity for advancement and hence, may result in low employee morale, which may be evidenced by excessive absenteeism, high turnover, low quality of product and general dissatisfaction and discontent among employees.

8.2.1.3 Operating

This step involves scheduling work operations, and assigning workers to jobs in such a manner so as to meet short-term as well as long-term levels of output, that it is consistent with the forecasted demand.

8.2.1.4 Controlling

The controlling mechanism is to be developed at the same time as the designing of operating systems and must be integrated with the system. The controlling process ensures that the operating system attains the desired results.

8.2.1.5 Updating

This means continuous revision of operating methods and systems in order to meet the dynamic social and technological environment. This updating is necessary in response to:

- Changes in customer demand and preferences
- Changes in technology
- Competition
- Changes in organizational objective

8.3 PRODUCTION PLANNING AND CONTROL

The production function comes into operation as a combined result of materials, machines, human resources and other factors. While managing the individual factors in isolation are significant in themselves, the efforts must also be directed towards their combined results.

The process of production planning and control consists of five phases. They are:

1. Routing
2. Scheduling
3. Dispatching
4. Inspection
5. Expediting or follow-up

8.3.1 Routing

Routing involves the determination in advance of the exact path along which materials will flow and the sequence of operations that will transform the raw materials into finished goods. It is a planning stage and requires the adoption of procedures that will determine the entire manufacturing path for the materials, tools, machines, equipment and the manpower and specify where and how these are to be used. It determines in advance:

- quantity to be manufactured
- requirements of inputs including capital, personnel, machines and materials
- type, number and sequence of operations that are designed to produce the output
- establishment of work stations and assembly points along the route of the product
- the proper feeds and speeds of machines and the time required per operation
- the economic lot size to manufacture, and
- preparation of routine sheets which detail, the "what, who, how and when" of the entire process of production.

Routing, requiring advance planning, ensures optimum allocation and utilization of all inputs to be processed in the production system. Also, once the system has been defined, routing becomes a routine work and it is easily monitored and any mistakes become easily traceable.

8.3.2 Scheduling

Scheduling is also a part of the planning process and deals with timing of operations. It determines when and at what rate the materials will be processed as prescribed in the "route sheet". It assigns the starting and the finishing times for each operation as well as group of integrated operations, if such operations are interdependent upon each other. Scheduling is done by using "time and motion study" techniques. Proper and optimal scheduling becomes extremely necessary where several parts or components are manufactured independently and separately and assembled into the finished product. Since these separate parts may require different times of completion, it is necessary to synchronize their operations in such a way that they become available for assembly when needed. This ensures the availability of manpower, materials and other requisites at the appropriate time and the utilization of these resources timely and effectively.

8.3.3 Dispatching

Dispatching is the action stage. It is the actual issuing of orders and assignment of work to the workforce. It determines as to who will do what. Dispatching is done by a dispatcher whose duties include:

- assignment of work to machines or work places
- issuing of authority to get necessary tools, materials, fixtures, gauges etc.,
- guiding and controlling the progress of material at each operation and making any adjustments that may be necessary,

- issuing of inspection orders,
- recording and reporting of idle times of machines and operators, and
- recording and reporting of actual output results.

8.3.4 Inspection

Inspection aims at maintaining quality standards of products and minimizing wastage and spoilage. This function encompasses: (i) inspection of raw materials for quality, (ii) inspection of machines and tools for their adequate performance, and (iii) inspection of finished product. It pursues the production process step by step to compare and evaluate the performance relative to the set standards.

8.3.5 Expediting or Follow-up

Expediting is basically a watchdog function to ensure that production is completed on scheduled time, and that it is not held up for any reason, or in that case, corrective measures are taken. This responsibility is assigned to specialists, known as expeditors, who are in close touch with daily plant operational conditions. An expeditor serves as the feedback link between the work performance and the functions of routing and scheduling. A responsible expeditor ensures that delays due to breakdown of equipment, lack of proper tools, insufficient material in process and excessive rejections and wastage are minimized. He also looks for any errors in routing, scheduling and dispatching, that cause delays, so that these can be checked. Such remedial action ensures accomplishment of goals. The current trend in the field of manufacturing is towards a closer control over all the operations. Mechanized materials handling, sequential manufacturing processes, centralized dispatching and recording, automation and extensive use of computers for monitoring the operations have made it possible to keep the process under tighter control.

Review Questions

1. What is productivity? Explain the importance of productivity.
2. How productivity is different from production?
3. What are the external and internal factors affecting productivity?
4. Explain some of the reasons for low productivity.
5. What is productivity index?
6. Explain some of the techniques used for measuring productitivity.
7. Explain how low productivity can be eliminated?
8. Explain some of the techniques used to improve productivity.

9. What are the steps involved in operations management?
10. What are the five phases of production planning and control?
11. Why operations can be considered a system?
12. Why is operations management important to efficiency?
13. What are the major considerations in process selection?
14. Define and describe—routing, scheduling, dispatching.

Caselets

PRODUCTIVITY

ABC Company Limited was about to install a new incentive plan for the workforce in all its plants. The plan envisages 22 to 25% increase in weekly earnings for high performing workers. The rationale of the new plan as stated by the CEO is as follows, "The plan discourages the workers from too much socializing. Output is satisfactory now, but it could improve if you talk less. We need more commitment to high performance."

Question 1: Analyze the company's productivity problem from the viewpoints of classical and modern organization theory.

Question 2: Suggest a solution to the company's problem and explain the theoretical problems that underlie your answer.

PRODUCTION SCHEDULING

You are appointed as the General Manager of a large company. After an extensive study of operations, you have approved the installation of new machines and a new scheduling system. This was expected to result in substantial increase in production and decrease in manufacturing cost. To the surprise of everyone, the production did not increase as expected. In fact, production dropped, quality declined, and worker's complaints increased. You have reasons to believe that the new scheduling system may be the culprit. However, your immediate subordinate insists that the new system is operating as intended. The President called you and reviewed the production figures for the last quarter. He was concerned with the effectiveness of your investment decision to acquire new machines. He indicated that you should resolve the problem without delay.

Question 1: Identify the problem in this case.

Question 2: What steps you should initiate to solve the problem?

CHAPTER 9 Information Technology and Management

Managers at all levels are finding that computer based information systems provide the information necessary for effective management. The management information system (MIS) is rapidly becoming indispensable for planning, decision-making and control. How quickly and accurately managers receive information about the rights and wrongs, largely determines how effective the control system will be.

9.1 EMERGING E-BUSINESS

One of the most exciting inventions in the recent past is the Web browser, which opened up the Internet. The explosion in the number of users is increasing the traffic on the Internet, which in turn, is putting pressure on telecom infrastructure; the infrastructure itself is growing and data traffic will be more dense in the future. Any country which wants to take advantage of the information revolution will have to improve its mobile communication and telecommunication networks. The barriers of organizational size, capital, and access to markets, have vanished with the advent of the Internet.

9.1.1 E-COMMERCE

E-commerce or electronic commerce, is conducting business communications and transactions via computers and over networks. It is the buying and selling of goods and services through digital communication. E-commerce also includes transactions on the World Wide Web and the Internet, and modes such as electronic funds transfer, smart cards, and digital cash. E-commerce covers outbound processes that concerns customers, suppliers and external partners, including sales, marketing, order-taking, delivery, customer service, purchasing of raw materials and supplies for production and procurement of indirect operating expense items, such as office supplies. It involves new business models and the potential to gain new revenue or lose some existing revenue to new competitors. There are two components to it: (i) online shopping, and (ii) online purchasing.

Online Shopping: It refers to the scope of information and activities that provides the customer with the information they need to conduct business and make an informed buying decision.

Online Purchasing: This refers to the technology infrastructure for the exchange of data and the purchase of a product over the Internet. Online purchasing is a metaphor used in business-to-business e-commerce for providing customers with an online method of placing an order, submitting a purchase order, or requesting a quote.

9.1.2 E-Business

E-business is_derived from e-commerce. It refers to conducting business on the Internet, and not just buying and selling but also servicing customers and collaborating with business partners. The term conveys that the business conducts its business entirely online. E-business includes e-commerce and also covers internal processes such as production, inventory management, product development, risk management, finance, knowledge management and human resources. E-business strategy is more complex, more focused on internal processes, and aimed at cost savings and improvements in efficiency and productivity. E-business goes far beyond e-commerce or buying and selling over the Internet, and deeper into the processes and cultures of an enterprise. It is the powerful business environment that is created when we connect critical business systems directly to customers, employees, vendors, and business partners, using Intranets, Extranets, e-commerce technologies, collaborative applications, and the Web.

9.1.3 Common Features

E-commerce and e-business both address technology infrastructure of databases, application servers, security tools, systems management and legacy systems. Also, both involve the creation of new value chains between a company and its customers and suppliers, as well as within the company itself.

9.2 INFORMATION TECHNOLOGY (IT)

Information is a valuable corporate resource. The Internet has provided the platform to design, develop, and deploy business applications. Information Technology (IT) helps business at four levels. At the operating group level, IT aids in developing and supporting systems and procedures. At the departmental level, IT ensures a smooth flow of information across departments and can guide organizations to adopt the most viable business practices. At the interface level, IT has two important roles. First, it ensures flow of information across the operating groups and second, it develops and maintains an enterprise-wide database. At the strategic level, IT provides critical strategic advantage to the organization. IT strategy should evolve from the mission of the organization.

9.2.1 Elements of Information

Before using an information for decision-making, the following elements need to be considered.

9.2.1.1 Nature of Information

Data are raw i.e. unanalyzed numbers and facts about events. Information results when data are organized or analyzed in some meaningful way. Thus, the operations manager at the desk might compare one week's output to the previous week's or to production quotas for monitoring and controlling performance.

9.2.1.2 Information Quality

The more accurate the information, the higher its quality and the more securely managers can rely on it when making decisions. The cost of obtaining information increases as the quality desired becomes higher. If information of a higher quality does not add materially to a manager's decision-making capability, it is not worth the cost added.

9.2.1.3 Information Timeliness

For effective control, corrective action must be applied before there is too great a deviation form the plan or standard. Thus the information provided by an information system must be available to the right person at the right time for appropriate action to be taken.

9.2.1.4 Information Quantity

Managers are often inundated with irrelevant and useless information. If they receive more information than they can productively use, they may overlook information on serious problems.

9.2.1.5 Information Relevance

The information that managers receive must have relevance to their responsibilities and tasks. For instance, the personnel manager probably does not need to know inventory levels.

9.3 MANAGEMENT INFORMATION SYSTEM

MIS is a formal method of making available to management the accurate and timely information necessary to facilitate the decision-making process and enable the organization's planning, control, and operational functions to be carried out effectively. The systems model of management shows that communication is needed for carrying out the managerial functions and for linking the organization to its external environment. The MIS provides the communication link that makes managing possible. The MIS has to be tailored to specific needs and may include routine information such as monthly reports; information that points out exceptions, especially at critical points; and information necessary to predict the future.

9.3.1 Designing a Management Information System

Successful MIS is the result of a deliberate step-by-step process (Figure 9.1). The logical stages for developing a MIS are:

1. System analysis: Make a preliminary survey and analyze the present system and its problems. At this stage, the system analyst is concerned with the organization's present position in relation to the information needs. By knowing the actual position the system analyst can attempt to plan its objectives.

2. State explicitly the objectives for the new system: After the system analysis stage, objectives are established. If these objectives are to be realistic, they must include standards for accuracy; the desired timeliness required, for example, hourly, daily, monthly, quarterly; the cost and the estimated budget; and the desired flexibility.

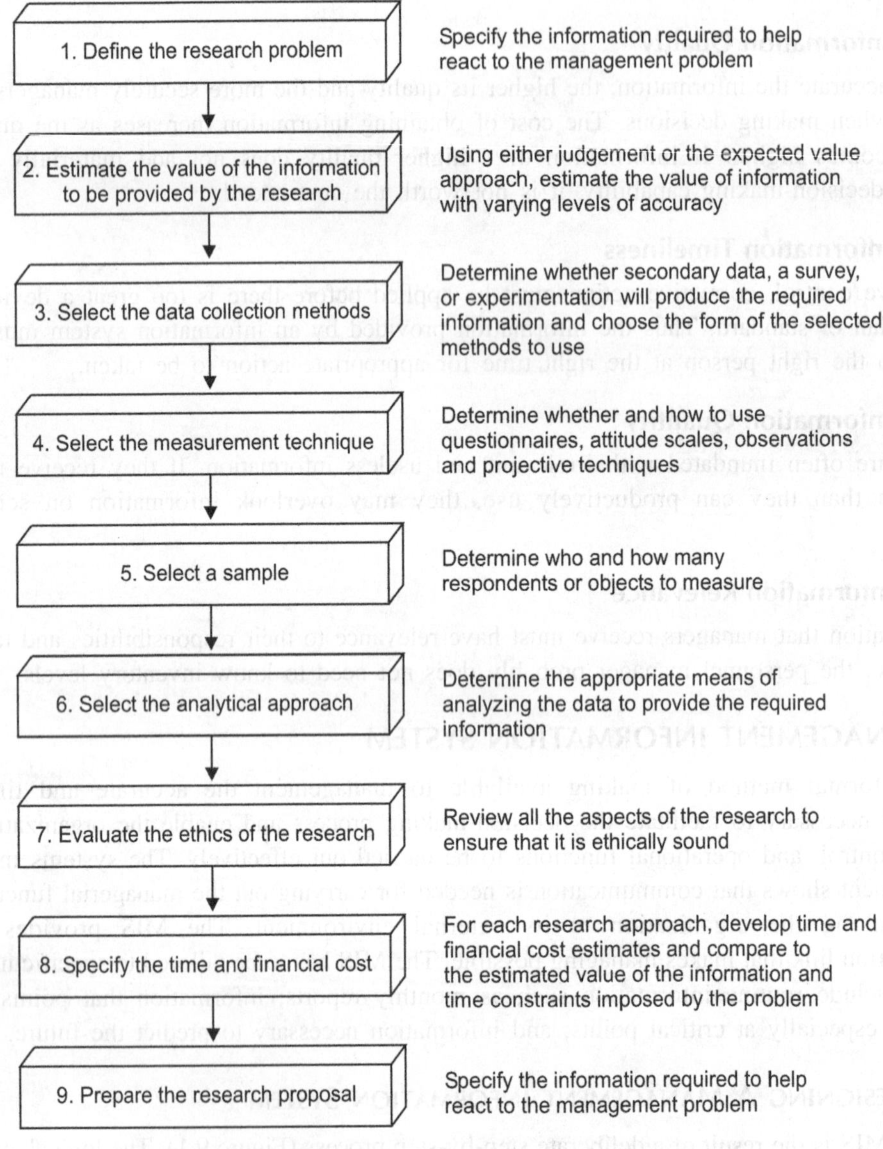

FIGURE 9.1 MIS Research Design Process.

3. Construct a conceptual design: At this stage, the designer must discover the actual needs of each manager. It is here that trade offs among competing needs and budget resources are measured and agreed upon. The users and the designer should participate as a group at this point. One approach is to locate the critical success factors (CSF) or the limited areas for which information is needed if the organization is to be competitively successful. The design should satisfy the routine information requirements that each worker needs to perform a job.

4. **Specify in detail how the system will work:** In this stage, the detailed requirements are outlined. Flow charts and process charts are useful to visualize the information needs. It is only at this stage that the organization is ready to select the computer hardware and the necessary capabilities. The software may be selected from among the commercially available ones or alternatively programs tailored to fit the needs of the organization may be developed.

5. Develop the system: At this state, integrated information system is developed containing every detail including computer programs and then pilot runs are conducted to debug the programs and procedures.

6. Test and implement: At this stage the new system is often introduced alongside the old system until the new system becomes settled. Part of this stage is the continuous evaluation of the system to meet new needs.

9.3.2 GUIDELINES

Some guidelines for successful MIS design have evolved from past experiences:

1. The design of a management information system should be determined by the users-managers (including top management) and not delegated to a functional computer specialist, such as a director of computer services. The computer specialist may be a most valuable member of the design team for selecting the proper hardware and software and for programming the computer, but only the managers have the knowledge about exact information needs. Experience shows that even managers don't use certain information that they initially demand for. This happens because what one perceives initially as a need is often changed by acquisition of that need. Only then does the person start to understand better the real needs. Thus, this guideline emphasizes "information needed", and not just "information wanted."
2. All users of the information system should participate in the development of the new system. This participation is especially useful in weakening the resistance to change to computerized systems. Moreover, the user knows what information he or she needs, when it is needed, and how it will be used.
3. The cost of the system should be evaluated on a cost-benefit basis. In this evaluation it should be made clear that the cost savings of information already offered is not the only benefit. Typically, the sophisticated computerized management information system supplies new, relevant, needed information not previously available to the managers.

4. The management information system should not merely increase the quantity of information. It should select, condense, and interpret information, so that managers receive only the required information.
5. Adequate training to all users should be provided during development and prior to final implementation. Also, written documentation should be made available for routine use by managers and others.

9.4 TYPES OF INFORMATION SYSTEMS

There are several types of information systems in use. Six of these are discussed below.

9.4.1 Transaction Processing System (TPS)

A transaction processing system(TPS) is an information system which records transactions that take place between two or more business entities. These systems keep track of such basic business activities as sales, cash deposits, flow of materials, payroll transactions and so on. A sales transaction, for example, may include the customer's name, type of merchandise purchased, price paid and the mode of payment such as cash or credit card. The primary purpose of he systems is to record, process and store information about transactions that take place in various functional areas of business for future retrieval and use.

9.4.2 Management Information System (MIS)

Management information systems are general purpose systems that provide managers with vital information about organizational activities. It is an organized collection of people, procedures, databases and computers that provide routine reports to decision-makers. The input to an MIS comes primarily from transaction processing system and the output is simply a summary report of these transactions. For example, a bank manager may get a summary report of the daily transactions of deposits and withdrawals at his branch.

9.4.3 Decision Support System (DSS)

Decision support systems provide managers with data and tools for making decisions on specific semi-structured and unstructured problems. For example, if one company wants to acquire another company, then this would be a unique problem rather than a routine problem requiring a unique solution. A DSS accesses and processes vast amount of internal and external data and integrates these data with various decision-making models, in order to produce alternative solutions to given problems. Then the decision-maker can select the best alternative. While MIS primarily draws information from internal transaction system, a DSS is more capable of analyzing internal as well as external information in an integrated way. A typical marketing decision support system is shown in Figure 9.2.

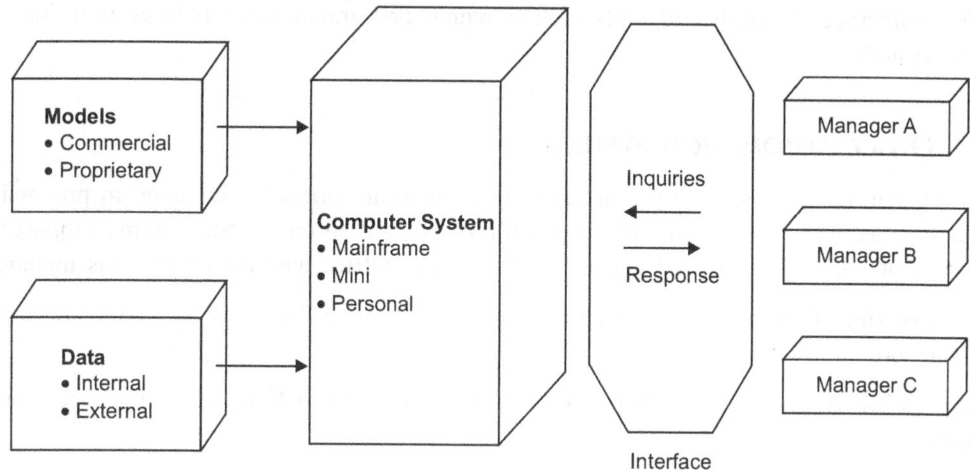

FIGURE 9.2 A Typical Marketing Decision Support System (MDSS).

9.4.4 Executive Support System (ESS)

An ESS is a "specialized" decision support system, primarily designed to be used by top executives of a company. The information is gathered from internal and external sources. This information is analyzed with the help of sophisticated softwares and top management engaged in long-range planning, crisis management people, and other strategic decision-makers use the output in a summarized form. Top-level managers expect an ESS to provide them with information needed to:

- Understand their organization's position in the industry.
- Build communication based networks with people inside and outside the organization.
- Monitor situation of special interests through specified details.
- Deal with multiple problems simultaneously.

9.4.5 Expert System (ES)

Expert systems are information systems in which computer programs store data and rules to replicate the abilities and decisions of human experts in specialized fields. They are built on a framework of known facts and responses to situations. They may incorporate such knowledge and problem solving skills as that of a nuclear scientist or a physician. An ES has three main components. They are:

(i) A knowledge base: It serves as a storehouse for knowledge and experience of experts in a given field. For example, the experience of a car mechanic would serve as a knowledge base for an expert system designed to solve car problems.

(ii) Inference engine: It is a set of programmed rules of interconnection between different parts of knowledge to solve a given problem. It selects the appropriate knowledge and application related to the specific problem.

(iii) User interface: It consists of tools such as menus and graphics that help users to interact with the system.

9.4.6 OFFICE AUTOMATION SYSTEM

Office automation systems serve the needs of those who are primarily involved in processing of data, such as, word processing specialists, file clerks and so on. These systems support the automation of various managerial and clerical activities Office automation systems include:

Word processing: Creating written documents such as letters and reports on a computer using a software programme.

Desktop publishing: Using software with sophisticated publishing capabilities to create documents.

E-mail: Sending mail electronically from one computer to another.

Video conferencing: Using group oriented systems that allow users in different parts of the world to discuss matters in a televised face-to-face communication.

Facsimile transmission: Using faxes in transferring information over phone lines to user anywhere in the world.

Review Questions

1. What is information and why is it important to effective managerial planning, decision-making and control?
2. What four factors determine the value of information?
3. What are the five components of an information system?
4. Compare and contrast the information needs of operational, middle level and upper level managers?
5. Why do people sometimes resist the implementation of a new computer system? How can their resistance be addressed?
6. Compare and contrast decision support systems, expert systems, and conventional management information systems.
7. Differentiate between information and data. How is data converted into information?
8. What are the various characteristics of useful information?
9. What type of information is needed at the top level of management as compared to the information needed at operational level of management.

10. Explain in detail the following information systems
    - Transaction processing systems
    - Decision support systems
    - Expert systems
11. Explain what you understand by MIS and its significance to the managerial decision-making process.
12. What are the specific benefits of a well-designed MIS and how such a design can be developed?

CHAPTER 10 Modern Management Concepts—A Primer

Companies must be flexible enough to respond rapidly to competition and market changes. They must continuously benchmark to achieve best practices. They must outsource aggressively to gain efficiency and they must nurture a few core competencies in the race to stay ahead of their rivals. The quest for productivity, quality, and speed has spawned a remarkable number of management tools and techniques like TQM, benchmarking, business process reengineering and partnering, outsourcing, and change management. The management tools have taken the place of strategy. A few of them are outlined below.

10.1 BUSINESS PLAN

The concept of a business plan and the information that it must contain is briefly discussed.

10.1.1 PURPOSE

The fundamental purpose of the plan is to convince other people who own capital to invest in your business. First, they must be sure that the business you propose will make sufficient money not simply to sustain itself but also to repay any loans. If the investors are being offered shares in the business rather than simple repayment, they will be concerned that the business has the potential to grow in the medium to long term. The investors will need to know who would want to buy the product and how many customers there are, and why they should buy the products of this company rather than those of a competitor.

10.1.2 CONTENTS

The precise details of what will go into the plan depend on exactly what the product in question is and how the business will be established. However, a content should include the following:

(i) Summary of business: This should give an overview of the business. The customers should be described along with their reasons for wanting the product or service. The total market for the product and the total investment required should also be given.

(ii) Description of product: The report should not include technical calculations, rather a description of the products' usage, its life and the ways in which it might change should be provided. Most importantly, the factors differentiating the product from its substitutes should be mentioned.

(iii) Market: The market for your product must be described. It includes the market size, how it breaks down, the spending power of each segment, the preferences of each segment, and the competitors and external influences, such as new legislation etc.

(iv) Management: You must describe how your business will be operated. For example, how will sales target be achieved; how will the product be manufactured; what are the processes that will be undertaken; who will be the suppliers; where will the business be based etc. All these operational details associated with running your business must be described.

(v) Financial details: This section must include the financial documents, such as, a discounted cash flow forecast which shows the net present value of the total incomings, total outgoings, loan repayments, and profit. Also included must be a monthly cash flow forecast, the balance sheet, and the profit and loss account. These should be presented for the next three years at a minimum and, more usually, five.

10.1.3 Preparation of Plan

The preparation of a good business plan is a major undertaking often lasting a year or so. It is advisable to get help on the areas where knowledge is weak rather than trying to research everything oneself—for example, taxation and VAT, legal implications of trading, legal requirements of accounting, product liability and insurance. For many people who want to establish a business, these subjects are a mystery. There are many sources of help for individuals desiring to start a business. The business plan cannot foresee all the problems and changes that the new business will face, and one cannot know the future. For this reason, the business plan will need upgradation with passage of time. However in practice, this is difficult to achieve.

10.2 BENCHMARKING

According to the American Productivity and Quality Center (1992), benchmarking is a systematic and continuous measurement process; a process of continuously measuring and comparing an organization's business processes against business process leaders anywhere in the world, to gain information which will help the organization take action to improve its performance. Benchmarking may form the basis of a renewed development in a company, as this tool helps to identify the processes in which the best possibilities of improvements lie.

10.2.1 Types of Benchmarking

Benchmarking is of three types:

1. Internal benchmarking
2. Competitive benchmarking
3. Functional/generic benchmarking.

10.2.1.1 Internal Benchmarking

The objects of analysis of internal benchmarking are department, divisions, or sister concerns of the parent company, in order to identify the best performance of a given activity within the company. In many companies, the same activity is displayed in many different places, for example, order booking, stocking, distribution, and product development. In this case, it would be natural to start seeking the 'best practice' internally in the company. The advantages are: (i) to ease the admittance to information and data, and (ii) to open up the possibility of a deep understanding of how benchmarking can be implemented. Internal benchmarking improves the internal level of performance and the internal customer satisfaction through reduction of the variations in quality and productivity.

10.2.1.2 Competitive Benchmarking

The company compares itself directly with present and potential competitors within the same range of products. Gathering information about the behaviour of competitors is always in supreme interest of a company. The advantage of competitive benchmarking is that at a very early stage, the company's attention is drawn to the expectations which the customers may rightly have from it. Furthermore, the results have a high degree of comparability as the products and thus the basic production structures are identical. The disadvantage is that the gathering of data is difficult. In many cases, direct information from the competitors is unattainable.

10.2.1.3 Functional or Generic Benchmarking

The potential comparative partner is any company which has obtained a reputation of being excellent within the area which is benchmarked. The company does not necessarily have to limit itself to its own trade but keep its eyes open to 'best practice' everywhere. The advantage is that the probability of finding world-class practice grows as the number of potential benchmarking partners is expanded. Another advantage is that the collection of data is considerably easier than in competitive benchmarking. It can be seen that usually the procedures found internally can, to a large extent, be transferred directly. The probability of finding world-class practice internally is usually small. It is the exact opposite of functional benchmarking. Here, the probability of finding world-class practice is large. Competitive benchmarking lies in the middle of these two extremes.

10.2.2 WHAT CAN BE BENCHMARKED

The purpose of Table 10.1 is to show that at a superior level, three main areas exist which can be benchmarked and that in principle, all of these three main areas can be combined by one or more of the three types of benchmarking.

The parentheses in the Table imply that difficulty in applying especially competitive benchmarking can be expected.

Table 10.1 Types of benchmarking and what can be benchmarked?

Type/what	*Quality*	*Productivity*	*Time*
Internal benchmarking	√	√	√
Competitive benchmarking	(√)	(√)	(√)
Functional benchmarking	√	√	√

It can be argued that only two main areas can be benchmarked—quality and productivity—as time will always be a part of either quality or productivity.

10.2.2.1 Benchmarking of Productivity

Regarding benchmarking of productivity, a common productivity measure is ordinary net profit per employee. It can be expressed as:

$$\text{Ordinary net profit per employee} = \frac{(\text{turnover} - (\text{purchase} + \text{expenses} + \text{depreciation} + \text{interests}))}{\text{average number of full time employees}}$$

The potential benchmarking partners can be identified by means of the above measure.

10.2.2.2 Benchmarking of Quality

Benchmarking of quality will either be a natural extension of time or productivity being applied first in connection with benchmarking, or it can be the area which, for some reason, has been focused on in the beginning. Benchmarking of quality can be divided into: (i) external quality i.e. customer satisfaction, the technical quality of the product etc. and (ii) internal quality i.e. employee satisfaction, process quality etc.

10.2.2.3 Benchmarking of Employee Satisfaction

In relation to employee satisfaction, it may be interesting to look into the following questions.

1. How is employee satisfaction measured?
2. How are measurements applied?
3. How are employees educated and trained?
4. How is it ensured that employees are involved in quality improvements?
5. How is employee involvement measured?

10.2.2.4 Benchmarking of Process Quality

Benchmarking of process quality can be divided into a row of key processes which, in relation to a production company, may further consist of the following key processes.

- Research and development
- Production and distribution
- Administrative supporting processes

In relation to *research and development*, it is important to look into the following questions:

1. How is research and development carried out?
2. How is design review carried out?
3. How are customer demands translated into constructive demands?
4. Does the company have a system for shortening the time for development?
5. How is the quality of the development work measured?

In relation to *production and distribution*, the following questions may be important:

1. How are the processes designed?
2. How can times of delivery be minimized?
3. How can process quality be measured?
4. How are the measuring applied?
5. How are continuous improvements ensured?
6. How are defects and problems dealt with?
7. How is quality audit performed?
8. How are quality plans made?

Finally, in relation to *administrative supporting processes* the following could be important:

1. How can supporting processes be identified?
2. How can the quality of supporting processes be measured?
3. How are measurements applied?
4. How can continuous improvements of the supporting processes be ensured?
5. How are defects and problems dealt with?
6. How can quality audits be performed?
7. How can quality plans of supporting processes be made?

The questions mentioned above are not exhaustive. There will be a number of things which can be benchmarked, all depending upon the exact company and the market in question.

10.3 BUSINESS PROCESS REENGINEERING

One of the important tasks of a manager is to ensure that all the processes are adding value and if not, then they must be obliterated; and this is the basic philosophy of business process reengineering (BPR). It is a process of rethinking and redesigning those processes which create value to the customer. BPR is defined as “the fundamental rethinking and radical redesign of business processes to achieve dramatic improvement in critical, contemporary measures of performance such as cost, quality, service and speed”.

BPR only eliminates unwanted work. It does not aim at getting rid of people. BPR is not simply reconstructing or centered on how work is done or how an organization is structured i.e. it should not be confused with mere automation. BPR offers a radical new principle that the new design of work is based not on classical hierarchical management or division of work and specialization but on end-to-end processes and creation of new values for the customers. BPR is primarily meant for: (i) total customer satisfaction, (ii) keen competition, and (iii) introducing planned change. Today, customers are well informed; they have knowledge; they are demanding more; they are sophisticated; they know their needs and they give written and precise specifications of the product required. Besides they have wider choices and greater range of alternatives. Competition is not local and gentle but global and intense.

10.3.1 Restructuring

Restructuring requires a business enterprise to determine its core competencies and decide in which areas it should continue to operate and diversify, and from which sectors it should get out. Only after the company decides its core competencies, it can look around to customers and their desires, their expectations, alternatives available to them etc. and then put its vision and mission into reality through the involvement of all its employees in reconstruction and reengineering.

10.3.2 Relationship between Reengineering and Restructuring

Some people feel that reengineering is nothing but restructuring. However, restructuring is one possible outcome of reengineering. In fact, reengineering could have many outcomes such as:

- Redefinition of roles and responsibilities
- Organization-wide information systems implementation
- Training for achievement motivation
- Business process obliteration
- New process innovation
- Business network redesign
- Business domain redefinition

Although reengineering of only a single process may not lead to significant improvement in the overall performance of the company, but the improvement relating to that particular process may be dramatic.

10.4 CHANGE MANAGEMENT

Every organization makes minor structural adjustment in reaction to changes in its environment. Planned change is the deliberate design and implementation of a structural innovation, a new policy or goal, or a change in operating philosophy, climate or style. Many large organizations have explicit change management programs to increase the ability of the organization to anticipate and learn from the changes that are occurring.

10.4.1 Concept of Change

The following are the characteristics of change:

1. Change results from the forces which are both outside and inside the organization. It disturbs the existing equilibrium in the organization.
2. Change takes place in all parts of the organization, but at varying rates of speed and degrees of significance.
3. Change may affect people, structure, technology and other elements of the organization.
4. Change may be reactive or proactive. Reactive change occurs due to the pressure of external forces and proactive change is initiated by the management itself to increase organizational effectiveness

10.4.2 Planned Change

Planned change encompasses the application of systematic and appropriate knowledge to human affairs for the purpose of creating intelligent actions and choices. The basic reasons for planned change are:

- To improve the means for satisfying economic needs of members.
- To increase profitability.
- To promote individual satisfaction and social well being of the employees

10.4.3 Process of Change

Most efforts for introducing change fails for the reason, that people are unwilling to alter long established attitudes and behaviour. The process of change involves the following:

1. Unfreezing: It involves making the need for the change so obvious that the individual, group or organization can readily see and accept it.

2. Changing: During this process, change agents will foster new values, attitudes and behaviours through the process of identification and internalization.

3. Refreezing: It means locking the new behaviour patterns into place by means of supporting or reinforcing mechanism, so that it becomes the new norm.

10.4.4 Elements in Change

It is important to recognize that there are some opposing forces that act to keep an organization in a state of equilibrium. Driving forces operate to bring about change in the organization whereas restraining forces are active to maintain present equilibrium. While planning a change, the manager should identify:

1. What forces are likely to push the change, and
2. What forces are likely to restrain it?

If the driving forces are stronger than the restraining forces, changes will be accepted by the people and vice versa. The manager should try to strengthen the forces which favour change and attempt to weaken restraining forces by removing the hindrances that block change.

10.4.4.1 Sources of Resistance

The sources of resistance are grouped into three broad categories: (i) organizational culture, (ii) individual self interest, and (iii) individual perception of organizational goals and strategies.

Organizational culture: Employees stay with an organization because their job helps them meet their life goals and because their personalities, attitudes and beliefs fit into organization culture. Indeed, many employees identify with their organization and take its gains and losses personally. As a result, they may feel threatened by change.

Self interest: The employee expects adequate pay, satisfactory working condition, job security, power and prestige. When change occurs, employees face a potentially uncomfortable period of adjustments to settle into a new organizational structure or a redesigned job.

Perception of organization goals and strategy: Mission statements can guide employee action in the absence of formal policies and procedures. This powerful force for stability can make it difficult to change.

10.4.4.2 Overcoming Resistance to Change

The management can use the following strategies to overcome resistance by the people to introduce change successfully.

1. Effective communication: The manager must inform the workers the justification of change and its benefit to them as well as the organization. Two-way communication will go a long way towards removing fears and apprehension of the workers and bringing understanding between the management and workers.

2. Education and training: The successful implementation of change is based on the subordinates who must be indoctrinated in new relationships, taught new skills and helped to change attitudes. The educational process can be aided by training classes, meetings and conferences.

3. Negotiation: Negotiating with those resisting change and offering them incentives may be a useful tactic for overcoming resistance. For example, union agreements, promotion of nominee of the union, increased economic benefits to the employees and so on. In many cases, it is possible to avoid major resistance through negotiations with those resisting the change.

4. Threat: Managers may force people to go along with a change by explicit or implicit threats involving loss of jobs, denial of promotion etc. They may also dismiss or transfer employee who stand in the way of change. However, such coersive methods are risky and may make it more difficult to gain support for future change efforts.

5. Facilitation and support: These include listening, providing guidance, allowing off time after a difficult period and offering facilitative and emotional support. Facilitative support means removing physical barrier in implementing change by providing appropriate training, tools, materials, etc. Emotional support is provided by showing personal concern for the subordinates during the periods of stress and strain.

10.4.5 MANAGEMENT OF CHANGE

The following guidelines should be followed to successfully implement a change.

1. Identification of need for change: The information regarding change comes from the external and internal control systems. It is essential to lay down the objectives of change. This will help in determining time, phase and quantum of change.

2. Determination of elements to be changed: After identifying the objectives of change, it is necessary to determine the elements which require to be changed. Change may be required in the elements like structure, technology and people. Structural changes are related to job design, departmentation, span of control etc. while changes in production techniques constitute technological change. Changes in organizational members are brought about by inducing changes in their attitudes, behaviour, interaction, and informal groupings.

3. Planning of change: This involves finding answers to questions such as—when to bring about change, who will be affected by change, how to introduce change or who will introduce change. It is of importance to prepare change agents, namely, individuals who are designated for bringing a change in the organization.

4. Soliciting workers participation: Participation will give a feeling of importance to the people involved. They are likely to be more committed to the change, if they are convinced about the rationale of change.

5. Implementation of change: Management should make every effort to let people know about organizational change. Internal announcement may be made through the medium of conferences, meetings, and bulletins. In order to successfully implement the change, subordinates must be taught new skills, helped to change attitudes, and given the information they need to understand where they fit into the picture and how they will be expected to operate under the new set up. The management should provide effective leadership to the workers.

6. Appraisal: The follow-up action is called for to see that changes are taking place as planned. The feedback information from each and every department affected by the change efforts must be continuously monitored.

10.5 CUSTOMER RELATIONSHIP MANAGEMENT

Customer relationship management (CRM) solutions provide customer-oriented services for planning, developing, maintaining and expanding customer relationships with special attention paid to the new possibilities offered by the Internet, mobile devices, and multi-channel interaction. CRM enables a company to capture a consolidated customer view through multi-channel interactions in a datawarehouse solution. CRM can then be used to strategically implement acquired customer knowledge in every area of the company, from the highest management level to all employees who come into direct contact with customers. CRM, thus, enables an organization to address its customers' preferences and priorities much more effectively and efficiently. CRM is a tool that can help organizations to profitably meet the lifetime needs of customers better than their competitors.

CRM involves:

- Automating processes in sales, marketing, and service functions.
- Increasing the efficiency of these processes to improve customer satisfaction.
- Conducting interactions with customers on a more informed basis.
- Individually tailoring interactions with customers on a more informed basis.
- Individually tailoring interactions to suit the specific customer's needs.
- Compiling information that increases understanding of customer behaviour and then analyzing the acquired information to generate customer intelligence that can be used by the marketing function to find brand new customers, retain existing customers, and cultivate a deeper share of wallet from all customers.

The ability of a CRM solution to measure, predict, and optimize customer relationships is directly proportional to the quality and comprehensiveness of the information provided to the analytical solutions.

10.5.1 Benefits of CRM

Customer relationship management provides the company with the following benefits:

1. Extending/widening customer relationships–This involves acquiring new and profitable customers, which, in turn, requires the company to determine the following:

- Products and services of interest to the potential customers that can be supplied by the company.
- Type of customers that will contribute to the profitability and long-term growth of the company.

2. Lengthening relationships with existing customers–This involves focusing on profitable customers to retain them. Recently, companies have shifted their focus from individual transactions to designing their market offerings and prices in order to make a profit over the customer's lifetime. This means that a company will sometimes underprice to gain new customers and it will be generous in its pricing and services to existing customers with an eye toward retaining them for the long run. This requires the company to determine the following:

- Customers that make significant contribution to profits and hence, should be retained.
- Customers that might switch because they are not satisfied with the company's products and/or services or, because they have started to find the competitors' products and services more attractive.

The emphasis, traditionally has been on pre-selling and selling rather than caring for the customer afterwards. A highly satisfied customer stays loyal longer, buys more new products and upgrades, talks favorably about the company to the prospects, is less sensitive to price, offers ideas for new product and service to the company, and cost less for the company to serve them than new customers.

3. Deepening customer relationships–This involves transforming unimportant (less profitable, short-term) customers into highly profitable, long-term business partners. This, in turn, requires the company to determine the following:

- Customers whose share of wallet can be and should be increased. Share of wallet is the ratio of the expenditure of a customer on a specific product group with a specific supplier to the total expenditure of that customer on that specific product group.
- The opportunities for up-selling and/or cross-selling additional products and services that would be of interest to customers.

CRM also enables a company to keep customer information consistent throughout the organization and make it available across all touch-points where the company interacts with customer. CRM can be described as Web-enabled sales and marketing tool that synergistically combines the functionalities of database marketing, one-to-one marketing, and sales force automation (SFA). CRM enables companies to provide excellent real time customer service by developing a relationship with each valued customer through the effective use of individual account information. CRM holds that a major driver of company profitability is the aggregate lifetime value of the company's customer base.

10.6 EMPLOYEE EMPOWERMENT

Empowerment means encouraging and allowing individuals to take personal responsibility for improving the way they do their jobs and contribute to the achievement of organization's goals. It requires the creation of a culture which would encourage people at all levels to feel that they can make a difference and also help them to acquire the confidence and skills to do so. The finest example of employee empowerment is total quality management (TQM) which is an employee-driven process for ensuring the best possible quality products and services for the satisfaction of customers. TQM empowers employees at all levels in order to tap their full creativity, motivation and commitment. The other practices which encourage employee involvement include suggestion system, job enlargement, job enrichment, quality circle, self-managed team, participative leadership, etc.

Empowerment brings about far reaching changes in the organization. In essence, it leads to development of mature human resources, effective communication, readiness for change and an atmosphere of trust in the organization. It has been observed that leaner organization has been accompanied by decentralization, larger spans of control for remaining managers, and expanded role in decision-making at lower levels of the organization.

10.6.1 IMPLICATIONS OF EMPOWERMENT

A glimpse of the implications of empowerment can be had from Table 10.2.

Table 10.2 Implications of empowerment.

From	*To*
• Fear	• Challenge and adventure
• Learning is a responsibility	• Learning is an adventure
• People take little initiative	• People solve their own problems
• Scant training and development	• Continuous development
• Change avoided	• Change welcomed
• Feedback is seen as criticism	• Feedback is seen as essential
• Training and development is the responsibility of personnel	• Training and development is everybody's responsibility
• Lack of vision	• Strong focused and shared vision
• Problem avoiding	• Problem solving
• Closed communication	• Open communication – sharing of information – sharing of ideas – sharing of skills
• Suspicion	• Trust

Thus, it can be seen that many responsibilities have been shifted from managers to work-groups in the form of employee empowerment.

10.6.2 Features

Companies with the culture of empowerment reflect the following features:

1. Everyone in the organization is valued and encouraged to make personal contribution.
2. Individuals are constantly aware not only of what they are seeking to achieve, but also why they are seeking to achieve it and how it fits with the wider corporate goals.
3. The culture is likely to be cooperative and purposeful rather than towards finding faults.
4. Individuals have a real willingness to take personal responsibility for their own success, for the success of the team in which they work and also for the organization as a whole.

10.6.3 Significance

The significance of empowering workers and groups arises because of the following factors:

1. Increasing pace of change, turbulence in environment and the changing expectations of customers require speed and flexibility in response which is incompatible with the old style of functioning.
2. The impact of downsizing, delayering and decentralizing means that the old methods of achieving coordination and control are no longer appropriate.

3. Organizations require cross-functional working and greater integration in their processes if they are to meet the customers' needs.
4. Employees now have greater awareness and are more concerned with the satisfaction of higher level needs. Empowerment can be used to satisfy such needs of employees and thus motivate them.
5. Empowerment provides opportunities to the lower level employees to develop their competencies. Thus, it can be used as a source of discovering managerial talent for the organization.

10.7 ENTERPRISE RESOURCE PLANNING

Enterprise resource planning (ERP) is an enterprise-wide system which encompasses corporate mission, objectives, attitudes, beliefs, values, operating style and people who make the organization. It is the method of effective planning of all the resources in an organization. The main function of ERP is transaction management both within an operating group and across operating groups. ERP calls for setting up an enterprise-wide network wherein all the divisions of a company are interconnected so as to enable real time connectivity and accessibility. ERP defines the business model and the IT needs of an organization. Functionality relationships in areas of finance, sales and marketing, distribution, manufacturing, purchase, human resource, and payroll are required. Similar relationships in the areas of supply chain management, distribution channel, field service are also necessary. ERP is capable of managing a range of business processes like order entry, procurement etc. and requires electronic data interchange (EDI) for the same. ERP implementation involves logistics and statutory requirements and commensurate technology in the business organization. ERP offers advantages like reduced inventory holdings, improved direct labour deployment and utilization, controlled purchase costs, and managed overtime. ERP also brings reduced tariffs and interactions, minimizes obsolescence, and provides information for running the business and achieving excellence in serving the market and the clients. ERP systems are usually customer order-driven and hence they provide an environment which fosters customer orientation. By defining operating groups and core activities, ERP systems tend to work around the outcomes rather than procedures. In the process the system can streamline and redefine systems and procedures thus, paving the way for quality systems. ERP systems are often integrated with finance and therefore are able to replicate the activities in the books of accounts, thus giving a clearer picture of the costs. The biggest benefit of ERP is the complete integration of the business process, which is best for coherency and harmony in activities. Selection of an appropriate package is the most critical factor. The cost of the package and ability of the vendor to bring out new versions of software are equally important.

10.8 GLOBALIZATION

Globalization deals with the integration of various country-strategies and the subordination of these country-strategies to one global framework. It is conceivable that a certain company may have a globalized approach but prefer to leave the details to local subsidiaries. There are few companies that may want to globalize all of their marketing operations. The difficulty then is to determine which marketing operations will gain from globalization.

10.8.1 Reasons for Globalization

Several factors may drive companies toward the pursuit of a global marketing strategy.

1. Globalizing for internal efficiency: By coordinating its operations for maximum efficiency, a company reduces costs and thus becomes more competitive. Some companies may encounter new technological breakthroughs that represents substantial costs. These upfront research and development costs cannot be paid off by one or a few markets alone. Consequently, companies become global out of a need to gain more volume.

2. Globalizing to compete in homogeneous markets: Theodore Levitt encouraged companies to pursue globalization of products by looking at the similarities of their markets as opposed to differences. As a result, companies will gain economies of scale through cost reductions because the multitude of model variations may drive up costs and prevent internal efficiency from standardizing volume. Lower prices can be offered as a result of standardization.

3. Globalizing for added synergies: While the international firm tends to see its investments in each market as separate and non-connected, the global company aims at managing the interdependence between various foreign subsidiaries. Leveraging strong positions to help weaker markets, also called cross-subsidization, is a move away from the traditional principle that each subsidiary should financially stand on its own. Cross-subsidizing foreign subsidiaries allows the global company to selectively slow down a competitor's development in markets where it is most difficult for it to strike back. The global company will try to maximize its profit for the entire system of subsidiaries whereas the traditional MNC aims at maximizing profits for each subsidiary independently.

10.8.2 Levels of Globalization

Globalization exists at various levels, especially, at customer level, market level, industry level, and competitor level.

10.8.2.1 Globalization at Customer Level

Global customers can be defined as group of customers with homogeneous needs and seeking similar benefits and product features across many markets or countries. A global need is an indication of a global product category. Companies facing global product categories realize that the products or services offered by them are present in most markets. In fact, there are few products that are so unique that they only exist in particular country segments. Global segments are relatively homogeneous groups of customers in various countries with similar needs, interests, and preferences, although they may not be majority segments in many markets. Such global customer segments will exist only if there is a presence of global product category.

Once the presence of the product or service across many markets has been ascertained, the company can look at the reasons for its products being purchased. The question shifts at this stage to the benefits sought by the customers. If a company markets a product that is purchased for similar reasons across the world, the company faces a global benefit which implies going beyond the more general global product category. Global benefits deal with the communications and branding of a product and lead to different global marketing strategies. True global products are more common in the industrial markets and less so in the consumer markets. A global product is described as consisting of largely the same features and functionality, although there can be differing degrees of globalization.

10.8.2.2 Globalization at Market Level

Global markets are characterized by customers who are both aware of and search out alternatives beyond their own country borders. In a globalized market, customers search the world for bargains or the best products and will buy from far away if a superior product is available. On the contrary local markets are characterized by customers who will only buy locally, and not go to great length to chase a bargain, and therefore ignore alternatives elsewhere. Furthermore, many firms are facing customers who negotiate purchasing contracts for multiple countries or regions rather than buying on a country-by-country basis. Global markets are much more pronounced in standardized products or components and markets of most commodities face them on a daily basis.

10.8.2.3 Globalization at Industry Level

Globalization has occurred at the industry level if the key success factors, which are the basic competitive requirements a company must meet, are relatively similar across many countries. This will indicate that the experience in cooperating and competing in that industry is transferable. Rather than relearning how to penetrate a given industry when entering a new market, the company may be able to fall back on previous experience. A second important development that is typical of globalized industries is the presence of critical input variables (CIV). When CIV are present, additional investments into opening new markets are relatively small and major benefits accrue to an integrative and global approach in that industry.

10.8.2.4 Globalization At Competitor Level

Here it must be noted that if a company faces the same competitors country after country, it may not mean that the competitors are actually competing with a coordinated strategy. This means that the mere presence of the same competitor may signal a different competitive environment. However, true globalization at the competitors' level occurs when the company faces not only the same competitor but also the same competitive strategy. Global presence, in the first instance, may signal eventual global competitive strategies in the future and this must be taken into consideration. Under globalized competition, companies will need to review traditional assumptions on how to assign roles to subsidiaries in various markets. Issues of cross-subsidization for competitive leverage may apply now and measurement of market share in global terms may also become necessary if the company faces global competition.

10.8.3 Global Strategies

Global strategies can be of various kinds concerning mainly three areas—marketing, product, and branding. They are outlined below:

10.8.3.1 Integrated Global Marketing Strategy

When a company pursues an integrated global marketing strategy, it means all aspects of the marketing strategy have been globalized. Globalization includes not only the product, but also the communications strategy, pricing, and distribution, as well as such strategic elements as segmentation and positioning. Such a strategy may be advisable for companies who face completely globalized customers along the lines.

10.8.3.2 Global Product Strategy

Pursuing a global product strategy implies that a company has largely globalized its product offerings. Although the product may not need to be completely standardized worldwide, key aspects or components may, in fact, be globalized. Global product strategies require that product use conditions, expected features, and required product functions be largely identical so that few variations or changes are required to be made. Companies pursuing a global product strategy are interested in leveraging the fact that all investment for producing and developing a given product have already been made. Global strategies will yield more volume which will make the original investment easier to justify.

10.8.3.3 Global Branding Strategies

Global branding strategies consist of using the same brand name or logo worldwide. Companies want to leverage the creation of such brand names across many markets because the launching of new brands requires a considerable marketing investment. Global branding strategies tend to be advisable if the target customers travel across country borders and will be exposed to products elsewhere. Global branding strategies also become important if target customers are exposed to advertising worldwide. This is often the case for industrial marketing customers who may read industry and trade journals from other countries.

10.9 INTERNATIONAL BUSINESS MANAGEMENT

International business implies being engaged in transactions across national boundaries. These transactions include the transfer of goods, services, technology, managerial knowledge, and capital to other countries. The interaction of a firm in a host country can take many forms, for example:

1. The exportation of goods and services

2. Entering in a licensing agreement for producing goods in another country. The parent company may also engage in management contracts that provide for operating foreign companies.
3. Forming a joint venture with a firm in a host country.
4. Multinationals may set up wholly-owned subsidiaries or branches with production facilities in the host country.
5. Thus, it may be concluded that in developing a global strategy an international firm has many options.

10.9.1 STAGES OF INTERNATIONALIZATION

Originally, international business was chiefly a matter of international trade i.e. raw materials were imported by the developed countries from the less developed countries and finished products were exported through various marketing channels to other countries. Gradually, after passing through various stages, this system developed into a full fledged internationalization activity. The stages involved are discussed as follows.

Stage 1: Despite the long and interesting history of international chains, little attention was paid to the management aspects. Early companies operated as political subdivisions of colonial firms, long before management became a separate discipline.

Stage 2: International development involves international finance and investment. Those countries with available capital sought to invest funds outside the home countries. These investments were treated strictly from the financial view point and involved the flow of funds through banks, investment firms, and governments. The management of the operations was chiefly within national boundaries with the flow of goods treated solely as imports and exports.

Stage 3: Beginning in the twentieth century, some large firms entered a stage in which the management of the overseas operations were controlled by subsidiaries, that handled all international businesses. The headquarters of these subsidiaries were usually located in the home country with only warehouses, service offices, and sale agencies, located overseas.

Stage 4: During post-world war period, the international companies appointed vice presidents of international operations as members of the domestic companies. They acted as contact and liaison personnel to maintain relationship with the various subsidiaries involved in international manufacture and trade.

Stage 5: This stage saw evolution of global company in which the overseas operations were integrated into a single organizational structure.

10.9.1.1 Unifying Effects

Unifying influences occur when the parent company provides and shares technical and managerial know-how, thus assisting the host company in the development of human and material resources. Whatever the interaction, policies must provide for equity and result in benefits for both the parent firm and the host company.

10.9.1.2 Potentials of Conflicts

Many factors can cause conflicts between the parent firm and the host country. Nationalistic self-interest may overshadow the benefits obtained through cooperation. Socio-cultural differences can lead to breakdown of communication and hence, misunderstanding. The international corporations must develop social and diplomatic skills in its managers in order to prevent such conflicts and to resolve those that unavoidably occur.

10.9.2 Multinational Corporations

Multinational corporations have developed different orientations for operating in foreign countries, ranging from ethnocentric to geocentric. This means that the total organization is viewed as a dependent system in many countries. The relationship between headquarters and subsidiaries are collaborative with communication flowing in both the directions. In brief, the orientation of the multinational corporation is truly international and goes beyond a narrow nationalistic viewpoint.

10.9.2.1 Advantages of Multinationals

1. The MNCs can take advantages of business opportunities in many different countries.
2. Companies with worldwide operations sometimes have access to natural resources and materials that may not be available to domestic firms.
3. Finally, the large MNCs can recruit management and other personnel from a world-wide labour pool.

10.9.3 Managerial Functions in International Business

The practice of carrying out the managerial functions of planning, organizing, staffing, leading and controlling differs considerably in domestic and international enterprises, as discussed below.

Planning: Planning requires setting objectives and then selecting strategies, policies, programmes, and procedures for achieving them. An important activity for the MNC is the assessment of opportunities and threats in the external environment. This is a complex task even for a domestic enterprise. Therefore, they form global strategic partnership.

Organizing: Organizing structures are established to achieve corporate objectives. The company can select from a great variety of structures. Managers may be put in charge of a product line, which is marketed worldwide. The truly multinational firm may integrate domestic and international business into a global structure, giving equal importance to domestic and foreign business activities.

Staffing: Managers of the MNCs can be classified in three ways.

1. They may be nationals, selected from the country in which the headquarter is located. These managers, because of their experience, are usually familiar with the parent company's policies and operations.

2. A firm may select managers who are nationals of the host country. These managers are familiar with that country's legal, political, and cultural environment. They also know local customers, suppliers, and government officials and public in general.
3. The source for managerial personnel consists of third country nationals. These are managers who have a nationality that is different from the parent company or the host country. Such managers may have gained experience by working at the company headquarters as well as in different countries. Thus, they would have developed behavioural flexibility that eases their adaptation to different cultures. These managers may be truly trans-cultural.

Leading: Leading involves motivating and communicating. Motivating and leading demand an understanding of employees and their cultural environment. Communication in multinational firms with subsidiaries and affiliates are different.

Controlling: Controlling is an essential managerial function that is influenced by several environmental factors unique to international enterprises. For example:

1. Revenues, costs, and profits are measured in different currencies.
2. The ratios between currencies are subject to considerable fluctuations.
3. Accounting practices and financial reporting often differ from country to country.
4. Due to the complex nature of measurement, there is a time loss in the measurement of performance which may delay detecting deviations from standards and initiating corrective action.

10.10 MANAGEMENT BY OBJECTIVES

The concept of 'management by objectives' (MBO) was introduced by Peter Drucker in 1954. He believed that what the business enterprise needs is a principle of management that will give full scope to individual strength and responsibility and at the same time provide a common direction to vision and effort, establish teamwork and harmonize the goals of the individuals with the common organizational goals. The performance that is expected of the managers must be derived from the performance goals of the business; their results must be measured by the contribution they make to the success of the enterprise.

Thus, the system of management by objectives can be described as a process whereby the superior and subordinate managers of an organization jointly identify its common goals, define each individual's major areas of responsibility in terms of results expected from them, and use these measures as guides for operating the unit and assessing the contribution of each of its members.

10.10.1 Benefits of MBO

Management by objectives is a comprehensive management planning and control technique and is bound to affect the entire organization structure, culture, and style. Management by objectives calls for regulating the entire process of managing in terms of meaningful, specific, and variable objectives at different levels of management hierarchy. It stimulates meaningful action for better performance and higher accomplishment. It is closely associated with the concept of decentralization.

The practice of management by objectives can be beneficial for an organization in the following ways.

1. It causes improvement in productivity due to the fact that management concentrates on the important task of reducing cost and harnessing opportunities rather than dissipating energies on less important matters.
2. It develops a greater sense of identification, by the management team, with the objectives of the enterprise wherein controls are reckoned as tools of 'self-control' rather than devices to be used against managers.
3. It improves communication and organization structure which helps in locating weak and problem areas.
4. It serves as a device for organization control and integration.
5. It stimulates the subordinates' motivation
6. It provides a realistic means of analyzing training needs and opportunities for growth on the basis of measurement of performance against accepted standards.

10.10.2 Setting of Objectives

The first step is to establish verifiable objectives for the organization and for various positions at various levels. In order to set objectives of the enterprise, a detailed assessment has to be made of the various resources at its disposal. This detailed analysis would lead to highlighting of desirable objectives, both long-range and short-range. An attempt should be made to set specific goals in various key areas on which the survival and growth of the business depends. The following activities are concerned with the setting of objectives.

10.10.2.1 Revision of Organization Structure

When the goals for each individual are reset under MBO there is a considerable change in the job description of various positions. This may call for a revision of the existing organization structure. The organization charts and manuals should be suitably amended to depict the change brought about by the introduction of management by objectives. The job description of various jobs must be defined with their objectives, responsibilities, and authorities. They must clearly lay down the relationship with other job positions in the organization.

10.10.2.2 Establishing Checkpoints

Management by objectives ensure periodic meetings between the superior and the subordinate to review the progress towards the accomplishment of targets of the subordinate. For this, the superior must establish checkpoints as standards of performance for evaluating the progress of the subordinates. The standards should be defined quantitatively as far as possible and the subordinate must understand them fully. The key result analysis should contain the following information.

- The overall objectives of the subordinate's job.
- The key results he must achieve to fulfill his objectives.
- The long- and short-term priorities of tasks he must adhere to.
- The scope and extent of assistance he may expect from his superior and related departmental managers and the assistance he must extend to other departments.
- The nature of information and reports he will receive to carry out self-evaluation.
- The standards by which his performance shall be evaluated.

10.10.2.3 Appraisal of Performance

While informal performance appraisal of a subordinate is done by his immediate superior almost everyday, formal appraisal at periodic interval, usually once or twice a year, does ensure that a thorough evaluation of a manager's performance is done and his achievements are carefully analyzed against the background of prevailing circumstances and given objectives. The design and format of the Performance Review Form will depend on the nature of the enterprise.

The important benefit of MBO is that it does away with the judgmental role of the supervisor. The performance of every individual is evaluated in terms of the standards or end results clearly agreed upon by the superior and the subordinate. Wherever MBO has been introduced it has led to greater satisfaction, more agreement, greater comfort and less tension and hostility between the superiors and the subordinates.

10.10.3 LIMITATIONS OF MBO

The limitations which make the implementation of MBO difficult are as follows:

1. Poor planning: One of the major weaknesses often associated with MBO is poor planning of the programme prior to implementation. Implementers must know how to involve personnel at all levels of management and obtain their support.

2. Lack of training: There is generally a lack of training and knowledge on the part of the supervisor in implementing the programme. Many are prone to sit down with the subordinate and dictate the goals and targets, with no input entertained from the subordinate, and demand that those targets be met in a specified time. Whether they are realistic goals or not does not concerns them. In this type of environment there cannot be a two-way communication.

3. Lack of follow-up: Lack of follow-up by the superior at the appropriate time is another hurdle in the successful implementation of MBO. It is most easy to procrastinate. The superior must get to the subordinate at the appropriate time. The subordinate should be prepared to tell the boss exactly what has been accomplished and how.

4. Inflexibility: Management by objectives may tend to introduce inflexibility in the organization. Since goals are set in every six months or one year, the superior may not like to modify them in between because of fear of resistance from the subordinate. There may arise a need to revise the goals at lower levels to achieve the long-range objectives of the enterprise. The manager must handle such a situation properly.

10.10.4 Making MBO Effective

The following elements can help to make MBO effective:

1. Top management support: The active participation of top management is essential for MBO implementation. If the top managers use the objective as an instrument for managing, this practice will also be followed down in the organization.

2. Education about MBO: The organizational members must be adequately educated about the philosophy of MBO. MBO can produce the anticipated results only when its purpose is precisely defined and technique chosen are appropriate to the purpose.

3. Active participation in goal setting: There should be a face to face communication between the superior and subordinate in setting the goals, discussing the subordinate's problems and resetting the goals, and reviewing his performance. Thus, there must be an effective two-way communication in the organization.

4. Decentralization of authority: The subordinates who have accepted the challenging assignments through discussion with the superior must be given adequate authority to accomplish their goals. MBO will not work if the manager is not willing to delegate sufficient authority to the subordinates as the subordinates will not be willing to accept new assignments without commensurate authority and may even resist the setting of clearly defined goals.

5. Orientation of executives: The philosophy of MBO is to be implemented by the executives. They must be adequately oriented about the value of MBO. They should be imparted adequate training for the effective implementation of management by objectives.

6. Integration of MBO programme: MBO should not be implemented as an isolated programme. It must be integrated with all the organization programmes including human resource planning, human resource development, product planning and development, production control, financial planning etc.

10.11 OUTSOURCING

Outsourcing in its simplest sense, is the transfer of operational responsibility of either business processes or infrastructure management to an external service provider. The outsourced process or function is generally considered to be non-core in nature by the customer, but the function can range from high volume or repetitive, such as electronic processing, to a more customized service, such as technology help desk outsourcing.

Increasing competition and rapid changes in business world have made organizations rethink about their strengths and core competencies. They are increasingly focusing on their core business processes and outsourcing the non-core ones to outside service providers. Companies can outsource any function—from logistics to human resources to information technology to payroll processing or even to manufacturing. Outsourcing is one of the most rapidly growing areas.

Definition: Outsourcing can be defined as strategic use of outside parties to perform activities traditionally handled by internal staff and sources. It is contracting out company's non-core and non-revenue producing activities to specialized service providers. Traditionally, organizations used to hire contractors to do particular type of work or help it level off peak workload. However, it is fundamentally different from contracting as outsourcing is a strategic management tool that involves organization restructuring unlike in contracting. It allows the organization to concentrate on its core competencies.

10.11.1 PHASES IN OUTSOURCING

Organizations that outsource their functions generally move through three phases.

- Internal analysis and evaluation
- Needs assessment and vendor selection
- Implementation and management

10.11.1.1 Internal analysis and evaluation

One of the prerequisites to successfully implementing outsourcing initiatives is the tone of the management. Top management has to be fully involved as outsourcing involves considerable restructuring of the organization. In this phase the management develops an outsourcing strategy and an understanding of services it needs to outsource. After identifying the goals and core competencies, the next step is to gather fact and figures related to these activities in order to compare the cost of conducting these activities in-house with outsourcing. This enables the company to answer non-financial questions like how critical are these functions/activities, or what are the dependencies on these activities, or does this activity tends to become a "mission critical" activity, and reach on decisions whether to outsource or not. Long-term cost and investment implications, work morale and support should also be considered.

10.11.1.2 Needs Assessment and Vendor Selection

The objective of this phase is to develop understanding about the needs of the organization. It involves not only searching for information within the organization but also looking at experiences of companies who have outsourced similar services. This phase also involves selecting vendors who can fulfill these services. It requires the following activities to be carried out.

Request for proposal (RFP): Once the company has analyzed its requirements, the next step is "request for a proposal" (RFP). Request for proposal should be structured in a manner so as to facilitate assessment and comparison of various vendors.

RFP should:

- Define complete requirements in measurable terms
- Describe the problem that needs to be resolved
- Describe the type of relation the company is looking for
- Specify service level

RFP is very important part of this overall process as it lays down companies' expectations. Clearly documented RFP helps understand what the company is looking for and evaluate if they can provide those services.

Vendor assessment and selection: Once the company receives proposals as a result of RFP, it needs to evaluate it. Often establishing cross-functional team with experts in legal, finance, human resources and the specific function being outsourced is helpful. While evaluating a vendor, the company should look at factors like vendor's financial stability, cultural lift, and proven track record. If possible, contacting vendor's existing clients can provide valuable information.

Contract: After the selection of the vendor is finalised, the company should negotiate and sign a contract at a reasonable price. Both parties should make sure that they understand the performance measurement criteria and its evaluation. The contract should clearly define the expected service levels and consequences of not meeting them. For a successful implementation of contract, both the parties should communicate regularly and openly and express mutual desire to succeed.

10.11.1.3 Implementation

Final phase involves implementation of outsourcing. Clearly defining and identifying tasks, and establishing time frame are helpful during this phase. Mechanism to monitor and evaluate performance should be established. This is important not only during but also after implementation to make sure the outsource arrangement is delivering what it is supposed to. Another important ingredient of this phase is to help people affected with outsourcing, in managing new relationships and change. Often training and education can address these issues. Ability to identify, communicate and resolve issues promptly and fairly will help company achieve mutual benefits and make a relationship last long.

10.11.2 Benefits of Outsourcing

Outsourcing brings many advantages to the organization; some of them are:

1. Focus on core competencies: Outsourcing allows management to focus on important and strategic issues. It frees management from repetitive and mundane tasks, and allows them to concentrate on their core competencies.

2. Best practices and improved business processes: Outsourcing allows organizations to adopt "best-in-class" practices. Vendors providing outsourced services are considerably strong and focused on processes. To remain competitive, they are continuously looking to improvise their services and adopt best practices for efficiency. This in turn helps organizations achieve faster, efficient and more economical business process.

3. More competitive approach: Organizations can respond more effectively to changing demands. Outsourcing allows companies to gain more scalability and greater leverage in responding to changes.

4. Reduced cost and advanced technologies: Outsourcing enables companies to implement latest technologies. As mentioned earlier, vendors who provide these services often implement latest technologies and thus companies can take advantage of these technologies, which they might not be having if they were conducting activity in-house. Vendors can also achieve economies of scale. This helps drive down overall cost in the system, thus enabling companies to realize more productivity and efficiency.

10.11.3 ISSUES IN OUTSOURCING

1. Loss of expertise: Outsourcing can lead to decrease in in-house expertise. Outsourcing of an activity or function also increases organization's vulnerability as it becomes partially or totally dependent on a service provider.

2. Policy/procedure: Organizations need to modify existing policies and procedures or develop new ones to coordinate with service providers. Quality control policies and problem resolution procedures need to be in place to address any situation concerning quality of services being provided by the service providers.

3. Staff morale: Staff morale play a very important role in outsourcing arrangement. These issues can range from layoffs to reallocation or retraining. Companies should address these issues effectively using change management techniques. As mentioned earlier, training and education of employees to help them adjust to new methodologies and environment can address these issues.

10.12 QUALITY CIRCLE

Quality circle is a small group of employees doing similar or related work who meet regularly to identify, analyze and solve product-quality problems and to improve general operations. The quality circles are relatively autonomous units (ideally about 10 workers), usually led by a supervisor or a senior worker and organized as work units. The workers, who have a shared area of responsibility, meet weekly to discuss, analyze, and propose solutions to ongoing problems. Some typical efforts in improving production methods and quality involve reducing defects, scrap, rework, and downtime, which are expected to result in cost reduction as well as increased productivity. In addition, the circles intend to focus attention on the self-development of workers and the improvement in working conditions. Through this process, there is an improvement in workers' morale and motivation, stimulation of teamwork, and also recognition of their achievements.

The technique of quality circle has been refined over the years. The objectives are:

- Overall improvement in quality of products manufactured.
- Improvement in production methods and productivity of the enterprise.
- Self-development of the employees who take part in quality circles.
- Encouragement of innovative ideas among the employees.
- Building high morale of employees by developing team spirit.

10.13 SUPPLY CHAIN MANAGEMENT

The supply chain includes the organization and processes for the acquisition, storage, and sale of raw materials, intermediate products, and finished products. Supply chain product flow is linked by physical, monetary, and information flows. In the broadest sense, it encompasses all logistics activities, customer-supplier partnerships, new product development and introduction, and inventory management facilities. Four different view of the supply chain reengineering have been proposed below.

1. The strategic view: The supply chain design offers a different way to carry and business. It is a chain of resources used to support a product's market positioning in terms of the largest customer, pricing and promotion mix. The end result is improved margins on product sales.

2. The functional view: The supply chain consists of the individual organizations needed to procure material, convert it, and sell it. It is supported by material, transportation, and other groups. The end result is lower costs in the dominant functions.

3. The logistics view: The supply chain is the physical path of a product through a set of facilities linked by a transportation network. They include factories, warehouses, sales offices, trucks and ships, and distribution centers. The objective is lower logistics costs.

4. The information management view: The supply chain is integrated by the movement of information among various participants. An integrated supply chain has a common information base and the mechanics in place to share this information among the participants. The objective is low information processing cost.

10.13.1 Reengineering of Supply Chain Management

Supply chain reengineering effort will have four characteristics:

1. Has the potential to shift the basis of competition
2. Involves multiple enterprises in the supply chain
3. Has an aggressive, not incremental, quantified improvement objective
4. Will incorporate a balanced approach encompassing the four views described above

10.13.2 Reengineering Issues with Supply Chain Management

- Human Resources—training and organization value department
- Project Management—communication and lack of management tools. Failure to assess project performance
- Management Support—goal setting, sponsorship, continuity of involvement
- Change Management—addressing organizational resistance
- Tactical Planning—resource commitment and financial justification
- Process Delineation—measurable goals, scoping of process, scoping of effort, and incrementalism
- Strategic Planning—alignment with strategy and business vision for the project
- Time Frame—timeliness of implementation, ability to assure schedule performance
- Technological Competence—capabilities in technical areas of project

10.14 TOTAL QUALITY MANAGEMENT (TQM)

Total quality management (TQM) refers to meeting the requirements of customers consistently by continuous improvement in the quality of work of all employees. For achieving total quality, three things are essential:

1. Meeting customers' requirements
2. Continuous improvement through management process
3. Involvement of all employees

Total quality management is a dynamic concept as the quality standards do not remain the same for ever. They are to be modified or changed to meet the requirements of customers and to make use of new technology. Even the ISO:9000 series standards have a provision of revision, modification or deletion of quality standards after every five years. Without the active involvement of employees, high quality standards cannot be achieved. Further, the whole concept of TQM is directed towards meeting the requirements of customers.

10.14.1 Elements of TQM

There are three essential elements of TQM which are discussed below.

1. Meeting customer requirements: TQM aims at satisfying the requirements of customers, which never remain constant but keep on changing with time, environments, circumstances, needs, fashion, etc. Thus, meeting the changed requirements of customers is a continuous goal of the producer.

2. Continuous improvement: The change in customer requirements may be in terms of desire for better quality products/services, bigger size, reduced cost, etc. A product has to cope up with new requirements. A new process may have to be developed, or it may require a new design. The production process has thus to be attuned and accelerated to meet these changing requirements. The management has also to take care of competition in the market so that customers do not shift to other producers.

3. Empowerment of employees: The enhancement of skills of employees will not only improve quality but also bring down the cost of production through efficient use of machine and materials and reduction of wastages. The employees must also be conscious about the need for improvement in the quality of work. Quality circle is an outstanding example in this regard. **TQM** should be the concern of all managers and workers in the organization if it is to serve its purpose fully. Each and every employee must be encouraged to become involved in implementing the TQM programme. TQM is a philosophy that calls for development of a company-wide culture for quality. A positive attitude towards customer and continuous enhancement of quality must be ingrained in the minds of the employees.

Review Questions

1. Explain the purpose and the detailed formulation of a business plan.
2. Define benchmarking and describe its importance.
3. Explain how benchmarking is done for: (i) productivity, (ii) quality, (iii) employee satisfaction, (iv) research and development, (v) production and distribution, and (vi) administrative supporting process.
4. Define business process reengineering and explain its importance.
5. Discuss in detail the relationship between reengineering and restructuring.
6. Differentiate between the external and the internal forces that induce change in organizations?
7. Explain some of the reasons for resistance to change. What can the management do to overcome such resistance?
8. Define customer relationship management and explain the procedures for developing a CRM solution for an organization of your choice.
9. What is the meaning of empowerment and what are its positive and negative implications?
10. What is ERP? What are its main functions? How does an ERP model satisfy the IT needs of an organization?
11. What are the reasons for companies going global?
12. Explain the globalization process at: (i) customer level, (ii) market level, (iii) industry level, and (iv) competitor level.
13. Define in the true sense, the concept of international business. Who would be considered as an international manager?

14. How do the management functions differ in the case of international management as compared to purely domestic management?
15. What do you understand by management by objectives? Discuss its various phases.
16. Write an explanatory note on management by objectives approach to performance appraisal.
17. What is outsourcing? Discuss in detail the benefits of outsourcing to an organization.
18. Discuss the concept of quality circle? Explain the importance of forming quality circles in organization for improving productivity.
19. Explain the term supply chain management. What are the characteristics of reengineering on supply chain management?
20. What do you understand by total quality management? How does this concept differ from managing quality of the product by quality control techniques?
21. What are the major ingredients of total quality management? Are some ingredients more important than the others? Explain.

APPENDIX 1

Henry Fayol's Principles of Management

1. Division of work: The object of division of work is to get better result with the same effort. It is accomplished through reduction in the number of tasks to which attention and effort must be directed.

2. Authority and responsibility: Authority is the right to give orders and responsibility is its essential counterpart. Whenever authority is exercised responsibility arises.

3. Discipline: Discipline implies obedience and respect for the agreements between the firm and its employees. Establishment of these agreements, binding a firm and its employees from which disciplinary formalities emanate, should remain one of the chief preoccupations of industrial heads. Discipline also involves sanctions judiciously applied.

4. Unity of command: An employee should receive orders from one superior only.

5. Unity of direction: Each group of activities having one objective should be unified by having one plan and one head.

6. Subordination of individual interest to general interest: The interest of one employee or group of employees should not prevail over that of the company or broader organization.

7. Remuneration of personnel: To maintain the loyalty and support of workers, they must be provided with a fair wage for services rendered.

8. Centralization: Like division of work, centralization belongs to the natural order of things. However, the appropriate degree of centralization will vary with a particular concern, so it becomes a question of the proper proportion. It is a problem of finding the measure that will give the best overall yield.

9. Scalar chain: The scalar chain is the chain of superiors ranging from the ultimate authority to the lowest ranks. It is an error to depart needlessly from the line of authority, but it is an even greater one to keep it when detriment to the business ensues.

10. Order: A place for everything and everything in its place.

11. Equity: Equity is a combination of kindness and justice.

12. Stability of tenure of personnel: High employee turnover increases inefficiency. A mediocre manager who stays is infinitely preferable to an outstanding manager who comes and goes.

13. Initiative: Initiative involves thinking out a plan and ensuring its success. This gives zeal–the energy to an organization.

14. Esprit de corps: Union is strength, and it comes from the harmony of the personnel.

APPENDIX 2

The Hawthorne Experiments

The human relations movement grew out of a series of studies conducted at the Western Electric Company, from 1924 to 1933. These eventually came to be known as the 'Hawthorne Studies' because many of them were perormed at Western Electric Hawthorne plant near Chicago. The Hawthorne Studies began as an attempt to investigate the relationship between the level of lighting in the workplace and worker productivity.

In some of the early studies, the Western Electric researchers divided the employees into test groups, who were subjected to deliberate changes in lighting, and control groups, whose lighting remained constant throughout the experiments. The results of the experiments were ambiguous. When the test group's lighting was improved, productivity tended to increase, although erratically. But surprisingly, when lighting conditions were made worse, then also there was a tendency for productivity to increase in the test group. To compound the mystery, the control group's output also rose over the course of the studies, even though it experienced no changes in illumination. Obviously, something besides lighting was influencing the worker's performance.

In a new set of experiments, a small group of workers was placed in a separate room and a number of variables were altered–wages were increased; rest periods of varying length were introduced; the number of working days and work weeks were reduced. The researchers, who now acted as supervisors, also allowed the groups to choose their own rest periods and to have a say in other suggested changes. Again, the results were ambiguous. Performance tended to increase over time, but it also rose and fell erratically.

In these and subsequent experiments, Mayo and his associates decided that a complex chain of attitudes had triggered off the productivity increases. Since they had been singled out for special attention, both the test and the control groups had developed a group pride that motivated them to improve their work performance. Sympathetic supervision had further reinforced their motivation. The researchers concluded that employees would work harder if they believed management was concerned about their welfare and supervisors paid special attention to them. This phenomenon was subsequently labelled as the Hawthorne Effect, since the control group received no special supervisory treatment or enhancement of working conditions, but still improved its performance, some people (including Mayo himself) speculated that the control group's productivity gains resulted from the special attention of the researchers themselves.

The researchers also concluded that informal work groups–the social environment of employees–have a positive influence on productivity. Many of Western Electric's employees found their work dull and meaningless, but their associations and friendships with co-workers, sometimes influenced by a shared antagonism toward the "bosses", imparted some meaning to their working lives and provided some protection from management. For these reasons, group pressure was frequently a stronger influence on worker productivity than management demands.

Bibliography

1. Adam Everett E., Jr. and Ronald J. Ebert, *Production and Operations Management*, Englewood Cliffs, N.J., Prentice-Hall, Inc. 1978.
2. Anderson, David R., D.J. Sweeney, and T.R. Williams, *Essentials of Management Science Applications to Decision Making,* St. Paul, Minn., West Publishing Co., 1978.
3. Awad, Elias, *Introduction to Computers in Business*, Englewood Cliffs, N.J., Prentice Hall, Inc., 1977.
4. Barndt, Stephen E. and Davis W. Carvey, *Essentials of Operations Management*, Englewood Cliffs, N.J., Prentice Hall, Inc., 1982.
5. Buffa, Elwood S., *Modern Production Management*, 5th ed., New York, John Wiley & Sons, Inc., 1977.
6. Byars, Lloyd L., *Strategic Management: Planning and Implementation*, New York, Harper and Row, Publishers, Inc., 1984.
7. Comerford, Robert A. and Dennis W. Callaghan, *Strategic Management: Text, Tools, and Cases. Boston*, Kent Publishing Co., 1985.
8. Daniels, J.D., E.W. Orgam and L.H. Radebaugh, *International Business: Environments and Operations*, 3rd ed., Reading, Mass., Addison-Wesley Publishing Co., Inc., 1982.
9. Davis, Keith and Robert L., Blomstrom, *Business and Society; Environment and Responsibility (Revised)*, New York, McGraw-Hill Book Company, Inc., 1975.
10. Diebold, John, *Managing Information–The Challenge and the Opportunity*, New York, John Wiley and Sons, Inc., 1977.
11. Dilworth, James B., *Production Management,* 5th ed., Cincinnati, Ohio, Southwestern Publishing Co., 1979.
12. Doll, D.R., *Data Communications: Facilities, Network and Systems Design*, New York, John Wiley and Sons, Inc., 1977.

13. Ebert, Ronald J., and Terrence R. Mitchell, *Organizational Decision Processes: Concepts and Analysis*, New York: Crane, Russak, and Company, 1975.

14. Eells, Richard and Clarence Walton, *Conceptual Foundations of Business, 3rd ed.*, Homewood, III, Richard D. Irwin, Inc., 1974.

15. Glueck, William F. and Lawrence R. Jauch, *Business Policy and Strategic Management, 4th ed.,* New York, McGraw-Hill Book Company, Inc., 1984.

16. Holoien, Martin, *Computers and Their Societal Impact,* New York, John Wiley and Sons, Inc., 1977.

17. Hussain, Donna and K.M. Hussain, *Information Processing Systems for Management,* Homewood, III, Richard D. Irwin, Inc., 1985.

18. Laufer, Arthur C., *Operations Management: Manufacturing and Non-manufacturing*, New York, Random House, 1979.

19. Mason, R. Hal, Robert R. Miller, and Dale R. Weigel, *International Business,* 2nd ed., New York, John Wiley & Sons, Inc., 1981.

20. Massie, Joseph L., and John Douglas, *Managing: A Contemporary Introduction,* 4th ed., Englewood Cliffs, N.J., Prentice-Hall, Inc., 1985.

21. Mayer, Raymond R., *Production and Operations Management,* 3rd ed., New York, McGraw-Hill Book Company, Inc., 1975.

22. Mintzberg, Henry, *The Nature of Managerial Work,* New York, Harper and Row, Publishers, Inc., 1973; *The Nature of Managerial Work, Englewood Cliffs,* N.J., Prentice-Hall, Inc. 1980.

23. Mintzberg, Henry, *The Structuring of Organizations, Englewood Cliffs,* N.J., Prentice-Hall, Inc., 1979.

24. Moore, P.G., and H. Thomas, *The Anatomy of Decisions, Middlesex,* England, Penguin Books, 1976.

25. Moore, Franklin G. and Thomas E. Hendrick, *Production/Operations Management,* 8th ed., Homewood, III., Richard D. Irwin, Inc., 1980.

26. Peters, Thomas J. and Robert H. Waterman, Jr., *In Search of Excellence,* New York, Harper and Row, Publishers, Inc., 1982.

27. Pearce, John A. and Richard B., Robinson, Jr., *Strategic Management*, Homewood, III, Richard D. Irwin, Inc., 1982.

28. Pearon, Harold et al., *Fundamentals of Production/Operations Management,* 2nd ed., New York, West Publishing Co., 1983.

29. Robbins, Stephen P., *Essentials of Organization Behaviour,* Englewood Cliffs, N.J., Prentice-Hall, Inc., 1984.

30. Rugman, Alan M., Donald J. Lecraw, and Laurence D. Booth, *International Business*, New York, McGraw-Hill Book Company, Inc., 1985.

31. Schellenberger, Robert E. and Glenn Bosemand, *Policy Formulation and Strategy and Policy*, Boston, Houghton Mifflin Company, 1985

32. Sharplin, Arthur, *Strategic Management,* New York, McGraw-Hill Book Company, Inc., 1985.

33. Smith, Garry D., Danny R. Arnold, and Bobby G. Bizzell, *Business Strategy and Policy,* Boston, Houghton Mifflin Company, 1985.

34. Sprague, R.H. Jr., and E.D. Carlson, *Building Effective Decision Support Systems*, Englewood Cliffs, N.J., Prentice-Hall, 1982.

35. Thompson, A.A. and A.J. Struckland, *Strategy and Policy,* 3rd ed., Plano, Tex, Business Publications, Inc., 1984.

36. Wheelen, Thomas L., and J. David Hunger, *Strategic Management and Business Policy Reading*, Mass., Addison-Wesley Publishing Company, 1983.

37. Wren, Daneil, *The Evolution of Management Theory,* New York, Ronald Press, 1972.

38. Koontz, Harold, and Heing Weihrich, *Essentials of Management,* Tata McGraw-Hill, New Delhi, 1998.

39. Weihrich, Heing and Harold Koontz, *Management—A Global Perspective,* 10th ed., McGraw-Hill International Editions, 1996.

40. Bell, Gail Freeman, and James Blakwill, *Management in Engineering,* 2nd ed., Prentice-Hall of India, New Delhi, 1998.

Index